Absolution

By
Clara Viebig

Double 9
BOOKS

Absolution

by Clara Viebig

Copyright © 2023

All Rights reserved.

ISBN: 978-93-59951-37-9
Published by

DOUBLE 9 BOOKS

2/13-B, Ansari Road
Daryaganj, New Delhi – 110002
info@double9books.com
www.double9books.com
Tel. 011-40042856

ABOUT THE AUTHOR

Clara Emma Amalia Viebig was a German author who lived from 17 July 1860 until 31 July 1952. Viebig was the daughter of a Prussian government official and was born in the German city of Trier. Hermann Göring was related to her. Clara's father was transferred when she was eight years old, and the family relocated to Düsseldorf, where she attended school. She frequently returned to the Moselle countryside in Trier and the surrounding area, where she took many walks. She was moved to live on the estate of some relatives in Posen when her father died, where she attended the local Luisenschule. Clara moved to Berlin with her mother when she was twenty years old. She traveled to Berlin to study music, but instead discovered that the stimulation of the huge metropolis, along with the landscapes she had already visited, was directing her toward a literary career. In 1896, she married Jewish Publisher Fritz Theodor Cohn (a partner in Fontane and Company, afterwards Egon Fleischel and Company). Clara began a flourishing writing career the next year, and her works were well praised. She spent the majority of her time after her marriage in Berlin and its suburbs (Schöneberg, Zehlendorf).

CONTENTS

CHAPTER I

"The rats! Ugh, the rats!" cried beautiful Mrs. Tiralla, as she stood in the cellar with her maid. They had gone down to fetch some of the pickled cabbage from the tub in the corner in order to cook it, and the maid was carrying the lamp whilst Mrs. Tiralla held the earthenware dish. But now she let it fall with a piercing shriek, and lifted her skirts so high that you could see her gay-coloured, striped stockings, and her neat feet encased in shiny leather slippers.

"Where are the rats?" The maid laughed and showed all her big white teeth. "I can't see any rats. There are none here, Pani," and she looked at her mistress with a half stupid, half cunning leer on her face. "Pani must have been dreaming, there's not a living thing in the cellar except Pani and Marianna. Sh! sh! hark!" She bent her head and listened for a moment; then she shook it and laughed again. "Rats would patter, but there's no sound of anything."

She raised the lamp, so that the light shone all around. Gliding shadows fell on the black walls gleaming with moisture, and showed up the cracks in the rough masonry, the places where the bricks were crumbling away, and the dark corners in which hung big spider-webs. It was the old cellar of an old house in which the two women were standing, and a very neglected one to boot. It had never been cleared. Turf and coals, all higgledy-piggledy, were stored away near the tub containing the *Sauerkraut*; and amongst the many wine bottles that lay scattered about on the floor there were just as many empty ones as full ones. The shelves, which once upon a time had reached half-way up the cellar walls, had fallen to pieces, and were now nothing but a heap of rotting wood. All kinds of rubbish lay amongst the potatoes, and broken hooks, broomsticks, and old pieces of pot stuck out of the sand, into which, here and there, a bundle of herbs had been carelessly thrust, in order to keep it through the winter. The place had never been aired, as there was nothing but a very small grating right at the top, which was never opened; and it smelt foul. The lamp gave a dim light, as though stifled by the mustiness, and the two figures--the clumsy figure of the maid and the more dainty one of the mistress--were encircled by a vaporous, glimmering mist.

"But there are *rats* here, do you see, do you hear? Ugh!" Mrs. Tiralla again gave a loud shriek, her face was pale, and, opening her sparkling eyes wide as if with terror, she seized hold of the girl's arm. "There was one! Ugh! Horrid animal!" She shook herself and gave a jump, as if one of the long-tailed monsters were already creeping up her warm body.

"Holy Mother!" As though infected with the exaggerated fear of her mistress, the maid now also gave a shrill scream and let the lamp fall, as her mistress before the dish. It broke into many pieces and went out. They stood in pitch darkness.

"You stupid girl!" screamed her mistress nervously, and raised her hand as if to strike her.

The maid ducked down and jumped aside, as though she could see the lifted hand in spite of the darkness; her suppressed chuckling was heard in a distant corner of the cellar.

"If Pani is going to hit me, ha-ha! I shall stop here, ha-ha!"

"Nonsense. Hit you? I shouldn't think of such a thing," protested Mrs. Tiralla, trying to conciliate her. "Just come here. Give me your hand."

"Oh, no, no! I am sure Pani will hit me."

"Give me your hand, I say--at once. I'm not going to do anything to you, stupid. Marianna, where are you?"

Beautiful Mrs. Tiralla now seemed to be seized with real terror--a terror that was much more genuine than before. Her voice trembled with anxiety, her bosom heaved and sank rapidly; one moment she felt quite cold and the next her head burnt. Ugh! how dark it was. Just like a grave! She felt icy cold right down her back. Ah, how dreadful to be here in the dark, quite alone with *those* thoughts.

"Marianna!" She cried so loudly that it echoed from the vaulted roof. "Marianna, where are you?"

No answer.

"Marianna, I'll give you my silk apron which you like so much. Marianna, but where are you?"

"Why, I'm here. I only went a couple of steps away from you. Here, Pani, here." The girl's warm hand seized hold of her mistress's cold, moist fingers, "So that Pani doesn't knock against anything," she whispered in an ingratiating voice.

Thus hand-in-hand the two women groped their way in the dark, until they came to the cellar steps.

"Praise be to the Holy Mother and all the saints!" lisped Mrs. Tiralla as she felt the first step of the slippery stone stairs under her feet. Fifteen steep steps more, and then, thank God, they would be at the top. Then it would be light again. And the dark thoughts would remain below in the darkness. She did not shudder now, when she was almost at the top; on the contrary, she could hardly help laughing, for she had at last succeeded in thoroughly frightening Marianna, who now firmly believed in rats. So she made up her mind that she would not scold the girl on account of the lamp. The thing was now to go on talking and complaining a great, great deal about the rats, so that everybody would soon say: "There are so many rats at Starydwór, in Anton Tiralla's house, that they dance on his benches and tables, that they devour his wheat on the barn floor whilst it's being thrashed, that they've nibbled at the mistress's beautiful dress in her wardrobe--her blue silk one, trimmed with lace." That would be splendid, splendid!

Mrs. Tiralla squeezed the girl's hand with a deep sigh of relief. "You see now that there are rats, although you would never believe it before; oh, ever so many."

"When Pani says there are rats, then there are rats," said the girl in a submissive tone of voice.

Mrs. Tiralla did not notice the smile that made the big mouth under the snub nose still bigger, nor the cunning, lurking gleam that flashed in the small, deep-set eyes.

"Ha-ha!" laughed the maid to herself, "did the Pani really think she was so stupid? Rats *had* to be here. The Pani wished rats to be here; the Pani tried to make-believe that rats were here. Well, let people who were more stupid than she was believe it, for she, Marianna Śroka, was much too clever, nobody could humbug her. The mistress must have some reason for saying it, for there were no rats."

She pretended, however, to agree with her mistress, and when they saw daylight again she shuddered and said: "Pani is quite pale with fright. *Psia krew*, those horrible animals! They'll soon be eating the hair off our heads."

Mrs. Tiralla nodded. Then she said, "You can come to my room afterwards, and I'll give you the apron I've promised you."

"And the lace," said the maid, "the lace which the Pani showed me the other day, I'll put it on my apron."

"My lace on your apron!" Mrs. Tiralla's pale face grew red with anger. "Are you mad?" "Oh, only a little bit of it--there's only a little bit left. What can Pani do with such a little bit? It's not worth keeping." And then the girl gave a loud, bold laugh, and added, "Then I'll say that Pani has given me it, as the rats would otherwise have devoured it. There are so many rats, the rats devour everything here."

A thought flashed through Mrs. Tiralla's mind, "How impertinent she was! What did she suspect? What did she know?"

The two women stared at each other for a few seconds as though they wished to read each other's thoughts. But then they both smiled.

"The Pani can rely upon me," the servant's smile seemed to say. "I'll pretend to be stupid: I'll hear nothing, see nothing, know nothing, just as it suits the Pani."

And the mistress's smile said: "That girl is so stupid, there's no need to fear her. She doesn't notice anything, she believes what is said to her. And even if she should notice something, she can be bought at a pinch with an apron, a bit of ribbon, a morsel of lace, or half a gulden."

"Now we've broken the dish, and there's no *Sauerkraut* for dinner, Marianna," said Mrs. Tiralla.

"Never mind, Pani," and the black-haired girl laughed until her narrow, sparkling eyes quite disappeared behind her prominent cheek-bones. "I'll go down in the cellar by myself with another dish and fetch up some 'kapusta'; Pani needn't fear the rats. And if he," with a short nod in the direction of the nearest door, "should say, 'Why are the dish and the lamp broken?' I'll answer, 'Oh, an accursed rat jumped over our hands and bit the Pani's hand and my nose. There are so many rats in the cellar that you can't go down any more with safety." "That's right," said Mrs. Tiralla, and smiled contentedly. "There's so much vermin in this old house that it's quite dreadful. And we've cockroaches as well in the kitchen----"

"The walls are covered with them every evening," the girl chimed in eagerly. "The *gospodarz* had better come to my kitchen some evening, when the light's out, and see it for himself, and then *he'll* say, 'Ugh!' They fly at your head, and into your face, and against your nose, eyes, and ears. They crawl about everywhere--ugh!" She threw her apron over her head and gave a loud shriek.

"*Psia krew*, what a noise! Confound you, woman, can't you hold your tongue for five seconds, not for those few moments when I want to sleep?"

The door of the room was flung open and the master began scolding the maid in an angry voice. But when he caught sight of his wife behind the girl his tone became gentler, even anxious. "What is it, what is it?" For Mrs. Tiralla had also screamed, as if in sudden terror. "Why do you both scream so? My heart! why do you both scream so? What *has* happened? Why, you're quite pale. Tell me, my Sophia, what's happened to you?"

You could see that this big man, with his strong limbs and ruddy-brown face, was very anxious about his wife, and, after hitching up his trousers (for he knew that she disliked him to take off his braces and make himself comfortable. "Fie, what a boor you are!" she would then say to him), he quickly approached her. "What on earth has happened to you? Tell me."

The woman's black eyes stared at him out of her pale face. "Holy Mother, the rats again!" she stammered, and stretched out her hands as though she wanted to seize hold of something.

Then Mr. Tiralla burst out laughing. "Rats? But, my dear little woman, there are always rats where there are pigs; and why shouldn't there be some here on the farm? If it's nothing but that." He laughed good-naturedly. "I thought you must have seen the little Plucka, [A] or the 'Babok,' the black man, in the cellar. Why didn't you say, 'All good spirits praise God!' and then the rats would also have ran away?"

A *Plucka: a ghost with feet like a hen.*

"Don't blaspheme," she said in an icy tone. "God punish you for so doing." And when he playfully tried to embrace her, and pushed his enormous, hairy hand under her chin, she shrank back, and, holding her apron up to her eyes, she burst into tears. She sobbed bitterly.

It was in vain that the man tried to pull the apron away; she held it firmly pressed against her face. Her slender fingers, which for a farmer's wife were singularly soft, had an enormous power of resistance.

He felt quite dismayed. "My heart, my dove, Sophia, what is the matter with you?" He tried in vain to catch a glimpse of her face. "Confound you, woman, why are you grinning?" he suddenly roared, turning to the maid who was still standing in the same place with a broad smile on her face. "Drat you! it's you who have vexed the mistress."

"No, no, Panje, not I. It was the rats, I swear it. If only the *gospodarz* would go down into the cellar he would see for himself how they run on the floor and jump up the walls. And in my kitchen he can see the cockroaches-- hundreds of thousands, hundred thousand millions of them! Some day they'll fall into Pan Tiralla's food, and then the master will see them for himself."

"Just you try to do it!" Tiralla raised his heavy hand as if to strike the maid, but she evaded him as adroitly as she before had evaded her mistress. It was so ludicrous to see her duck down behind her mistress and make use of her as a bulwark, that the uncouth man roared with laughter. "You needn't fear, you idiot," he said good-naturedly. "I'm not going to hit you. I know very well that you're a little devil, but I don't for a moment think you'll put any dirt into my plate."

"Oh, no," she assured him ingenuously, "I won't do that," and she came out from behind her mistress.

He pinched her firm cheek with his hairy hand. It hurt, and his rough fingers first left a white, then a burning red mark; but she put up with it in silence. No, the *gospodarz* wasn't angry. He was really much better than his wife. All at once Marianna thought that her master was to be pitied. She drew a little nearer to him and threw him a glance full of promise from under her half-closed lids. If the old man wanted she was quite willing.

But Tiralla had only eyes for his wife. He continued to beg for a look from her. There was something ridiculous in the way this strong, already grey-haired man worried about this delicate, dainty little woman. "Sophia, my darling, what is the matter? Look at me, my dove, pray don't cry."

He succeeded at length in taking the apron away from her face. But when he tried to kiss her cheek her eyes sparkled, and she spat at him like an angry cat. "Oh, you've hurt me! Pooh, how you smell of manure and tobacco, and of gin, too. You stink, you boor!" And she spat on the ground.

"My darling," he said quite sadly, "what things you do say. I have only drunk one small--really, only one quite small glass--of gin to-day. I swear it by the Holy Mother."

"Don't pollute the Holy Mother by calling on her," she cried in a cutting voice. "Rather blaspheme her, that she sends you the sooner to hell, where you belong. I shall not shed a single tear for you, I swear that."

"What--what have I done to you?" the man stammered, quite terrified. "I've never done anything to you. I've bought you dresses, as many as you liked; I've taken you to balls as often as you liked; I've let you dance with whom you liked; I've never said 'no' when you've said 'yes'; and now you speak so horridly to me. You're ill, my dear; I'll send for the doctor."

"Yes, ill!" she cried, sobbing bitterly. "You've made me ill--you, you, you!" She rushed at him as though she wanted to scratch his face with her nails. "I don't like you! I detest you! I--I hate you!" she shrieked in a piercing voice. Her eyes sparkled; she clenched her hands and struck her breast, and then she thrust all her fingers into her beautifully smooth hair and tore it out. Her dainty figure trembled and swayed, and she turned so pale that he thought she was going to faint.

The servant opened her eyes in amazement. What was the matter with her? Oh, how stupid she was, how stupid! Why shout it at the master if he hadn't noticed anything? Ay, now she had told him plainly enough-- "I hate you!" And he, poor man (may God console him!), what did he do? Was it a laughing or a crying matter? Marianna Śroka did not know if she should think "Oh, you arrant fool!" or if she should wish, "If only he were *my* husband, or, at least, my lover." For the *gospodarz* was good, thoroughly good; he wouldn't stint, her--her and her two little ones. That woman was really too nasty. She didn't deserve such a good husband.

Hitherto her mistress had always had her sympathy, but in a sudden revulsion of feeling she now felt much more drawn towards her master. It was a shame how that woman treated him. She must really have bewitched him, that he put up with such things. It would be better if he took off his big, leather slipper, with the wooden heel, and hit her over the head with it and stunned her, rather than that he should beg and implore in that way. Oh, yes, of course there was no doubt about it, the master was enchanted; the big, stout man had been bewitched by that little woman, that lean goat. She was a "mora," who could change herself into a cat, or into one of those creatures that fly down the chimney on a broomstick. The priest ought to know it; he would soon put a spoke into her wheel. But there was a better plan than that. She, Marianna, would take the matter into her own hands, then she alone would earn the gratitude of Pan Tiralla. She would take the tip of her shift and rub the bewitched man's forehead with it three times, and then the spell would leave him. And who knows what then might happen? Perhaps he might turn the woman out of the house then, as she was so horrid to him, and always slept in another room, and banged the door in his face. Wasn't he as strong as an ox? Wasn't he rather a fine-looking man? Even if his hair were bristly and already grey, and his eyes rather watery, he was still a man for all that. And he had money--oh, such a lot. The servant's heart beat more rapidly when she thought of it. All the shops in Gradewitz could be bought up with it, and those in Gnesen as well, and--who knows?--perhaps even those in Posen. What a pity it was that this woman, this witch, would some day get all that money. The maid cast a sidelong look at her mistress, which made her pretty but coarse face positively ugly.

Mrs. Sophia Tiralla stood weeping. Her shoulders drooped so dejectedly, and her head was bent so low, that you would have thought all the cares of the world were weighing her down. Her husband had given up his useless attempts to approach her, he stood as if rooted to the spot, and his pale blue, sleepy eyes wandered from the woman to the maid, and then from the maid to the woman in perplexed surprise.

"If only I knew what was the matter, darling," he said at last in a dispirited voice. "Good heavens! what flea has bitten you?"

The servant burst into a loud guffaw. How very comical it sounded. She couldn't compose herself again, it really was too funny. A flea.--ha-ha, a flea! She thrust her fist into her mouth and bit it, so as to suppress her laughter.

Her mistress cast her an angry look. "How dare you? Go to your work. *Dalej, dalej.*"

The maid grew frightened. Ugh, how furious her mistress looked! Her glance was as cold as steel. "Let that wicked look fall on the dog!" she murmured, protecting her face with her arm. And then the thought came to her, "Oh, dear, now she won't give me that apron!" All the same, it was better to keep on good terms with the mistress, she was the one who ruled the house. So she whispered in a tone of excuse:

"I'm sorry, Pani, but it was so funny when *gospadarz*--big, fat *gospodarz*--compared himself to a tiny little flea. I couldn't help it, I had to laugh." And she gave a waggish laugh, in which Mrs. Tiralla this time joined. There was something merciless in the laughter of the two women.

But Mr. Tiralla did not notice the mercilessness of it in his delight at seeing his wife in a better humour. He took her by the hand as if nothing had happened, and drew her into the room.

And she allowed him to draw her in. If he, even now, didn't notice that she hated him, in spite of all she had done, didn't even notice it when she told him it to his face, then he should feel it. It was his own fault. A cruel smile played for a moment round her short upper lip, but then the tears again started to her eyes.

As she was sitting there with him--he had tried to draw her on his knee, but she had adroitly evaded him, and had squeezed herself in between the table and the wall, so that he could not reach her so easily--certain thoughts were chasing each other with frightful rapidity through her brain. She had often thought them out before, but they always made her tremble anew. A deep silence reigned in the room.

But Mr. Tiralla did not desire any further entertainment. It was enough for him if she were there, if he had the feeling that he only required to stretch out his arm in order to grasp her with his strong hand, to draw her to him, to caress her, even if she did not want it. After all, he was the stronger. He had thrown himself full length on the bench near the stove, but he could scarcely find room there for his huge limbs, which stuck out on all sides. He sighed. He had already tramped across his fields that morning, and had seen that the winter corn was getting on all right, had heard the busy flails keeping time in the barn, had looked for a long time at the cows chewing the cud in the shed, and had stroked his two splendid horses. That had, indeed, been a day's work. Now he had a perfect right to rest a little. Besides, there was snow in the air, a big, thick, grey silence outside; so it was much more comfortable to lie in the warm room until the *barschtsch*, and the cabbage and the sausages were brought in. And after dinner it would be nice to lie down again, until it was time to go to the village inn. There he would meet the gentry, sometimes even the priest. His Reverence didn't disdain to drink a glass with them now and then, and talk over the news, although he didn't care for it to be mentioned later on that he had been there. Quite a sociable man, that priest, and not so strict as Sophia by a long way. Mr. Tiralla felt quite friendly towards him. *He* wouldn't cast his wickedness in his teeth. Ah, Sophia really did exaggerate. Didn't he go to Mass every Sunday, and every festival, too? Nobody could really expect him to go to matins as well; hadn't he to get out of his bed much too early both summer and winter as it was? And weren't his particular saints hanging in his room; and wasn't he always ready to give what the Church demanded? There was no reason for him to be a hypocrite into the bargain; and when a man has got a pretty wife he wants to see something of her as well. So it would be difficult for her to blacken him in the priest's eyes, as he very well knew what a healthy man required.

Mr. Tiralla stretched his mighty limbs and opened his arms wide. Then he said, "Just come here, darling."

"What do you want?"

The man's spirit of enterprise vanished as he heard her icy tone. "Why don't you speak more kindly to me?" he said despondently. "You know I don't want anything from you. I--I only wanted to ask you if you would like a new dress for St. Stephen's Day? Or what would you say to a pair of earrings? Or would you, perhaps, like a new fur cloak when we drive to Posen to engage servants?"

"I don't want anything," she answered in the same cold voice.

"Just think it over, something will be sure to occur to you," he said encouragingly. "Only let me know what you want. Nothing will be too expensive for me if it's for you. Come, little woman, do come here." He again opened his arms.

But she did not move.

"Don't you want a new dress? I saw some beautiful materials in Gnesen. Rosenthal has a wonderful display in his window--oh my, such finery! Cherry-coloured cloth and black braid to trim it with. The prefect's wife wears such a dress on Sundays. Wouldn't you like to have the same, darling?"

Her eyes began to sparkle. New dresses! A dress like such a fine lady! She took a fancy to it; but only for a few moments, then the light in her eyes again died out. What was the good of that dress at the side of such a man? She shook her head energetically as she answered: "I won't have one."

He saw he would never attain his object in that way. Although Mr. Tiralla hated getting up he soon saw that he would have to squeeze himself down beside her behind the table or drag her out by main force. And then if she cried out, that lovely little dove, "Go away! Leave me, you beast!" then he would have to close her mouth with a kiss, by main force.

Mr. Tiralla cursed as he put one of his big feet down on the ground. It vexed him to have his peace disturbed in this way; but he could not resist her, she was too charming. He groaned as he rose from his seat.

She noted his approach with terror. Oh, now he would clasp those big white arms round her, which were all covered with downy hairs, those arms into which her mother had delivered her whilst she was still young and harmless, and had only thought of the dear saints, and had felt no desire for any man. Now she was no longer young and harmless, and--a sudden thought flashed through her brain--oh, perhaps she could persuade him to buy poison then! Poison for the rats! She had often broached the subject before, but he had never wanted to do it. He did not believe in the rats, and even if they were to jump over his nose he would not bring any poison into the house. The thought was repugnant to him. When she wanted poison for the vermin on the farm she had never been able to get it, except by producing a paper signed by Mr. Tiralla himself.

She shuddered. She shook as though with terror. "Oh, those rats!" Then she got up hesitatingly. She sat down again, as if undecided--she fell back almost heavily into her chair; but then she gave herself a jerk. She rose quickly, went up to her husband, and sat down on his knee.

The sudden change in her almost disconcerted him. But then he felt very happy. She had not been so nice to him for ever so long. She stroked his head, and he leant his forehead against her soft bosom, and felt it heave.

"How fast your heart beats."

"No wonder," she answered shortly. And then she kissed his bristly hair and fondled him. "My old man, my darling, you'll really buy me a new dress? Really?"

He nodded eagerly, he was too comfortable to speak.

"I should like," she continued, pressing his head still more firmly against her bosom, "I should like to wear such a cherry-coloured dress, trimmed with black braid, as the prefect's wife has. If she saw me in it in Gradewitz, or if your acquaintances in the town saw me, wouldn't they say, 'How well red suits Mrs. Tiralla. What a pretty wife Anton Tiralla has'!"

He smirked.

"But what good would it be to me?" she continued, and her voice sank and became quite feeble. "The rats would devour it."

"Drat the rats! Leave them alone!" He jumped up angrily, in spite of his great love for her; she had bothered him too often and too much with her rats. "To the devil with you and your everlasting rats!" Once for all poison should never come into his house; rather a thousand rats than one grain of poison. Where there's poison the Evil One has a hand in the game.

But she again forced his head down on her bosom. He *must* remain there. It was as if he were being bewitched by her hands as they played about on his head.

He stammered like a child. "Leave the rats alone. Give me a kiss--there, there." He pointed to the back of his ears, to this place, that place, and she pinched her eyes together and pressed her mouth to his hair.

She drew a deep and trembling breath, as if she were struggling for air. She opened wide her firmly closed eyes and stared at one particular point-- always at one point. It must be! Then she said with a voice that sounded like a caress, while her face, which he could not see, was distorted with aversion:

"Would you like to sleep, darling? There, lean on my arm. Let Marianna do the work alone, I'll stop with you. Oh, my darling, I'm so frightened."

She clung to him more closely, so closely that her warm body seemed to wind itself round him. "The rats, ugh!" She gave a trembling sigh. "Those horrid rats! We'll put poison, won't we, darling? Poison for rats; but soon, or I shall die of fright."

CHAPTER II

Mr. Tiralla's farm lay some distance from the village, near the big pines and deep morass of Przykop. Starydwór was a large farm, and there were many in Starawieś who envied Mrs. Tiralla. She had been as poor as a church mouse before her marriage--her mother was the widow of a village schoolmaster--and had not even possessed six sets of under-linen and a cart full of kitchen utensils, and now she had so much money! But however much her enemies might wish her ill, nobody had ever been able to say of her that she had been unfaithful to her old husband.

The farmer was already getting on in years when he married her, and was a widower into the bargain with a big son. "That couldn't have been an easy matter either for the little thing," said those who were friendly towards Mrs. Tiralla. But she had behaved very well; anyhow, Mr. Tiralla had grown stout, and used to tell those who had warned him against proposing to the girl of seventeen, "that his Sophia was the sweetest woman in creation, and that he was living in clover." And he still said so, even now, after they had been married almost fifteen years. She had bewitched him. Her big eyes, that gleamed like dark velvet in her white face, played the fool with him. He could not be angry with her, although she often tried him sorely. And, all things considered, wasn't it rather nice of her that she was so coy and reserved? The owner of Starydwór had, in the course of his life, come across enough women who had thrown themselves at his head. He could not even credit Hanusia, his first wife, with a similar modesty.

And his Sophia was pretty. It flattered the elderly man's vanity immensely that nobody ever spoke of her as "Mrs. Tiralla," plain and simple, but always as "the beautiful Mrs. Tiralla." When he drove with her through Gradewitz--he on the box, she on the seat behind, in her veil and feather boa--everybody stared. And even in Gnesen the officers dining at the hotel used to rush to the window and crane their necks in order to see the beautiful Mrs. Tiralla drive past. Then Mr. Tiralla would crack his whip and look very elated. Let them envy him his wife. *They* did not know--nobody knew--that he many an evening had received such a vigorous blow on the chest from her, when he had attempted to approach her, as nobody would ever have given such a delicate-looking woman credit for. On such occasions he would console himself with the thought that his Sophia never had cared for love-making. But she was a dear little woman, all the same, a beautiful woman, his own sweet wife, from whose hand the food tasted twice as good and agreed with him twice as well. And she was still as beautiful as on the first day; perhaps even more so now that she was over thirty, for she used to be much too thin and small, and did not weigh even seven stone. He could have carried her on his hand.

He would have loved to deck her out in gay colours, like a show-horse, but she had the tastes of a lady. That was because she had had a good education. She spoke German very fluently, and could also write it without a single mistake. She knew quite long pieces of poetry by heart. She could speak of Berlin, although she had never been there, and that made a wonderful impression upon her husband. Gnesen and Posen and Breslau were also big towns, but Berlin--*Berlin*! He felt very ignorant compared with her, although in his youth he had gone to the Agricultural College at Samter, and had understood pretty well how to make something out of the five hundred acres he had inherited from his father. The children--the son of his first wife and little Rosa--would never be obliged to earn their living among strangers. And, what was of more importance still, his beloved Sophia's future would be secured if he died before her, for he had made a will in her favour, as he had promised her mother he would.

Mrs. Kluge had been able to close her eyes in peace, fully satisfied with having brought about this splendid match for her pretty daughter, for it was her wisdom and circumspection which had paved the way for it. Mrs. Kluge was of a better family than most of her neighbours. She had originally come from Breslau, but after her marriage with the schoolmaster from Posen she had had to wander about with him from one miserable Polish village to another, and had always been very poor. However, she had never allowed her little Sophia to play in the street with the other children, and the child had always had shoes and stockings to wear--rather suffer hunger in secret than go without them.

When Sophia grew older, and the time drew near for her to receive the Holy Sacrament for the first time, she became the priest's avowed favourite. Mrs. Kluge was a pious woman, perhaps the most pious woman in Gradewitz, and whilst making dresses for the farmers' wives in order to support herself and her child her lips used to move the whole time in silent prayer. It was owing to her dressmaking that she had become acquainted with farmer Tiralla's wife--maybe also owing to her piety. For did it not seem as if it were Providence itself that had brought Mr. Tiralla as well as his wife to her room when she was making Mrs. Tiralla's last dress? He had driven his wife over--she was in delicate health at the time--and, as it was bitterly cold, he had come in as well, and had left the horse standing outside. He could hardly get through the low door, and had quite filled her small room. Little Sophia was handing her mother the pins whilst the dress was being tried on, and had received a shilling and a look from Mr. Tiralla which had made her blush and lower her dark eyes without knowing the reason why.

Sophia Kluge was modest; no young fellow in the neighbourhood could boast of being in her good graces. She did not even know why the lads and lasses used to steal out into the fields in the evenings, and why their tender songs should rise so plaintively to the starry skies. Sophia, with the black eyes and white face, which no sun, no country air had ever tanned, for she had always remained at home with her mother, was a pious child, so pious that the priest, still a young man with saint-like face, took a great deal of notice of her. He would send for this girl of eleven to come to him in his study, which the old housekeeper only got leave to enter three times a year. There he would speak to her of the joys of the angels and of the Heavenly Bridegroom, and enrapture himself and her with descriptions of heaven and of the streams of love which had flowed through the hearts of all the saints.

Mrs. Kluge was proud of the preference shown to her daughter; but the salvation of her soul did not make her lose sight of her earthly lot. She had suffered many privations in her life, and had had to give up very much, and she wished her daughter to have some enjoyment even on this earth. It seemed to her like a sign from the saints that Mrs. Tiralla was prematurely delivered of a child and died before she had worn her new dress. Then Mr. Tiralla began to look out for another wife, and when he came in person to pay the outstanding account for the dress, the clever woman noticed the complacent smile which he cast at the young beauty. She was well aware of her daughter's beauty, and knew how to value it. When Mr. Tiralla said to her, "Your daughter is devilish good-looking," she had answered, "Ah, but she's still so young." And when he came once more and said, "*Psia krew*, how sad it is to live alone on such a dreary farm," the wise woman replied, "You'll have to marry again. There are plenty of widows and elderly spinsters who would be pleased to marry you." That had angered him. He neither wanted widows nor elderly spinsters, he coveted the youngest of them all.

Sophia had run to the priest and had wept and lamented when her mother had said to her, "Be happy, Mr. Tiralla wants to marry you." No, she wouldn't have him, she didn't want to marry at all.

Even now, after the lapse of fifteen years, Mrs. Tiralla's heart swelled with bitterness when she lay awake at night and thought of the way she had been treated. Her mother had begged and implored her with tears in her eyes. "We shall then be out of all our misery." And when the girl continued to shake her head she had boxed her ears--the right and the left indiscriminately--and had told her in a peremptory voice, "You *shall* marry Mr. Tiralla."

And her friend, the priest? Ah! Mrs. Tiralla once more pictured herself in that quiet room in which, with hot cheeks and enraptured gaze, she had so often listened, on her knees, to the legends of the saints. Once more she held the hem of the cassock between her fingers and watered it with her tears. She had wept, had resisted: "No, I will not marry him, I cannot!" Had not the priest always told her--nay, positively adjured her--to remain a virgin, to remain unmarried, and in this way secure for herself a place in heaven? She had kissed his hands, "Help me, advise me!" Then, she did not know herself how it had happened, then she had suddenly jumped up from her knees, confused and trembling, and had rushed to the door and had hidden her face in a tumult of undreamt-of feelings, which had almost stunned her with their sudden attack. All at once she was no longer a girl, she was a woman, who, trembling, ardent, feverish with desire, had become self-conscious. How blissful it was to be a--*his* chosen one. To sit all one's life in that quiet room with the saints. In the girl's confused dreams the figure of her Heavenly Friend seemed to mingle with that of her earthly one. Oh, how exquisite he was, how beautiful! His hands were like ivory, his cheeks like velvet. And his kiss----

Instead of him Mr. Tiralla had come----

Mrs. Tiralla had placed a footstool in her bedroom under her picture of the Saviour carrying His flaming heart in His hand. The priest of her youth had left Starawieś long ago--he had asked to be removed from the neighbourhood--but she still prayed a great deal.

It was the morning after Mr. Tiralla had drunk a glass too much in his joy at her unusual display of tenderness, and as she got out of bed her first glance fell on the picture opposite. She crossed herself, and then, gliding on her bare feet to the footstool, she knelt down and prayed for a long time.

Mr. Tiralla had promised her faithfully, as he yesterday lay in her arms, that he would fill up the paper to-day and would drive over to Gnesen and fetch the poison for the rats himself. How was it that she felt so quiet about it? She could not understand it herself. Even if her heart did beat a little faster, it was not from fear, but only from expectation of something good, joyful, long hoped for. Fifteen years--ah, fifteen long years.

She continued to murmur words of prayer, whilst her thoughts were with her husband on his way to the chemist's in Gnesen. But suddenly she pressed her lips tightly together. Her mouth looked very inflexible. She forgot that she was praying--her heart was filled with fierce curses and accusations. Her mother, who had sold her--sold her like one sells a young calf (why not call a spade a spade?)--was dead.

Mrs. Kluge had not long been able to enjoy the thought that the little house which she had formerly rented at last was hers, and that she had no longer to make dresses at any price for the farmers' wives, who were everlastingly grumbling. She had not long been able to enjoy the thought, and that served her right!

The woman's eyes gleamed as though with satisfaction. Her mother had had to leave everything behind which she had stipulated for as payment for her daughter. Now she had long ago turned to dust. But the other culprit, the buyer? Oh, Mr. Tiralla had grown stout, *he* did not look as though he also would soon be lying under ground.

"Holy saints! Holy Mother!" She raised her hands in prayer. She did not exactly know how she was to put her prayer into words, it would sound too awful if she were to say, "Let him die; he *must* die!" It was as though she were going to expose herself in her nakedness to the Holy Virgin and all the saints. No, that would not do.

She let her hands fall in her perplexity. What now? But then it suddenly occurred to her, why need she tell everything to the saints? Why trouble them? Surely it would be enough if she secured their help. So she prayed: "Holy Mary, pure Virgin, oh, bring about by means of thy divine power and that of all the saints that he really goes to Gnesen, that he at last fetches the poison--the poison for the rats. I entreat thee, I implore thee!"

She wrung her hands and wept bitterly; she hit her breast with such force that she hurt herself. What she had suffered from her husband, and would suffer again and again. He would not leave her in peace, and she hated him, she loathed his eager, outstretched hands. If only she could have gone into a convent, how happy she would have been there. All that filled her once more with horror. She had been so terrified on her wedding night, when her husband, intoxicated with joy and wine, had embraced her; so terrified when she felt she was about to become a mother against her will; so terrified when the nurse had laid the little live girl on her bosom. She had pulled herself together and endured it when she felt the little seeking mouth at her breast, although it was as if a stream of icy-cold water were running down her. But then, when her husband had appeared, had placed himself near the bed in which she lay so feeble, so weak, so at his mercy, and had said with such a satisfied smirk, "*Psia krew,* we've done that well!" then she could not restrain herself any longer. She had uttered a cry, a feeble, plaintive, yet piercing cry, and had reared herself up with her last strength, so that the little creature on her breast had begun to whimper and whine like a young puppy. The nurse had hastened to the bedside, quite terrified, and had made the sign of the cross--"All good spirits!" No doubt she thought that the "Krasnoludki," the wicked dwarfs, wanted to steal the new-born child. She had quickly thrown her rosary round the infant's neck, and had sprinkled the bed with holy water. But the young mother had burst into tears--into hopeless, never-ending tears. Then Mrs. Tiralla had been very ill, so ill that her anxious husband had not only sent for the doctor from Gradewitz, but also for the best physician in Gnesen. Both doctors had assured him, however, that there was no danger, that his young wife was only very weak and nervous.

Mr. Tiralla could not understand why.

* * * * * * * * * * * *

Mrs. Tiralla now got up from her prayers. It was high time to urge her husband to start for Gnesen. Perhaps he was still lying in bed. She dressed in angry haste. She did not arrange her thick hair with her usual care--her hands were trembling, she was in a hurry. No sound of wheels reached her attentive ear, the man could not be taking the carriage out of the coach-house. Her husband must still be sleeping.

Hastily throwing on her skirt, and without waiting to fasten her blouse, she ran across the stone passage to the room into which she had been drawn as a trembling bride, and in which her little girl had been born. There he was, still lying in the big bed, snoring.

"Get up!" She seized him by the shoulder and shook him.

His hair stood up like bristles around his forehead. "How horrible he looked!" she thought. And what did the room smell of? Drink. That disgusting smell came from him.

No feeling of compassion softened her eyes. She stood bolt upright at the side of the bed and scanned him from top to toe with sparkling eyes. He would soon lie there again.

A triumphant cry rose to her lips, but she suppressed it. Silence, silence. What would that inquisitive maid think if she rejoiced in this way? She seized hold of her husband once more with renewed strength, and shook him so vigorously that he started up.

Mr. Tiralla stared around with eyes that were still quite dim. Who was there? Why didn't they leave him in peace? He wanted to sleep longer.

"Get up!" she shouted to him. "You've to go out. It is time, high time!"

"Who must go out? Not I," he stammered drowsily, and fell back on his pillow.

He was so heavy that she could not lift him; her shaking and her cry of "Get up!" were of no avail. Then, in her anger, she poured some icy-cold water on his face. That helped.

He opened his eyes, suddenly quite wide awake. "Ah, my dove, are you coming to me?" he said tenderly, and stretched out his arms.

She hit him across his fingers. "Leave that nonsense!" she said coldly. But then her voice grew softer. "You've promised to drive to Gnesen, remember. It's time!"

"To Gnesen--Gnesen? I'm not going there. What have I to do there?" He had no idea of what he had said. What he had promised the day before in his transport of joy was now quite forgotten.

She saw with despair that she would have to start afresh. She sat down on his bed, and, clenching her teeth, threw her arms round him and began to coax him. "You promised me--to go--to the chemist's--about the rats--you remember--the rats."

"What do I care for rats?" he exclaimed, laughing boisterously. "As long as the rats don't jump on my bed they don't disturb me." And he gave her a resounding kiss.

She submitted to it with closed eyes; she was deadly pale. Suddenly she twisted herself out of his arms, and, looking at him fixedly with her black eyes, she said slowly and very softly, but every syllable was distinct: "If you don't go to Gnesen now, I'll jump into the Przykop. I'll drown myself in that big pool under the firs. I can't stand this any longer. If *you* don't go, then *I* will."

The man grew disconcerted. Why did she emphasize the words so strangely? What did she mean by it? Such nonsense! But then he made up his mind to go. He scolded and cursed as he got out of bed. "*Psia krew*, what nonsense it was to get poison for the sake of those few rats; they could easily be killed with a cudgel." He proposed to her that he should spend a whole night in the cellar hunting for them.

But she persisted in her demand. "You've promised me to do it! You've sworn it! I'll never believe you again if you perjure yourself in this way. I'll never allow you even to touch my fingers again if you keep your promises so badly."

"Well, well, all right then, I'll go," he said at last. Why did she make such a fuss of it? He put on his boots in a very bad humour.

She assisted him to dress; she held his coat for him in her eagerness to help him.

But as he was putting his arms into the sleeves of his coat he drew them out again. "I won't go, all the same. What's the good? We'll set traps--yes, we will. Call Jendrek, he can go and buy them--two, three, as many as you want. He can fetch them at once from Gradewitz. Call him!"

She did not move; she was so startled that she trembled. Was he to escape her even at the last moment?

He stamped his foot. Wasn't she going? Was *he* to call the man? He walked angrily to the door.

Then she barred his passage; she fell on his breast half unconscious and quite exhausted. "I--I'll--if you'll do this to please me--I'll--I--will also do something to please you."

Mr. Tiralla drove to Gnesen. Mrs. Tiralla herself had helped to harness the horse, and had stroked it tenderly whilst she did so. Jendrek had felt hot and cold and covetous as he listened to the soft words the beautiful woman had lavished on the dumb beast.

"Run, my pretty horse, run," she whispered softly to the animal, then she leant against the stable wall. She was hardly able as yet to stand upright; her knees still trembled under her; her heart still fluttered like that of a bird whose cage door had been opened and then closed again, just as it was going to fly out. She did not recover until her husband came out of the house booted and spurred. And whilst the man held the horse's head until his master had mounted the box, she went close up to the carriage, and, holding out her hand to her husband, said "Good-bye." There was something sympathetic in the tone of her voice, and as she looked at him her eyes, which were often so cold, seemed to promise him something.

He cracked his long whip and urged the horse on. "*Huj, het!*" If only he were home again! But if she had the thing so much at heart he could easily please her by driving to Gnesen. She was such a sweet little woman, was his Sophia.

Mrs. Tiralla stood looking after her husband for a long while. For the first time in fifteen years she felt something like affection for him--affection and gratitude. Then she drew a long breath and went back into the house.

It was very quiet, as quiet as if Mr. Tiralla had never filled it with his loud voice and broad figure. The maidservant was in the field fetching potatoes, the men were in the barn, Rosa was at school. She was quite alone.

"Ah!" The woman raised her arms with a deep sigh and ran through the room as if she were flying. How happy she felt--ah, how happy! She had not felt so happy for years. She walked round the big room and examined it. She would place a sofa there, where the big bed stood. It was the biggest and best room in the house; she would make a drawing-room of it. Or perhaps Mikolai would like to have it when he came home after serving his three years in the army? She would not make a point of having the room, she was quite satisfied with her own bedroom.

She sat down near the window and gazed dreamily into space. She could generally see the village, with its sunken cottages and thatched roofs all covered with moss, and the new brick walls of the fine-looking inn through the open yard door as in a frame, but to-day there was nothing to be seen. Everything was hidden by the driving snow-flakes. Oh, what a storm, what a lot of snow! If that continued Mr. Tiralla would be delayed on the way, he would not be able to come back so soon. Hark! was not that the sound of a bell--the bell on the horse that she herself had harnessed? She jumped up, startled. Surely he would not turn back on account of the storm without effecting his purpose?

She pressed both hands against her throbbing heart and listened. Then she smiled reassuringly. Ah, that was no bell outside, that was here--here, in both ears! Now it began to ring violently. All at once her face was suffused with a burning blush, and she had to hold her head with both hands in order to support it. Oh, how frightened she felt. What had she done? What was she going to do?

She looked round the room with terror in her eyes; the silence, the emptiness now alarmed her. What was she to say when his son came back from the army? What was she to tell him about his father? Would he believe her? Wouldn't he point at her with his fingers and say, "She's done it"? Oh, what was the meaning of this great fear? Where did these thoughts come from all at once? She had never had them before.

Jumping up from her seat near the window she ran into the kitchen; the emptiness of the house tortured and tormented her to such a degree that she could not bear to be any longer in her husband's room. But the kitchen was also empty, the servant had not yet returned. Mrs. Tiralla cowered down near the fireplace, shivering with cold. How far could he be now? Could he be in Gnesen? Oh, no, the horse did not trot so quickly; still, it might be possible. Hadn't she given it sugar, and stroked and patted its head? It would be sure to trot well. And if he had already got to Gnesen, if he had already been to the chemist's, if he had even got the poison, the poison for the rats! Ah! She could not help it, she had to scream aloud with fear. What had she done?

"Alas, alas!" She buried her head in her hands and moaned. But she had done nothing so far, not committed any crime. Why was she so terrified?

But she was going to do it!

She rose from her prostrate position, and, with a confident gesture, stroked back the hair from her forehead. She was going to do it, for she had prayed for it. There was no going back, the saints had heard it. Had not the priest always told her in years gone by, when she was still a child, that what she asked for would be granted? Her prayer was now before the highest throne. There was nothing to be done, it was to be. If the saints had not wished it to be so her husband would not have gone to Gnesen, in spite of all her urging, in spite of all her caresses.

This assurance calmed her. She began to bustle about in the kitchen and look into all the corners to see if the maid had not again put something aside for one of her followers. She was such a flighty person. Indeed, if she had not looked upon it as the duty of a Christian not to thrust the girl back into the misery from which Mr. Tiralla had rescued her, she ought to be turned out of the house--the sooner the better. She had still not had enough, even with those two brats. It was really a disgrace to have such a person in the house.

All the same, Mrs. Tiralla was glad, and gave a sigh of relief when Marianna came into the kitchen with her basket full of potatoes. She was happy at the thought of no longer being alone in the empty house, and quite forgot to scold the maid when the midday bell rang and there were no potatoes boiling on the fire.

The servant had seen Mr. Tiralla drive off--he had gone to Gnesen, Jendrek had told her--why should she hurry then? She could easily manage the Pani. If she agreed to everything she said the Pani would be quiet and not scold. But why on earth was the Pani always talking about rats? The master was to fetch poison, she had made a point of it, for when had she ever been so tender to him before? Hadn't she, Marianna, overheard her yesterday at the door? Ay, how she had flattered him! She had purred like a cat when it curls itself up on your lap. Poison for rats! Alas!

When the maid had seen her master drive off that morning she felt as if she must call out to him, "Stop! Don't go!" But she had held her tongue; what business was it of hers? If he were such a fool, well, it would be his own fault. Then her flirtation with Jendrek had made her entirely forget her master, until it all occurred to her again when she saw her mistress in the kitchen.

"The master has gone out," said Mrs. Tiralla, and although Marianna did not question her, she added hastily--"gone to Gnesen." Then she said with a blush, which the lie brought to her cheeks, "He wants to look at some winter materials for a suit at Rosenthal's."

The maid still said nothing, only nodded and began quickly to peel the potatoes that were in the basket.

"He'll probably go to the chemist's as well to fetch some poison for the rats."

She could not help it, the words were forced out against her will. She had to say it. The maid's silence brought them out. Why was she so quiet? What was she thinking of? Mrs. Tiralla was seized with a fit of trembling.

The maid raised her head. "Then Pani must be very pleased." Then she sighed and lowered her head again. "Poor master!"

"Why, what do you mean? 'Poor master!' Why do you say that?" Mrs. Tiralla trembled more and more.

"Well, isn't it 'poor master' to have to drive out in such awful weather? Who knows when poor master will be back again?" Marianna smiled.

Was it a malicious or a harmless smile? Mrs. Tiralla racked her brains to find out. Oh, she was quite harmless.

Still, she could not rid herself of the fear which had taken possession of her. She would have to take care how she behaved to the maid. Even if her flightiness were ever so objectionable to her, she would have to keep on good terms with her. So whilst the maid stood stirring something on the fire, in deep silence, Mrs. Tiralla went into her bedroom and brought out a gay-coloured Scotch shawl, which she had been fond of throwing over her own shoulders. "There," she said, putting it on the girl, who was still standing in the same place near the fire, "it's cold, and I see you've nothing to warm you."

"*Padam da nog!*" Marianna turned round as quick as lightning, and, stooping down, kissed her mistress's knee. "Oh, what a fine shawl, *what* a fine shawl! May the saints reward Pani for it. May they bless her to the end of her days." Then, kissing the shawl, she danced round the kitchen with it. "How it suits me! Oh, and it's so nice and so warm! Oh, and so gay!" She laid her finger on the gay colours and was as happy as a child.

"Oh, no, she had nothing to fear from her!" All at once Mrs. Tiràlla recovered her spirits. She was still young enough to understand the poor girl's delight at her gay shawl, and she laughed to see her joy.

'Mid laughing and joking the two women prepared the dinner.

When Rosa came home from school late, and very tired and worn out with wading through the snow, her mother, who was in a good humour, gave the hungry child a treat--a golden coloured omelette with raspberry jam. Then the two women made a strong cup of coffee for themselves and put one aside for Mr. Tiralla as well, and warmed his bed with hot bricks. He was to have a warm bed after his long drive.

CHAPTER III

Röschen--she had been christened Rosa, but he always called her Röschen--was her father's favourite child, and his exact image, as Mrs. Tiralla used to say in a peculiar tone of voice. Yes, the girl had the same blue eyes as her father, although they were not so pale and watery as his, and the same coloured hair, for his must also have had a reddish tinge before it became grey. And that was why Mrs. Tiralla so often turned away when the child had wanted to get on her lap and, with clumsy little fingers, stroke her cheek.

However, Mrs. Tiralla was in a more affectionate mood to-night. The little girl looked up in astonishment when she felt a soft hand on her head; but then she clung to her mother, and her dull eyes gleamed with joy and gratitude.

Mr. Tiralla had come back from Gnesen, and it seemed to the woman as if a star were now standing over the house, showing her distinctly the way she was to go. She felt happier than she had been for a long time.

Her husband had handed her the packet from the chemist's as if it had been a box of sweets he sometimes brought her from town. It was nicely done up in striped tissue paper with a piece of red string round it. But, on taking off the string, she had caught sight of a grinning death's head and cross-bones on the lid, and had read the word "Poison." She had screamed and let the box fall on the table.

"There, you see, now you're afraid of it as well," said Mr. Tiralla.

How little he knew her. She and fear?

"How am I to prepare it? How am I to prepare it?" she cried in an eager voice.

He showed her how. He felt very important, for the chemist had warned him to be exceedingly careful. He would not have given such a thing to anybody else but the well-known Mr. Tiralla, the man had said, not even if they had brought a paper from the doctor. She was to strew some of the white powder, which looked as harmless as sifted sugar, on a small piece of raw meat; and put it in the corners. There would be no rats left in the cellar then. Or she could strew some of the wheat which was in the paper bag, and which you could hardly distinguish from ordinary wheat, as it only looked a little redder.

"But I implore you to be careful, my dove. Swear that you'll be very careful, Sophia." Mr. Tiralla was seized with a sudden fear, and wiped the perspiration from his forehead. He felt burning, although the cold snow still clung to his fur collar and cap. He took oft his top-coat and stretched his limbs as though he felt oppressed, whilst she stood motionless at the table and stared at the packet with gleaming eyes.

"Which is the most efficacious?" she asked in a dreamy voice, "the powder or the wheat?"

"They're both equally efficacious," he assured her uneasily. "The wheat is bad enough, but you've only to swallow a little of that white stuff--oh, you needn't even swallow it, hardly touch it with the tip of your tongue, and you're done for. It's a deadly poison--strychnine." He shuddered. "Oh, how could I bring such a thing home with me? I am possessed by the devil. Give me it!" He snatched the packet out of her hands and ran to the stove, in which big logs of wood were crackling and spluttering.

"Are you mad?" She saw what he was going to do--he intended burning it. She was at his side in one bound, and, tearing the packet out of his hand, she hid it in her pocket.

"Give me it, give me it!" he cried.

She laughed at him and pressed her hand tightly against her pocket.

Then he began to wail and lament. Alas, alas, what had he done? How could he ever have been so foolish as to bring such a thing into the house? He would never have another peaceful hour, he would always be thinking that an accident might happen.

"But why," she asked in a calm voice, looking at him fixedly with her black eyes, "should an accident happen?"

"Alas, alas!" he moaned, and buried his head in his hands.

She had to comfort him. Her words calmed him; he was like a child. Then he asked her to stroke him; she did that also. At last he wanted to be helped to bed; he must have been drinking, although he denied it. The maid had to come as well; and whilst she took off his riding-boots he put his heavy head on his wife's shoulder, and she had to hold him in her arms.

When they had got him to bed they both looked very hot and flushed, for he had been pinching them in fun and had pretended to be quite helpless.

Then he sent for Röschen, whom he had not seen the whole day, for she was already on her way to school when he was still snoring in bed, and when he drove to Gnesen she had not yet returned. And now he longed for some one to fondle him. And the little girl knew very well what her father wanted; so she climbed up on his bed and laid her thin little arms round his neck and pressed her cool cheek to his. Then he talked to her in whispers and called her by an the pet names he could think of. She was his little red-haired girlie, his star, his song-bird, the apple of his eye, his sun, his balm of Gilead, his guardian angel, the key which was to open the door of heaven for him. And the child smiled and stroked him with her soft hands. She loved him so. He gave her everything her mother would not give her.

Still, she loved her mother in secret. Didn't everybody call her "the beautiful Mrs. Tiralla"? Didn't the schoolmaster, who was always so harsh, often send a message to her mother, and even pardon her faults and favour her just because she was the daughter of the beautiful Mrs. Tiralla? Rosa knew that she was not pretty; at least, she did not consider herself so when she plaited her curly, reddish hair before the looking-glass. Her mother's hair was as black as ebony and as smooth as silk, and her yellowish complexion and the tinge of red in her cheeks seemed twice as beautiful as her own freckles.

The growing child longed to be beautiful, although she did not exactly know why; and it disheartened and depressed her that she did not grow better-looking, in spite of all her fervent prayers. She used to kneel down at her bedside every evening in the little room she shared with Marianna and raise her hands in earnest supplication. She did not even know herself what all the things were which she prayed for.

Marianna was also a devout Christian, and, when they both lay in their beds, she would tell the listening child all about signs and wonders, about spells and miraculous cures, and about the strange things that happened in the neighbourhood.

Hadn't farmer Kiebel heard the sound of a horn behind him in the wood not far from the new Jewish cemetery when he was driving back from Wronke to Obersitzko after the last fair! "Toot, toot, toot!" He had got down and had drawn lots of crosses in the snow with his whip in front of the trembling horses and all around the cart; and then the black huntsman had rushed past him with horns blowing, dogs barking, and making a fearful noise. His cloak had flapped so much that it had almost blown Pan Kiebel down from his cart; but the crosses in the snow had protected the pious man, and the black huntsman had had to ride on.

And there was a mountain at Ossówiec, where the witches had met last June, and where they would soon meet again in December, in order to deliberate where they should go in the shape of dust and wind. But if you painted "C.M.B.," the initials of the three Kings of the East, on all the doors and walls, no witch would be able to get in and throw something into your plate. Or you need only say to yourself, "God bless it," before you began to eat or drink, and then no witchcraft could harm your food, for the saints would hold their hands stretched out over the plate.

Those who regularly prayed to the Holy Mother or to the saints had no need to fear the devil, who, four weeks ago, had come to miller Kierski at midnight--the man who lived at Latalice, north of Gradewitz, and was always swearing and drinking--and had almost wrung his neck off. He had been left on the dunghill behind his barn, where he lay quite stiff and blue in the face; and if St. Peter's cock had not flown on to the roof of the mill and crowed three times, so that the devil thought it was the miller's cock crowing in the early morning, the miller would have been found as dead as a door-nail, with his face turned round to his back; and his soul would already have been in hell.

Marianna firmly believed that ghosts were screaming in the pines outside, and that witches were dancing in the wind that howled round the farm; but above all she believed that the devil was running about on the Przykop like a will-o'-the-wisp, and was longing to get into the house, in order to fetch a soul to hell.

But even if she had not so firmly believed it, it would have amused her to whisper all kinds of strange stories to the trembling child, who had long ago crept into her bed and was clinging to her. Her stories became more and more marvellous, more and more weird. The night time, the moaning of the wind, the plaintive cry of the screech-owls perched in the old pines in the morass; above all, the darkness of the room, the deep silence, the loneliness, gave wings to the maid's fancy. Everything became instinct with life: a creature sighed in every tree, a voice spoke from every stone, something gasped for air under every clod of earth, something lurked in every pool. The branches that tapped against the window-panes were the fingers of the dead, the stars that shot across the heavens were wandering souls, and the clouds and winds were full of prophecies.

Once when she was a child, Marianna told Rosa, she had run in amongst some corn in order to pluck some ears and make herself a wreath of the red poppies. And there she had been seized by the "Zagak," a big man with a cudgel in his hand and a hat full of holes on his head, and with shoes through which all his toes were peeping. If a cart with creaking wheels had not happened to drive past at that moment, in which a farmer was sitting, singing a hymn, the "Zagak" would not have let her go. But she got off that time with a fright and a torn skirt. She still shook when she thought of the "Zagak"--ugh! How fortunate it was that he could not get at her here in her warm bed. The woman shuddered voluptuously, and she and the child clung still more closely to each other.

Then Röschen's little fingers clutched hold of Marianna's coarse ones, and both began to pray with all their might. What else could they do in the solitude and darkness of the night, surrounded by evil spirits that crept out of every corner, even out of the human breast? Prayer alone saved. And they prayed and prayed.

Big drops of perspiration and tears rolled down Röschen's delicate little face and her limbs trembled.

Oh, if only the Holy Virgin would come and take her under her blue mantle. She was so terrified and in such pain. Her head ached; her back and her chest as well; her throat was so swollen that she could hardly swallow; her eyes burned as if with fever.

"Holy Mother!" The child could hardly look over the feather-bed, as she tried to pierce the darkness with her terrified eyes, so high had it been drawn up. "All good spirits praise God! Dear Holy Mother, hail, Mary!" Oh, there she was, there she stood in the darkness and nodded to her.

The darkness was no longer dark, the tapping of the fingers against the window-panes and the soughing of the wind round the house had all at once lost their terror. Oh, how sweet the Holy Mother looked, how mild, and so beautiful. She took the terrified child under her protection and smiled at her, until her burning eyes dosed, until a glorious dream came to her in her slumbers and filled her soul with a sweet terror.

Was it any wonder, then, that Rosa Tiralla should cease petting her father when he suddenly began to moan and cry out, "Oh, what have I done? Oh, how terrified I am! I shall never have a quiet hour again. The devil has a hand in such a game!" and should say to him in a very earnest voice, "Why are you so terrified? Call on the Holy Mother; she wears a blue mantle, and she will wrap you in it. I'm often terrified, but then my fear disappears. Shall I call on her?"

"Yes, oh, yes." At any other time Mr. Tiralla would have burst out laughing, but to-day he nodded eagerly. And then he whispered in the child's ear, but so softly that his Sophia, who stood listening near the table as if ready to pounce on them, could not hear a single word. "I'm so terrified, I don't know why. Pray, pray."

Rosa slid down from the bed, and, kneeling on the skin rug, pressed her folded hands against her pale lips. She prayed fervently. They were the same old prayers which had been repeated mechanically so many times before; but they gained solemnity in the child's mouth. Her thin voice sounded deeper and more sonorous; the lamp-light shone on her reddish hair, that curled around her temples until it looked like a halo.

Mrs. Tiralla raised her head and glanced at her daughter; glanced at her and started, forgetting for a time the thoughts which had raged within her with such force that she had grown weak and incapable of making any resistance. Ah, yes, there was Rosa and there was Rosa's father. But Rosa was not the exact image of her father, all the same; she had also inherited something from her. Mrs. Tiralla suddenly felt twenty years younger as if by magic. She pictured herself in the priest's quiet study and heard once more the wonderful stories with which he had captivated her so irresistibly. She had always listened to him in silence, but she had grown hot and red. She still felt how the blood used to rush to her head as though she had been drinking wine.

Oh, yes, the girl must go to a convent, there was no doubt about that. They would cut off her curly hair, that gleamed in the lamplight, when she took the veil; the linen band would cover her brow and her cheek. Only her small nose and her blue eyes would be seen. Oh, how sweet Rosa would look in a nun's dress. She would blossom like a rose in the Saviour's garden. Mrs. Tiralla was seized with a sudden love for her daughter, and she went up to her and laid her hand on her head.

Rosa was very happy. Her mother had even kissed her when she had said good night, and she felt as if a flame of light had flashed through her. She did not care to hear any of Marianna's stories to-night, although she generally begged for some. "I only want to pray," she said. And she prayed that her mother might always smile at her. She admired her so, her slender figure, her beautiful hair, and her velvety eyes. Nobody was as beautiful as her mother, only the Holy Virgin.

Rosa's eyes closed whilst she was still praying, and in her slumber she suddenly saw the Holy Mother standing by her bedside. She had exactly the same face as her own mother and wore the same dress, a dark blue skirt and a bright red, striped blouse. And the Holy Mother bent over her, so that she felt her warm breath on her cheek; she was probably listening if she were asleep. Then the Holy Mother left her and listened at the bed where Marianna had been snoring for a long time; and then she went softly out of the room. Oh, how beautiful she was. The little girl fell soundly asleep with a prayer on her lips.

But Marianna was not asleep, even though she had pretended to be. What was her mistress doing, wandering about the house like that during the hours of the night? The country girl's hearing was as sharp as that of any denizen of the woods, and she could hear her going softly up and down the stairs and wandering restlessly through the rooms. Why wasn't the Pani asleep? And why had she come to their room? She must be up to something.

As soon as the child was fast asleep Marianna sat up in bed and placed her hand behind her ear. Now her mistress was in the kitchen. *Psia krew!* what was she rattling the coffee-mill for? Or was it the tin in which the sugar was kept?

"All good spirits!" The girl made the sign of the cross. Was the woman in league with the devil? The master had brought poison from Gnesen, poison for the rats. The servant's observant eyes had noticed the box on the table, the white box from the chemist's, with the black death's head on it. If now that woman downstairs were to put some of it in master's coffee or among the sifted sugar, of which he loved to pour half a basinful into his cup? Holy Mother!

The maid crouched down in her bed and drew the feather bed over her ears. She would neither see nor hear anything. What business was it of hers? The master was a kind man, but the mistress was really very kind too, and it was a difficult matter for such a poor servant-girl, who had already got two children on her hands, to side with either party. It would be much better to have nothing to do with the whole affair.

But in spite of putting both fingers in her ears, for the thick feather bed was not enough, she still heard her mistress wandering restlessly backwards and forwards. And that went on till dawn, and prevented her falling asleep. She generally snored the whole night through, but to-day she heard the cock crowing on the dunghill and the dull lowing of the cows before she closed her eyes.

She overslept herself. When she at last awoke from her uneasy slumbers she found Rosa standing before the little bit of looking-glass plaiting her hair, and from the yard came the clatter of wooden shoes and the rattle of the chain in the well as Jendrek drew up the bucket.

"Holy Mary!" cried Marianna, as she jumped out of bed. "Why didn't you wake me, you wretch?" she said to the child furiously.

"I was just--just going to do it," answered Rosa in a tone of excuse. As she stood there in her short petticoats and bare shoulders she looked very small and thin. "I was just going to shake you."

But you could see that Rosa had never thought of waking the servant, her thoughts were otherwise occupied. She was still dreaming with her eyes open. Oh, if only she could have told some one what she had dreamt--it had been so beautiful. The Holy Mother had let her hold the Child Jesus in her arms, and she had felt the soft, warm little body on her breast. How it had clung to her. Rosa smiled blissfully to herself as she looked in the tarnished bit of looking-glass, all stained with soap-suds.

Marianna ran down into the kitchen without washing herself or doing her hair. Oh, dear, there stood her mistress at the fireplace, her hair beautifully done and as neat as ever. Had she even made the coffee?

"The coffee is ready; you're so late," said Mrs. Tiralla. But she did not scold the servant for sleeping too long, she merely handed her the tray with the enormous coffee-cup on. "There, carry it in to him. I've already put sugar in it."

Marianna stared at her mistress in amazement. Her drowsiness suddenly disappeared; what she had thought of during the night suddenly occurred to her again. She stammered something and remained as if rooted to the spot, until her mistress said to her, laughing, "Take it to him. Why do you stand there like an idiot?"

No, it would be quite impossible for anybody to laugh like that who had put poison in the coffee. Marianna drew a breath of relief. But as she carried the tray across the stone passage she made the sign of the cross over it--"God bless it!"--as a kind of security. Now nothing could harm it. And as she smelt the warm, strong coffee, she could not help drinking some of it. She had had nothing to eat as yet, something warm would do her good. How strong the coffee was. It tasted quite bitter in spite of the sugar--pooh! But it was very good, all the same. She took another big gulp.

"*Psia krew*, you rascally woman! I suppose you're drinking some of my coffee, as I'm not getting it," shouted Mr. Tiralla from his bedroom. A boot, thrown by an expert hand, flew through the half-open door right against Marianna's apron. She gave a loud scream and let the tray fall; the sweetened coffee ran over her feet and along the stone passage.

"*Psia krew!*" A second boot came flying. The door was thrown wide open, and there was Mr. Tiralla sitting on the edge of his bed angling with his bare feet for his slippers, which had disappeared under the bed.

The maid stood on the threshold, soaked.

Mr. Tiralla burst into a loud laugh. "What a blockhead you are, to be sure!" he shouted, slapping his thighs. "Good heavens, was there ever such an idiotic person! Don't stare at me so stupidly. Come, come, you needn't begin to cry directly. Go and fetch some more coffee."

"The Pani will hit me," the girl sobbed. "I'm so frightened, so terribly frightened."

"Sophia," shouted Mr. Tiralla, who had had a very good night, "Sophia, this stupid girl has spilt the coffee; now don't hit her."

Mrs. Tiralla was already on the spot. She grew deadly pale and then burning red as she saw the sweetened coffee running along the ground like a brown stream.

The servant ducked down; now the mistress would be sure to hit her. But she did nothing of the sort. She did not even raise her hand in menace, she simply said, "It wasn't to be. Make him some more coffee." Then she fetched a cloth and wiped it up with her own hands, collected the broken bits of china, and said nothing more.

Marianna felt quite confused. She had never broken anything without being punished for it by her different mistresses. And to-day she hadn't even got a box on the ears nor been threatened with one. She went about like a dog on the scent; there was something wrong here. The place was haunted. She kept her eye on the mistress, but she was sitting in the room near the window reading. The master had gone into the fields to try to shoot a hare; and Rosa was at school. Oh, if only she had had a soul to speak to.

The maid felt oppressed, as though a very important secret were weighing her down. Besides, she really did feel as if she had a heavy weight on her chest. What could it be? She had to draw her breath the whole time, and she could not swallow; she felt as if she were choking. Oh, how terrified she was! And then she had such an awful thirst, her mouth was quite parched. She staggered to the bucket; she wanted to drink, but she could not. Holy Mother, why could she not swallow? All of a sudden she was seized with a fit of trembling, which grew so severe that she had to sit down on the floor just where she stood. Oh, how ill she felt. Her eyes grew dim, and she was bathed in perspiration. Now she could not breathe at all. She tried to scream, to cry for help; she could not do that either. She endeavoured to get up, but she was perfectly stiff; her head felt as if it were in splints. Her hands were clenched as though she were in a fit. Oh, God, have mercy! Was she going to die? How her limbs ached.

The maid lay there in a state of collapse, until she gradually recovered so far as to be able to rise, moaning and groaning, and stagger out of the kitchen into the yard. There she was very sick.

Jendrek came up to her and laughed as he saw her standing there. Ha-ha, had she been to a dance, unknown to everybody? But the harvest-homes were over, and Twelfth Day had not yet come round. "What had she been eating or drinking to make herself so ill?" he inquired in a scoffing tone.

She did not answer. All she could do was to raise her head a very little and give him a strange look.

He grew terrified when he saw how enormous the pupils of her eyes had become. Ugh! she did look awful. Instead of telling her how pleased he was to think that she for once in a way could sympathize with his feelings on a Monday morning, he grasped her by the arm and asked, "Is anything the matter? Tell me."

She groaned and gave a feeble nod. When he had asked her what she had been eating, the thought had pierced her stupefied brain that she must have been bewitched, that she must have eaten or dr----

"Poison, poison!" she suddenly shrieked, and throwing herself on the ground she rolled about and screamed, so that the man shrunk back in fright.

Mrs. Tiralla must also have heard the girl's shrieks, for she came out of the house at once. She ran up to the maid, but as the latter continued to scream "Poison, poison!" in a loud voice, and roll about as if she were mad, with her hands pressed against her body, the woman grew so deadly pale that Jendrek thought she would also fall down.

"Silence, silence!" she cried hastily, holding her hand before Marianna's mouth. But as the latter pushed her hand away and went on screaming, she looked round like a terrified animal at bay.

Jendrek felt quite anxious when he saw his mistress's eyes. "Shall I go to Gradewitz and fetch the doctor?" he asked timidly.

"No," cried the woman angrily. And then, rousing herself, she seized hold of his smock and cried, "Are you mad? She's only drunk, only drunk, nothing else."

"I'm not drunk!" screamed Marianna. Then she added in a furious voice, "That fool, that Jendrek, says I'm drunk; but let him sweep before his own door first. I've not drunk anything, not a drop, and that I'll swear." All at once Marianna recovered her voice. "That fool! It's poison that I've got in my body. I've been poisoned; I'm going to die--oh, oh!"

The man opened his eyes in amazement.

When Mrs. Tiralla noticed that he was listening intently to what Marianna was saying she grew as red as she before had been pale. Then, with a short, forced laugh, she said, "Nonsense. Poison? Where should you have got it from? You're raving, my girl. Come," she added, helping the girl to rise, "lean on my arm. You're already better, aren't you? I'll put you to bed. I'll make you a strong cup of tea. I'll give you a hot-water bottle. And then, when you're better, we'll see if one of my petticoats will fit you; you must be dressed more warmly." She felt the girl's thin skirt. "Why, she has nothing on. She must have caught cold. I'll take care of her. You are better now, aren't you? Holy Mother! Marianna, speak! You're better, aren't you?"

Marianna shook her head. She pretended to feel very wretched once more, and, rolling her eyes, she began to groan and lean so heavily against her mistress that they both stumbled.

Jendrek had to come to the rescue. They took the girl between them and dragged her into the house and up the stairs to bed.

When the man saw how kind his mistress was to Marianna, he stared at her in surprise. "What a good woman she must be," he thought to himself.

Whilst Mrs. Tiralla was rubbing the servant's icy-cold feet and hands she continued to repeat the same question, "You're better, aren't you?"

It touched Jendrek to see how anxious the good woman was. He thought that he would like to be ill as well; and he made up his mind that he would groan like that next Monday and scream, "Poison, poison!" and lie on the ground and roll about. It must be very nice to have your cheek and forehead stroked by the mistress's soft hands, as she was stroking Marianna's, and to see how she worried about you. And then she had run into the kitchen and brought her a cup full of good, warm tea, and had held it to her lips and said, "Drink, dear, drink."

But Marianna did not want to drink. She almost knocked the cup out of her mistress's hand. And when the latter tried to persuade her in her soft voice, "Do drink, it'll do you good," she answered pertly, "I'll take precious good care I don't. I shall not drink it," and turned her face to the wall.

Why on earth wouldn't she drink that good cup of tea? The man would very much have liked to know that.

But Mrs. Tiralla did not ask why. The cup rattled in her hand, and as she stepped back from the bed she trembled so that she had to sit down on the nearest chair. She closed her eyes for a moment. But when she opened them again and saw the man's questioning looks, she gave him a sweet, almost timid smile, and said, "I'm not very strong. Such things affect me so. Oh, what a fright it gave me."

As they were going down the steep, dark stairs, she felt for his arm. "Lead me, Jendrek, I can't walk alone. Oh, poor Marianna!"

CHAPTER IV

The winter was long in Starydwór, and the winter was the season of the year which Mrs. Tiralla liked least, for her husband would spend almost the whole day at home. He grew more and more lazy; he would not even go out shooting. "Why should I shoot hares?" he would say. "I can buy them very cheaply; any 'komornik' will kill one for me. I would much rather stop at home with Sophia."

Beautiful Mrs. Tiralla had grown thin during the course of the winter, "as slender as a fairy," said Mr. Schmielke, the tax-collector. The gentry used to meet at the inn every evening and discuss the most important events of the day; and as nothing much happened in Starawieś, Gradewitz, and neighbourhood, they would speak of Mrs. Tiralla. This they did rather often, for the men considered her the most interesting topic of conversation in Starawieś, Gradewitz, and the neighbourhood.

"By Jove, how beautiful that woman is!" some one would exclaim; and then another would add, "What a pity that that old fool has got her."

"There's nothing to be done," sighed the tax-collector, who had served in the guards at Potsdam, and had always been accustomed to carry everything before him on account of his smartness. "Absolutely nothing to be done, gentlemen. I've already had a try; but, to tell you the truth, she has sent me to the right about. Ah, the fair Sophia!" He stroked his moustache and tilted his chair as far back as he could, in order to look into the tap-room and wink at the clumsy little country-girl who was helping the landlord behind the bar.

Mr. Böhnke, the schoolmaster, was very much put out. There was this Prussian, who had fallen from the clouds into their loyal Polish district, and at once imagined that he could win the most beautiful woman for himself. But such a rose was not meant for a fellow like him--a fellow with no education worth speaking of, for he had been nothing but a noncommissioned officer. "Pray don't speak so loudly. Don't shout out the names like that!" he exclaimed, jumping up from his seat and closing the door into the tap-room.

It vexed him to think that his pale face had grown scarlet. This Schmielke was certainly held in high esteem by everybody, and of course it would not be wise to quarrel with a representative of the Prussian Government. Still, it was very impertinent of him even to think of Mrs. Tiralla, of that educated woman, the daughter of a schoolmaster, extremely impertinent. Really, you couldn't help laughing at it. And he gave an angry laugh.

"You seem to be enjoying yourselves here," said a voice at that moment; and, looking round in surprise, the men caught sight of a head covered with a mass of white hair, that stood up like bristles round an angular forehead, and a pair of lovely brown eyes. It was the priest who had opened the door softly and had stuck his head in. "Let me see, who are you all? Mr. Böhnke, *dobri wieczor*." He nodded somewhat condescendingly to the schoolmaster who had jumped up from his chair, and then gave a very friendly nod to Mr. Schmielke, the tax-collector, who was leaning back in his tilted chair with two fingers thrust into the front of his uniform.

"How do?" said the tax-collector.

Ziëntek, who was a good Catholic, felt very much annoyed at his heretical friend Schmielke's off-hand behaviour. Ziëntek was a clerk at the post office in Gradewitz; but he enjoyed himself better in Starawieś, where he was not so well known, and often cycled over late in the evening. He had jumped up from his chair like the schoolmaster, although perhaps not quite so quickly, and had shaken hands with Father Szypulski, the priest.

Father Szypulski now stepped up to the table, for he saw that they were all good acquaintances, with whom he felt quite at home. He had been so lonely in his small study, where there was hardly room for so big and broad a man as he. He couldn't always be reading, and it was impossible to go to the neighbouring farmers for a game of cards, as the roads were at present in a frightful condition. He couldn't even get to his colleague in Gradewitz, which was only a few miles distant by the highroad. Besides, what would have been the good of it? They couldn't have gone to the hotel in the market-place, as there were always too many people about. Oh, there really were too many Germans amongst the settlers. And who would notice him going to the inn on such a snowy night if he took up his cassock? A few stupid peasants at the most, who would bend their heads so low when they greeted him as though their priest were a saint at least. And in the inn he would find human beings.

The priest no doubt felt that it was not quite the thing for him to sit in the inn, and that his superiors would have taken umbrage at it. But had he ever taken more than he could stand? So far nobody had ever seen him the worse for drink. He reviewed one colleague after another in his mind; where was there one who had not behaved like other men? And why had they sent him to such a remote post? so rural, so primitive. His scruples were gradually being lulled to sleep in the snowy winter days, that were not even brightened by a faint gleam of light--he hardly ever caught a glimpse of a paper, besides papers were pernicious reading--in that monotonous silence, that was not even enlivened by the whistle of an engine, for the railway was on the other side of Gradewitz.

"What are you talking about, gentlemen?" inquired the priest in an interested voice; and he was soon in the midst of the conversation about Mrs. Tiralla. He was her father confessor. "A good little woman, an exceedingly nice little woman," he said in a laudatory tone.

"I had a fearful to-do with Tiralla the other day, your reverence," said Kranz of the *gendarmerie*, who was sitting at the end of the table stroking his fierce-looking, greyish moustache. "I felt quite sorry for the woman. I had to speak. I didn't think it could be possible, but I was told of it, and I found out for myself that it was true--Tiralla lets the day-labourers kill hares for him. It makes no difference to him whether they're on other people's property or not. I taxed him with it, and he didn't even deny it, he simply laughed. But his wife turned as red as fire, she felt so ashamed of him. 'It's a disgrace!' she cried, and looked at me with eyes full of tears. And then she gave him a real, good scolding. 'Haven't I told you again and again that if you want to eat hares, you're to shoot them yourself? If you don't do so I'll throw them out of the kitchen next time you bring them, I swear I will.'"

"Bravo!" they all shouted. "Splendid!" There was only one more thing she ought to have done and that was soundly to box his ears, the scoundrel. They were so furious with him that they seemed entirely to forget that they lived in a country where hares are no man's property, so to speak, and are often killed by passers-by as they gambol about fearlessly in the immense, lonely fields that extend for miles.

The younger men's eyes sparkled as they listened. The tax-collector, the clerk from the post office, and the schoolmaster were none of them thirty. The forester, who was sitting next to the clerk from the post office, and Jokisch, the inspector of the settlement near the lake, could also be reckoned amongst her admirers, although they were married men; and the gendarme was still a good-looking fellow, in spite of his greyish moustache and an almost grown-up daughter.

"I knew all about those hares," said Bilkowski, the forester, laughing.

"You knew it?" The gendarme opened his eyes wide.

"Oh, I say, don't look like that. If I were to publish everything that happens here," and the forester shrugged his shoulders, "I should never get any further."

"But a man ought to--it's his duty--I'm obliged," and the gendarme, who had only been transferred to this post the spring before, pulled out an enormous note-book from his pocket with a determined look, and took out the pencil. "I always write everything down. Things were bad enough in Upper Silesia, but they seem to be worse here."

"Oh, you'll get used to them," said the forester reassuringly. "It's really very nice here. I shouldn't like to live anywhere else now. It was also rather difficult for me at first, and especially for my wife. She made enough fuss about it. But now I never hear anything more, and"--he paused for a moment, then added with a smile that was half embarrassed, half sly--"I only see what I want to see. What else is there for me to do? Am I to act in opposition to the nobility, who would continue to do exactly what they liked all the same, or am I to let the peasants kill me when they commit outrages in the royal woods? Of course I always go to the Przykop when I hear a shot; but if they don't shoot, if they only make use of their cudgels, what then?"

He was right. They all agreed that it was no easy matter to be a forester. Still the gendarme did not exactly approve of Mr. Bilkowski speaking so frankly. "But, my dear fellow," and Bilkowski patted him on the shoulder, "we're all in the same boat. Why shouldn't I speak frankly amongst friends?"

The priest cast a glance at the open door leading into the tap-room. Then he whispered to the schoolmaster, "Close it."

Böhnke hastened to comply with the hint.

"Do you think that the Tirallas would come to our Gardewitz ball?" asked the clerk from the post office, blushing like a young girl. "I'm getting it up, and if the Tirallas were coming I would arrange a cotillon with flowers. If we were to order them at a big shop in Posen we could get real ferns and wired flowers at sixpence a bouquet. Why, it would even be worth while writing to Berlin for them. If you want to give such a ball you must be prepared to spend something on it."

"When do you intend having it?" This was a matter that interested everybody, and the little man felt very important.

"On Shrove Tuesday, as usual. After that there's always such a long spell where there's nothing whatever to do. It'll be splendid, I can tell you, splendid! I hope Sophia Tiralla will come."

"Why shouldn't she, I should like to know?" Schmielke resolved at all events to secure her for the cotillon in good time, as that meant he would take her into supper as well.

They all had the same intention, and all had made up their minds to call on the Tirallas at the earliest opportunity. It was quite a different kind of thing to clasp a woman like that in your arms instead of Miss Stumpf, the baker's daughter, who was both clumsy and stout; or the stupid, snub-nosed Miss Musiëlak, the stationmaster's daughter; or even Miss Stanislawa, who was rather pretty, but whose father, Count Jagodziúski, was the town clerk, and was always borrowing money from them all. Could even little Jadwiga Hähnel, with the freckles, the rich mill-owner's only unmarried daughter, or the fair Marianna Rózycki, the butcher's daughter, who, after the first glass of beer, always fell violently in love with her partner, could they be compared with Sophia Tiralla? All the young ladies of Gradewitz, Starawieś, and neighbourhood were in turn reviewed, but the prize was unanimously bestowed on the fair Sophia.

"A pretty little woman, to be sure," said the priest.

"Have you noticed that as well, sir?" asked Schmielke pertly, with a sly wink.

The schoolmaster started angrily, another impertinence from that man. Even Ziëntek gave an embarrassed little cough; really, how could Fritz say such a thing?

But the priest did not appear to have taken it amiss, and laughed when he saw Schmielke wink. Why shouldn't he see it as well as the others? Did he think he was blind? He was fortunately still in possession of his eyesight, and there could surely be nothing wrong in his admiring a pretty creature.

The schoolmaster listened in amazement to this free and easy confession. How could his reverence say such things aloud? And in Schmielke's presence too, that heretic. It would of course be at once repeated and turned to account.

The others, however, were very much amused by the confession, and shouted and laughed loudly. Jokisch, the inspector, who had hitherto hardly opened his mouth--he had been too busy drinking--now raised his glass. "Long live our priest. We've the best in the whole kingdom. Let him live and let live."

They all clinked with the priest, and Jokisch was even so impertinent as to slap him on the shoulder as he said, "What a pity, sir, that you can't go to the ball."

"Do you think I couldn't dance, eh?" said the priest, eyeing his long boots, which resembled those of an officer in a cavalry regiment. "You needn't fear that I should be out of place there. What a pity"--he gave a little sigh--"but it would never do."

"Why not, I should like to know?" asked Schmielke, and laughed. "The youth does not know the reason why."

"Those are some fine ideas you've got," the schoolmaster blurted out. He had worked himself into such a passion that he could not restrain himself any longer. "You Germans seem to have some nice ideas of us. But, of course, you're a heretic." It sounded very venomous. "It's quite possible that your clergy do such things." "Now, now," said the priest, giving the schoolmaster a sign to be quiet. He felt annoyed that the differences of religion and nationality should have been brought up. How stupid of this Böhnke to make such a to-do. They had to live together and get on with each other. The first in the land were striving to do the same. Hiding his momentary embarrassment under a jovial laugh, the priest broke the silence that now reigned in the room by saying in a loud voice:

"I would advise you to take a glass of bitters, Böhnke, or some Glauber-salt. That would do you good."

A roar of laughter greeted this witticism.

The schoolmaster turned pale and bit his lips, for he dared not say anything; but he looked down on them all with supreme contempt. How far superior he was to them in education--even superior to the priest, who was only a peasant's son, whilst his father had been a schoolmaster. He was to have studied philology and have been master of a higher-grade school. But even with the less advanced education he had received at the seminary, he still felt himself far superior to all of them. And this he thought he could say without putting too high a value on his own capabilities.

Böhnke always kept aloof from everybody; he had no friends, he was harsh to the children, and was often bad-tempered. Rosa Tiralla was the only child to whom he spoke kindly; but she was quite different to the other children, much better bred. You could see that she had a nice mother, who was of good family. The schoolmaster took an interest in this woman. But it was not only her beauty that attracted him, he also felt that they were kindred spirits on account of her parentage. He was filled with jealousy and anger when he heard those ill-bred fellows calling her "Sophia Tiralla," plain and simple Why couldn't they say "Mrs. Tiralla"? That would have been the proper thing for them to do. The schoolmaster continued to bite his lips and stare in front of him, pale and morose.

But a spark had fallen into the straw, and the former peaceful conversation was at an end. Jokisch and Schmielke suddenly commenced quarrelling. Jokisch, who had already drunk too much, began to speak disparagingly about Mrs. Tiralla. She was one of those whom you couldn't trust out of your sight. He felt quite sorry for Tiralla, who wasn't a bad fellow, but imposed upon, imposed upon. "My wife says----"

"Tut, tut, your wife's jealous," said Schmielke teasingly, and laughed. "Naturally it can't be agreeable for her to have the fair Sophia as her nearest neighbour."

"What do you mean?" roared the man. "I suppose you mean to infer that I've been carrying on with her. I've not had anything to do with her; I wouldn't touch her with a pair of tongs." He grew more and more furious.

"H'm, your wife has taught you well, I see," remarked the tax-collector superciliously.

"Taught me--taught me? I've finished my training long ago," roared the inspector. "I needn't learn any more. I was inspector for five years at Count Bninski's, in Opalenitza; I needn't learn any more for your rotten Prussian crown land, especially in *that* neighbourhood"--he spat on the floor--"in *that*----"

A blow closed his mouth. The schoolmaster had jumped up from his seat; all his vaunted culture had disappeared. "Hold your tongue!" he shouted, facing the tipsy inspector like a turkey-cock that has been infuriated by a piece of red cloth. He was a delicate-looking fellow, a mere stripling compared with the broad-shouldered inspector, but there was a dangerous gleam in his eyes.

Jokisch had, indeed, gone too far. "*Psia krew!*" cried the priest, without knowing what he said, whilst the others shouted in the wildest confusion, "Prove it, prove it!" He was to prove that he had the right to say such things about Sophia Tiralla. They were all simply burning with curiosity. What did he know of her, what, what? That anybody knew such things about her only added to her charm and piquancy in their eyes.

"Well, fire away," said Schmielke in a jovial voice.

The priest also smiled. He had often before listened to two men quarrelling, for he knew very well that they would in the end always bow to his judgment, although the matter was no concern of his.

"I don't know anything," said Jokisch, all at once quite sober. Oh, what a fool he had been, suddenly flashed through his mind. If he now said something about her, wouldn't they all believe that he had burnt his fingers? So far nobody knew that he had tried to kiss her in the dark stone passage at Starydwór a short time ago, and that she had given him a sound box on the ears for it. He therefore entrenched himself behind his wife. "My wife says she's a very bad housekeeper. My wife says she's very unkind to her husband. She sleeps alone in her own room."

"Alone? I say, really?" They were all delighted to hear it, and their eyes again began to sparkle. And no wonder, he was such a horrid old fellow.

"My wife says she would like to poison him, judging from the way she looks at him." That was his highest trump card, but even that did not seem to excite any indignation, for every one present was busily occupied in devising a plan by which he could curry favour with the fair Sophia.

But the priest smiled. "You're biassed, Mr. Jokisch, biassed. There's nothing wrong with Mrs. Tiralla."

"She's a good woman, a really good woman," agreed the gendarme. "I came past the farm the other day on my way from the Przykop, and found the servant lounging at the gate--Marianna Šroka, from Althof, you know, a buxom lass, but awfully cheeky. 'Panje,' said she in a low voice, and crept close up to me, 'Panje, there's murder in that house.' She pointed to the Tirallas' house and made such eyes, she looked quite mad. She wouldn't let me go. Then I got curious, and felt I must go into the house. The woman came out of the room at once. 'Where's Mr. Tiralla?' I asked, and at the same moment I heard a voice saying, 'Who is it, Sophia darling? Come in, come in, it's very comfortable here.' He was in high spirits, and we were all very happy together, although Marianna kept rolling her eyes about and winking at me quite openly as if to say, 'Take care!' What a horrid person she is, a real serpent. And Mrs. Tiralla is just like her husband, and continues to warm such a creature at her bosom. She's a good mistress, you can take my word for that. 'Please,' she said, and 'Thank you,' when Marianna brought something up from the cellar. But that's just like that kind of person. She's as comfortable with them as she can possibly be anywhere, and still she abuses them. I said to Mrs. Tiralla, 'How do you like your servant?'--I wanted to introduce the subject, but she answered, 'Oh, she's very good, very good,' and praised her highly."

"A very nice feature," remarked the priest.

Everybody was filled with indignation against Jokisch. How dared he say a single word against Mrs. Tiralla, even when he was drunk? The schoolmaster had been quite right this time. Jokisch was to keep a civil tongue in his head. He was a henpecked husband, a tattler. All the bachelors jeered at the inspector. Little Zientek poured the dregs from his tumbler over his head, and when he resisted, and snorted and swore loudly as he hit about him, they drew the chair from under him, so that he sat down on the floor on which everybody had been spitting. On any other occasion the gendarme would have separated the men, but now he looked on with the utmost calm. It served the man quite right. The priest had at first watched the proceedings very doubtfully, and had kept an eye on the door to see if anybody were spying upon them. But when the others took their tumblers, and, following Ziëntek's example, poured the dregs over the man's head, he almost split his sides with laughing.

He saw, however, that it was about time for him to be going, so he got up from his seat and disappeared as quietly as he had come; and the men were laughing, quarrelling, and shouting so loudly that they hardly noticed his departure.

The schoolmaster felt like a hero, as he tramped home through the snow. He was her knight; he had just paid that vulgar, disgusting fellow out. Jokisch had received the first and last kick from him as they all together had conveyed the heavy man to the door. "Throw him out, that slanderer!" This time they had all made common cause, all except the gendarme, who had retired at the very last moment. He always did so when there was any quarrelling going on in the private room at the inn, otherwise he would have been obliged to write down the names of these disturbers of the peace.

The stars shone down on the schoolmaster as he walked home all alone; the cold wintry sky looked like a huge glass bell that had been put over the flat country. The stars gave light; he could easily discern the empty village street, which was as wide as the widest street in a big town--so wide that it made the low cottages on either side look twice as low as they really were. Böhnke stumbled along as though he were intoxicated. But that was not the case, for he never drank too much, whatever the others might do. He was tormented with an ambitious longing to win this woman. Mrs. Tiralla was always very kind to him; he thought he had noticed that she also looked upon him as a kindred spirit. To-morrow he would see little Rosa--that dreamy child who would sit with a vacant stare on her face and not know what the others had been talking about--and he would tell her to remember him very kindly to her mother, and to ask her if she wanted anything to read during these long winter days. She could take her choice among his books. He would gladly lend her them all, in spite of the many hardships he had had to undergo in order to procure them. She had certainly borrowed a volume from him almost three years ago; she had had it almost the whole time he had been in the neighbourhood, and he would probably never see it again. But he did not mind that. To-morrow he would again place his library at her disposal. The best thing would be to write her a note and give it to the child. He wrote a most beautiful hand, it looked like print. How the other people in this neighbourhood did scrawl!

The Gradewitz ball would cost him a lot of money, and he had hardly any. But what did that matter? He would go there, even if he had to borrow from the Jew. Happily there was always one thing he could do; if Isidor Prochownik dunned him, his daughter Rebecca should lose her place in the class--she should go down to the very bottom; but if the old man left him in peace Rebecca should have a very high place. He laughed to himself at the splendid idea. But then he turned scarlet, although there was nobody watching him, only the starry heavens above him, and around him the deserted, sleeping village. He was overcome with shame, for he felt that it was not right of him to move Rebecca up and down just to please himself. But then he stifled all qualms. What did it matter to that girl, who was so dirty, so stupid, so utterly neglected, even if she did go down to the bottom? It was of no importance to her. And he--he must go to the ball.

Böhnke dreamt that night of the beautiful Mrs. Tiralla. She wore a silk dress, and had given him a decoration in the cotillon. He stretched out an eager hand, and she pinned the gold paper-star on his breast. And then she clung to him, the silk dress gave way, and her white bosom opened like a book. "Read it," she said, smiling, "we two understand each other."

It was a confused dream, for then followed all kinds of nonsense which the young man could no longer remember when he awoke.

He went to school next morning feeling like a schoolboy who carries his first poem to his beloved one in his pocket, and is longing impatiently to give it to her. Although he had gone to bed very late the evening before, he had got up early and had twice written a note to Mrs. Tiralla. He had not been satisfied with it the first time, and had therefore written it again. Rosa was now to take it to her. But when he went into the schoolroom his eyes sought in vain for the pale, absent-looking face under the mass of curly hair. All the brown, snub-nosed, sly-looking faces were there, but Rosa Tiralla was wanting. This was a great disappointment. He was more harsh and impatient than ever that day; he required his questions to be answered at once, without any hesitation, otherwise he took the first book he could lay hands on and hurled it over the forms. He could scarcely contain himself, he felt so irritable. Why the deuce had that red-haired girl just stopped away that day?

As Rosa was again absent the next day and the day after that, and as none of the children could tell him the reason why, he came to a decision-- he would go to Starydwór. She must be ill. Would it not be the proper thing for him to make personal inquiries about his pupil?

The crows were cawing over his head as he endeavoured to find the path over the snow-clad fields. He could hardly see it, for there was only a very faint trace left of the cart that had taken the milk from Starydwór to Gradewitz early that morning. He shuddered as he wandered through the enormous white fields. It was true they were no more melancholy-looking at this time of the year than when full of turnips and ripe corn; but their uniform whiteness seemed to give them a larger and more desolate appearance. Even the hares, as they nibbled away at the few stalks that were left, and the birds of prey, as they lazily flapped their wings in the direction of the Przykop, did not enliven their desolation; for the sluggish inertness of their movements, which enabled passers-by to approach them quite closely, proved only too clearly how very rarely they were disturbed.

Was it because he was not warmly enough dressed that he trembled so? Böhnke put his hands to his face--ugh! how cold it was. His top-coat was certainly very thin, it was only meant for summer wear; but he really couldn't have put on that thick, rough coat he wore every day for school. He was wearing his best black coat and kid gloves; his fingers were quite numb. He would have liked to run, in order to get warm, but big lumps of snow clung to his boots like lumps of lead. When he came in sight of the trees in the low-lying Przykop, it was as though something were holding him back, and as though the wind were pushing him back so as to prevent him from going any further. And he was longing with all his heart to get to Starydwór as soon as possible.

To the left lay the settlement--the distillery chimney reared its head in the air like a big white asparagus--and there Jokisch lived. But he would not live there much longer. When the land had been parcelled out and the settlers had come, he would go. Thank God! Böhnke was filled with a vague jealousy; they were neighbours, he and she, and he considered every neighbour dangerous. Jokisch was certainly a fine-looking man, and Böhnke felt firmly convinced that he also found Mrs. Tiralla very fascinating, in spite of all he had said to the contrary, for who would not? Perhaps that was the very reason why he had been so angry with her.

Then the schoolmaster began to run. Who would hinder him in getting to Starydwór as quickly as possible? There it lay.

The old farm, which had been in the hands of the Tirallas for over a hundred years, had rather an imposing look in the distance. Not much was to be seen of the farmhouse itself--it was very low, as though sunk in the ground--but the barns and stables, all roofed with new, red tiles, formed a wall round the square courtyard in front of it, and the whole together constituted a very fine property. But what good was it to her if she didn't love her husband?

The young man cast one more look at his clothes, and then, after flipping the snow off his trousers, walked through the open gateway, over which was a figure of the Holy Virgin sitting on a throne, which was protected by a grating. A couple of dogs rushed at his legs and barked; but he was not a coward, although he was no giant, and a kick soon frightened the curs away. A man stood in the stable door watching the schoolmaster as he walked up to the farmhouse.

What did the Starawieś schoolmaster want? Ha, ha, was he also coming to kiss the mistress's hand? Somebody had already been there yesterday, and the day before yesterday as well. How they all ran after her. But they had no luck, thought Jendrek with a broad grin on his face. The Pani bestowed the kindest look on him, and she gave him bacon every day in the kitchen, and an extra glass of gin as well. God bless the good woman!

Böhnke stepped into the stone passage, but nobody came. He gave a loud cough; he had never been there before, and did not know where to knock. He scraped his feet, and as there was still no sign of anybody he called out in a polite voice, "May I come in? Hallo! is nobody at home?"

Then he heard Mr. Tiralla's voice coming from the room on the right, "Come in, come in, it's very comfortable here."

The schoolmaster knocked at the door.

"Confound you! Come in, I say."

Böhnke went in, but he at once drew back. Oh, he didn't wish to disturb. But still he stood as though rooted to the spot, and stared and stared. There was Mr. Tiralla lying all his length on the bench by the stove with his head resting on his wife's lap.

Mrs. Tiralla blushed crimson as their eyes met. Then she lowered hers, and jumped up so hastily that the heavy man on her lap was in danger of falling on the floor.

"*Psia krew!*" cried the man, and then he laughed. Surely she didn't feel shy, weren't they husband and wife?

She answered nothing, but she glanced at her husband with such an expression of disdain, and then looked so hopelessly out of the window, that Böhnke at once knew that she was unhappy, and that her husband did not understand her. And he felt his heart beat.

"Oh, it's you, Mr. Böhnke," she said in a friendly voice, and held out her hand. It felt like velvet as it lay in his, but it was as cold as ice. He ventured to press it slightly; but she did not return the pressure, she only gave him a sad look out of her splendid eyes and smiled a little. Oh, that poor woman!

How he would have liked to give that abominable fellow a blow as he lay on the bench.

Mr. Tiralla was in a very good humour. He shouted to Marianna to fetch beer and gin, and then told his wife to bring out some food. Böhnke will be hungry--such a schoolmaster is always hungry--bring what you can find: ham, eggs, cake, sausages, cheese, and what else you've got in the larder. "We've got plenty." Then, without rising from the bench, he seized hold of the schoolmaster with the words, "Take a seat, pray," and forced him down on the nearest chair in spite of his resistance. "We're pleased to give you it. *Psia krew*, only no excuses."

Böhnke had stammered something about not wishing to give trouble, about not being hungry, about going away immediately. But the farmer had given a boisterous laugh as usual, and had said that the schoolmaster had better tell that to the marines, for he didn't believe it. He had probably been brought up in the same way as his wife, eh? She had always worn shoes and stockings as a child, and had been as dainty-looking as a doll; but her little bread-basket had been as empty as a barn before harvest. She had been as thin as a church mouse in those days.

The schoolmaster saw Mrs. Tiralla give her husband a second look, but there was more than disdain in her look this time--something else gleamed in the depths of those dark eyes. Then she turned away and went out of the room without saying a word.

"Heigh, Sophia, be quick!" shouted the man after her.

And then he began singing her praises to the schoolmaster. Mr. Tiralla loved to have visitors; he was so delighted to have an opportunity of talking about his wife and his happiness to somebody. He bragged about everything, and dilated loquaciously upon matters that a husband does not generally mention to other men. His Sophia had a wonderful figure, a wonderful figure! As slender as a birch! And she was so dainty, slim in the waist and still rounded, broad across the hips, soft and warm like a partridge or like one of those little pigs made of marzipan, which Wolkowitz, in Posen, used to put in his window at Christmas time. And her bosom! Would you believe that---- Lowering his voice but very little he was about to confide some more intimate particulars to the young man. But the latter tore himself away from the hand that was pressing him down on the chair. He had been fidgeting about on his seat for some time, but now he felt he could stand it no longer. A burning blush suffused his face--was it from shame or desire? Oh, that woman, that poor woman, at the mercy of such a man! He was filled with an inexpressible repugnance for this stout, coarse old man, who literally undressed his wife in the presence of others. Could anybody blame her if she disliked him as much as Mrs. Jokisch had said?

The farmer had not noticed that the schoolmaster was struggling with his feelings. It had not even struck him that he was silent. He had found him a modest young man who did not talk much, and that was a good thing, because then he was listening. Mr. Tiralla was very pleased with his visitor.

Marianna appeared with three bottles of beer under each arm and a small tray with glasses in her hand. She looked hale and hearty, and there was no trace left of that fearful indisposition which had attacked her at the commencement of the winter. She scanned the visitor with sparkling, roguish eyes. Would he in time become the Pani's lover? It wouldn't surprise her if she got hold of one now. But this man--she made a grimace of disapproval--this man wasn't half good-looking enough. And he didn't seem very enterprising either, for he had never even glanced at her, although she had more than once touched him with her sleeve and had reached right over him in order to place the glasses and the six bottles on the table.

"That's enough for the present," said Mr. Tiralla. "But listen, girl," he added, pinching her in the thigh so that she screamed aloud, "go down to the cellar and fetch us another bottle of Tokay. And where's the gin? You must have a glass to begin with, little Böhnke, or you'll catch cold. Hallo, you little devil, why are you still there?" he roared at the maid, who stood smiling and showing all her teeth. "Can't you understand me? Do you think I'm speaking German? Isn't it Polish I'm speaking? She's very stupid," he said apologetically, as the girl left the room with a bold laugh, "but she's faithful--and she's pretty."

He said this with a smile which horrified the schoolmaster anew. Had it come to that? The man was not even faithful to her? Poor, poor thing! He had never felt so sorry for anybody in his life, and he was not soft-hearted as a rule. He longed for her return. She probably felt ashamed of what had happened, otherwise she would have returned long ago.

Mr. Tiralla was also growing impatient. The gin didn't taste half so good if his Sophia hadn't taken the first sip of it, and he didn't care for the beer at all. He shouted again for the maid, and when she came with the bottle of Tokay and a large tray of eatables he said to her angrily, "Put it down. Where's your mistress? *Psia krew*, what's become of her?"

Marianna shrugged her shoulders. "I don't know why the Pani doesn't come. *Gospodarz* must know best himself."

"Confound you! Call her. She is to come."

The maid disappeared. A few minutes later she stuck her head in at the door and said with a sad look, "Pani can't come, the Paninka is worse again; oh, she's very ill." Then she withdrew as quickly as possible.

The glass which Mr. Tiralla hurled after her only hit the door, and then broke into a thousand pieces.

The schoolmaster could not stand it any longer. What was the good of staying there? Of course, she wouldn't show herself any more. Such bad luck! Why on earth should that stupid, red-haired child just get worse now? Or was it only an excuse? Oh, of course, it was an excuse. She would be sitting upstairs in a corner, bowed down with shame and weeping, weeping so much that her beautiful figure--broad across the hips, a waist as slender as a birch, slim and still rounded--shook with it. Although the young fellow tried his utmost not to think of it, he could not help it; he saw her the whole time just as the old man had described her to him. He changed colour; one moment he felt hot, the next cold. Mr. Tiralla went on filling his glass with beer, gin, and Tokay, the one after the other, and he drank more than he was accustomed to in his absent-mindedness. He was thinking of nothing but her. He could not believe that he was to leave the house without seeing her once more. So he sat and sat, until the sky grew darker and darker and the early afternoon turned into pitch-dark night. At last he rose from his chair with despair in his heart. He had attained nothing of all he had meant to attain; he hadn't offered her any books, he hadn't secured her for a dance at the Gradewitz ball, he hadn't even inquired about the child, which had been his nominal reason for coming to Starydwór. He felt furious with Mr. Tiralla; he was to blame for everything. Then he bade him good night.

Mr. Tiralla did not accompany him to the door--little Böhnke would be able to find it alone--so he groped his way through the dark passage to the front door, reeling a little as he walked. Suddenly a warm hand grasped his, some one chuckled near him in the dark, and the servant's deep voice said half compassionately, half mockingly, "Did you find it slow with Pan Tiralla? I'm sorry. Pani is upstairs with little Rosa. If Pan Böhnke wants to say good night to her----" she pushed him in the direction of the stairs and disappeared in the dark, chuckling.

Like a gnome, he thought--oh, no, like an angel. He was seized with a superstitious terror. Everything seemed so strange; the old house, the chuckling maid, the loud-voiced man, the beautiful woman. He began cursing all the drink he had had and cursing Mr. Tiralla. Oh, if only he had been as sober and as clear-headed as he generally was.

The old staircase creaked under his feet. What would she say? Wouldn't she consider him intruding if he came up to her? But weren't those groans that he heard above the creaking of the stairs? That poor, beautiful woman! He must go to her. Where was she?

Now he was at the top. Hark, wasn't that the child's voice?

"Mother," he heard Rosa say, "sweet mother, I really did see her, you can believe me. She was as beautiful, as beautiful as you. She had hair like yours, when you undo your plaits. And she gave me the Child Jesus to hold. I love it, I love it!" She repeated that several times with great fervour.

What nonsense was the child talking? Of whom was she speaking? The schoolmaster drew nearer to the door. Ah--he gave a start--ah, now she, Mrs. Tiralla, was speaking. But he couldn't very well understand what she was saying, she spoke so softly. And now and then she seemed to be sobbing. He knocked at the door and walked in. Rosa was lying in bed and her mother was sitting on the bed near her. They both stared at him in astonishment, but when he said with a voice that hesitated at first, but then grew firmer, that he felt he couldn't leave without hearing how she was, the child looked pleased.

"I'm very well," she answered, with a shy smile. "Very well, thank you, Panje Böhnke."

"She's feverish," said her mother. "She fainted the day before yesterday; Marianna came rushing down to tell us. We shall have to send for the doctor if she doesn't get better."

"No, no," cried the child, sitting up in bed and looking as though she were going to cry. "I'm not ill, mother darling, I'm not ill." She threw her arms round her mother and pressed her head against her breast.

The schoolmaster stepped up to the bed and laid his hand on the child's head. No, *she* wasn't feverish, but he began to feel so as soon as he came near that beautiful woman. He busied himself with Rosa; what was the matter with her, wouldn't she soon come back to him?

Rosa nodded, and then raising her head from her mother's breast, she pushed her tangled hair away from her face, which looked dazzlingly white in spite of the freckles. Even Böhnke, in his agitation, noticed how bright her dull eyes had become.

"She dreams so much," said her mother sadly. "She frightens us by screaming aloud in her sleep. And she talks in her sleep as well; Marianna is really terrified. Oh, those awful dreams!" She sighed.

But the schoolmaster did not inquire any further into the matter. Little Rosa's dreams did not interest him in the slightest, all he wanted to do was to give Mrs. Tiralla a proof of his devotion.

"Would the Pani like to borrow some of my books?" he inquired. "I shall be very pleased to bring some." And then wishing to give her a hint of how he understood and pitied her, he took heart and added, "If people live such a lonely life as the Pani does, and are so un----" he wanted to say "unhappy," or "so little understood," but he faltered, and his veiled eyes looked longingly at her. He did not know how it was, but he always lost his self-possession when he was near her.

She must have understood him in spite of his faltering, for she sighed and said, "Ah, yes, Mr. Tiralla doesn't care much for reading. He eats, drinks, sleeps, and----" she also faltered and blushed. And then she gave him a long look out of her black eyes, so that his heart stood still. "I shall be very grateful to you if you'll lend me some books," she continued in a soft voice. "Mr. Tiralla doesn't like to spend money on them. Oh, I'm so fond of reading beautiful tales, sentimental ones."

The man was in the seventh heaven. So she wanted books? That meant that he would often have a chance of coming to see her. For he would take good care not to give Rosa the books; he would bring them himself, and never more than one at a time. "I'll bring you some," he said, overjoyed.

"Oh, not so loud, not so loud," begged Rosa, and her face was burning. She had fallen back on the pillow, her eyes were wide open, but she spoke as though in her sleep. "I hear her, sh, mother, sh!"

What did she hear? The two looked at each other, whilst the howling wind outside seemed to creep along the walls of the house like clinging fingers. Böhnke shook his head; the child was really very peculiar.

But Mrs. Tiralla gave a slight shudder, and, bending over her daughter's bed, she said in a strangely soft voice, "Go on listening, Rosa dear, go on listening." Then she grasped the schoolmaster's hand and drew him out of the room. "Come. She is already asleep."

They stood outside in the dark. A murmuring sound was heard from the bedroom, a few joyful exclamations and then Rosa's voice rose clear and triumphant. Böhnke was full of amazement; what was the meaning of it all?

Mrs. Tiralla, who was still holding his hand, now whispered to him, "I've no friend. I stand quite alone. I often wish I were dead."

The young man pressed his burning, eager lips to her sleeve. He felt almost stifled with emotion and stammered something hardly intelligible. He was her friend, her faithful, devoted friend. He had already once been her knight, but if she commanded, he would also be her dog. For ever and ever.

If the schoolmaster had hoped for a proof of her favour he was disappointed. She only pressed his hand, and oh, how icy-cold hers was, and how firm. Her dainty hand could press as firmly as any man's. "I rely upon you, Panje Böhnke," she whispered, and then, raising her voice, she added calmly and distinctly, "Don't fall. Here's the staircase, here."

Mr. Tiralla's powerful voice was heard downstairs. "Where are you, Sophia? Let the devil take hold of you by the tip of your shift. Why don't you come to me, my little dove, my darling?"

"Good night," she whispered hastily, once more pressing the schoolmaster's hand.

He stood alone in the silent courtyard; there was no light in the stables and sheds, the cattle made no sound. He felt oppressed. Did he dread the walk through the lonely fields? Oh, no, on the contrary he was able to breathe once more when he reached the open fields, and the howling wind threw a whole load of snow into his face and over his clothes. "Ah," he drew a long, trembling breath. But all at once he felt terrified. There came a long-drawn, shrill whistle from the Przykop, a quite peculiar whistle. No bird screamed like that, and no human being either. A shudder ran down his back; he was seized with a superstitious fear, which he could not shake off again in spite of his common sense and his education. That was the witch that whistled in the pitch-dark Przykop.

And he made the sign of the cross as the peasants do when they hear the witch whistling, and spat on the snow that gleamed in spite of the darkness. When that's done, the witch has lost her power and you need not follow her.

CHAPTER V

Rosa Tiralla had seen visions; but whether they were good or bad visions nobody knew. Marianna Śroka cried loudly when she brought the news to the village, and her lover, Jendrek, confirmed it with a nod. The Paninka had seen something, the Paninka was bewitched.

Mr. Tiralla was deeply grieved about his Röschen, as deeply grieved as he could possibly be about anything. He had already been looking out for a husband for his little daughter--she would be fourteen next autumn, and a wife cannot be too young-and now she seemed only fit for bed. The strong man had never suffered from nerves--didn't even know what they were--but all sorts of things happened nowadays to alarm him. Rosa was so irritable that she cried if anybody spoke crossly to her. The doctor advised them not to treat her harshly, for she cried so bitterly that she became quite hysterical. And after the attack was over she was so feeble that she could not move a limb, and looked exactly like somebody who was going to die; so that her father in his terror used to say, "yes," and "my angel," "everything you like, my angel."--nothing but "my angel."

And Röschen imagined that she was always surrounded by angels. She thought her father, Marianna, and Jendrek were angels, but especially she thought her mother one. Pan Böhnke was also an angel. He often came to see her, and then he and her dear mother would sit by her bedside and talk to each other, and their voices would sound so soft and low that her eyes would close, and she would fall into a sweet sleep.

Mrs. Tiralla had never imagined that she could feel so much love for her daughter. She was really fond of her now. Marianna would on no account sleep any longer in the same room as Rosa; she said that it was impossible to close an eye the whole night through, and if she worked so hard during the day she really must rest at night. The truth was that when Marianna stole out of bed in order to go to her lover, the child would sit up in bed and call out, "Where are you going, Marianna?" and there was such a strange note of reproach and admonition in her voice, that the girl shuddered and did not venture to go to Jendrek. How had the child found it out?

So Mrs. Tiralla had her bed brought up to her daughter's room. Her husband cursed and raged, for hitherto he had at least had his wife next to him on the same floor. But she insisted upon having her own way. She said that Röschen wanted care, and mustn't sleep alone. And he saw that she was right.

At night, when the house was so quiet that the ticking of the big clock sounded like peals of thunder and her husband's snores like a saw-mill hard at work, Mrs. Tiralla would sit by her child's bed. She would hold her hand--a small, narrow, delicate-looking hand with blue veins--and they would whisper together about the joys of Paradise. Whilst all around was joyless--the dark night, the lonely farm buried in deep snow, the solitude in which a soul so often gets lost--those two would whisper together about the joys of Paradise--about nothing else.

The heavenly world in which Mrs. Tiralla had also lived as a child had once more drawn near to her by means of Rosa. She could very well understand what occupied the child's thoughts to the exclusion of everything else. And that was right, for she was to be a saint. Was she not almost one now? There was a rapt expression in Rosa's eyes, when she used to tell her mother about what she had seen, about the Holy Mother and the Child Jesus, and about her beautiful, beautiful guardian angel who always sat at her bedside when she was asleep. A short time before, she had suddenly awaked in the night, but had been too tired to open her eyes properly, and she had found the angel bending over her--such a beautiful angel in a long white garment.

Mrs. Tiralla knew all about it. It had been she, and the white garment was her nightdress, which was long and fine, like those worn by smart ladies. But she let the child remain in her belief. Why undeceive her? And after that she used to creep every night to Rosa's bed and disturb her sleep by laying her hand on her head and bending over her as if she were her guardian angel, to the child's and her own great delight. She loved doing it. She even practised her part, so that she grew more and more proficient in it every night.

In the daytime, Mrs. Tiralla would rummage in her drawers and show Rosa the things she had possessed as a child, precious relics which she devoutly kissed. These were consecrated beads, a consecrated palm branch, a little white china angel, a vessel for holy water and many gaudy pictures of saints, which her priest had once given her. Then she would relate something about each of these treasures as they lay on the child's bed. She would speak in a low, monotonous whisper, as though praying and with a dreamy smile on her face, and would gradually work herself up into such a state of eagerness and excitement that her radiant eyes would become veiled, and, bursting into tears, she would sink down on the child's bed. Then mother and daughter would weep in each other's arms.

Rosa's tears were tears of ecstatic rapture and longing, of a great longing for something she could not name--the dear Virgin, the dear little Child Jesus, the dear guardian angel and all the dear saints. She knew them all; she knew the history of every martyr that now wore a halo. Her mother had read about them aloud to her again and again from the book of holy legends that she had brought out of the gaily painted chest in which she, as a girl, had kept her belongings.

How splendid it must be to live like those holy women. If you were like St. Julia or St. Helena, or even St. Agnes, you would get leave to nurse the Child Jesus in Paradise, and rock it and sing it to sleep with hallelujah.

When Rosa was all alone she would try to sing the heavenly lullaby; she would try to take the highest notes with her small, weak voice, and make them sound soft and harmonious instead of shrill and piping.

Then the servants in the yard used to say, "St. Panusia is singing," and they would listen devoutly to the long-drawn song, sounding like a chant, that came from Rosa's bedroom.

But Rosa never felt quite satisfied with her lullaby, and often burst into tears. It must be because she didn't pray fervently enough, because she was far from being good and pure enough. So she wrote down all her sins on a piece of paper in her stiff, uneven handwriting, that she might not forget any of them--there was a long row of them--and she made up her mind to confess them all and get forgiveness for them as soon as the snow was so far melted that she could go to the priest.

She did not attend school at present, not being strong enough to walk all the way from Starydwór to Starawieś.

Mr. and Mrs. Tiralla were preparing to go to the Gradewitz ball in spite of the snow and the bad roads. They hoped they would be able to get through all right. Mr. Tiralla could never have brought himself to let an opportunity pass of gloating over the many eager eyes that would watch his wife in the mazes of the dance, whilst he sat comfortably in the corner of the ballroom with his glass and his cards.

Mrs. Tiralla was a very good dancer, and her heart beat as she unpacked the ball-dress her husband had ordered for her from a fashionable dressmaker in Posen. She could very well have worn her blue silk again if the rats had not been nibbling it! However, this filmy white gauze, with its long flowing sash and a small bouquet of artificial roses for the bodice and another for the hair, was certainly much prettier; there was an underskirt of silk, too, which rustled and swished every time she moved.

Mrs. Tiralla was dressing in the large sitting-room on the ground floor. The bedroom upstairs was too cold, so Marianna had brought the looking-glass down and had fixed it up on a table by means of some pieces of wood, and placed two lighted candles in front of it. Mrs. Tiralla was doing her own hair. The Gradewitz dressmaker would have been asked to do it, as she was also the hairdresser of the neighbourhood, but she had taken offence when she heard that Mrs. Tiralla had got her ball-dress from Posen.

Mrs. Tiralla did not crimp her hair as a rule, but to-day she got a waving-iron, and she and Marianna did it together. The maid was by no means clumsy, although she had such big hands, and she helped her mistress to pile up her wavy hair at the top of her head. But when at last it was ready, Mrs. Tiralla thought it so hideous, that she burst into tears and tore it down with an angry *"Psia krew!"* which made Rosa shrink. The child was crouching in a dark corner of the room with her hands clasped round her knees, gazing with admiration at the beautiful vision in the white embroidered petticoat.

Ugh! how difficult it was to please the mistress this evening; now she wanted this, now that. If Marianna had not consoled herself with the thought that she would soon be mistress of the house for a whole night, she would have cried instead of laughing pleasantly as she was doing now. "Pani must do her hair in her usual way," she said. "That suits Pani best of all."

"She is right," sighed Mrs. Tiralla, as she began once more to comb out her tangled hair, and she tore at it so savagely that at last her silky, black tresses clung to her white temples in big, smooth waves. Then she twisted the plaits in a huge coil at the nape of her neck; that was the way she had worn her hair in her girlhood, and that suited her best.

"By Jove, you look like a little girl, my love," smirked her husband from his seat, on the bench near the stove, where he was lying as usual in spite of his clean shirt, black coat, and hair covered with pomade. "Many people will envy me to-night."

She did not answer; she felt annoyed with him. Wasn't it disgraceful of him to lie there in his new, clean clothes, just as though he had his greasy, everyday coat on?

"How beautiful, oh, how beautiful," whispered Rosa, who had crept out of her corner and was kneeling before her mother with both hands raised as though worshipping her. Mrs. Tiralla had now put her ball-dress on, and the snowy-white gauze fell round her like a fleecy cloud. She thought herself that she looked beautiful, just like a young girl. Ah! A slight but burning pain made her tremble. How sad to think that all this beauty was to wither away at her husband's side--always at her husband's side. All at once she was seized with a violent fit of fury, one of those sudden attacks which deprived her for a time of her senses. "Get up," she said to Rosa coldly, as the child gently stroked her dress. "Get up. Why do you do that? You're soiling my dress."

Rosa began to cry.

"Why do you frighten her so?" exclaimed Mr. Tiralla reproachfully; he could not bear to hear his daughter cry. "Come here, my Röschen, my little lady-bird; leave your mother, she's in a bad humour to-day. Come to me, Röschen, my sweetheart, come; take hold of my coat, you won't soil that."

"Yes, go, go!" and the woman dragged her dress so violently away from the clinging hands that a flounce came undone. Then she grew still more furious, for now the dress would have to be sewn. She scolded Rosa in a loud voice, and the child gazed at her with a strange look in her dilated eyes. Could angels scold as well? Alas, she must have done something very bad, must have been a very good-for-nothing girl if the angel scolded her. She crept back into her corner sobbing in a subdued fashion.

"That's right, be angry, it suits you," said Mr. Tiralla, laughing.

Neither of the parents took any more notice of the child. The father rose from the bench when he heard the crack of Jendrek's whip, as the carriage drove up to the front door. It was late. If they wanted to be there in time they would have to start at once, as it would take quite two hours to drive to Gradewitz to-night with the roads in such a condition.

"*Dalej*, my dear," he said, holding his wife's fur cloak for her, in a sudden fit of politeness.

Marianna drew her master's thickest woollen socks over her mistress's dainty shoes. "Oh, what beautiful little shoes," she exclaimed ingratiatingly. "Pani mustn't walk in the snow with her beautiful feet."

As the woman bent forward in order to help the maid, her husband threw a look at her low-necked dress and smirked. Then he pressed a resounding kiss on her smooth, cool neck.

The maid screamed with laughter, and continued to do so long after the carriage had jolted out of the gate. She and Jendrek had accompanied them so far, each carrying a lantern for fear they should fall into any of the dangerous holes in the unpaved yard made by the pigs and poultry, and now covered with loose snow.

The child remained alone in the big, stifling room, into the dark corners of which the light from the two flickering candles on the table could not penetrate.

Mrs. Tiralla sat with closed eyes behind her husband, whose broad back kept off the wind. They could not have taken any other carriage, as it would have been upset on the bad roads. It was difficult enough even for this open conveyance, with its big, clumsy wheels, to get along, for sometimes the wheels would be high up, sometimes low down, it all depended on whether there was more or less ice in the ruts.

How awful it was to live in such a flat country. Mrs. Tiralla sighed, as she sat wrapped up in her fur cloak and many shawls. The schoolmaster was right, this was no place for her. Life in these surroundings made one feel quite strange. She had, indeed, been born for something else. Had not her priest said to her even in the old days when she was still so young, "Thou art chosen amongst many"? And what had been her lot? The woman flashed a furious look through her half-closed lids at the man sitting in front. Now he was taking her once more to be exhibited, just like a breeder who wishes to win a prize for the animal he has kept in such good condition.

Mrs. Tiralla was filled with a wild fury; she would have liked to hurl her husband out of the carriage. If only he were lying in the snow; if only the wheels would go over him; if only she could seize the reins and whip up the horses, "*Huj, het!*" Free, free! But--then her head drooped and a sudden sadness came over her--she had not the courage to do it. She had put the rat poison in the lumber-room in the old gaily painted chest from her girlhood, where nobody would look for it. She had told her husband that the rats had eaten it all, and he had believed her. He had not been surprised that they had not found any dead rats, for it is a well-known fact that animals hide in any hole they can find when they have been poisoned. There they die. If only she had not been so terrified when Marianna shrieked "Poison, poison!" How awful it would be if that big man were to roll his eyes and foam at the mouth and shriek, "Poison, poison!"

"Holy Mother!" she said to herself as she folded her hands under her fur cloak, "look down on me. Thou gracious one, lend me thy assistance in what I'm about to do." To do it alone was too great an undertaking; would she ever, ever find courage to do it again? It had not seemed so difficult the first time. But the saints had not willed it; the maid, that idiot! had upset the coffee, and her husband had not got a single drop of it. What a pity, thought Mrs. Tiralla regretfully. How could she have felt so happy that morning when she saw her husband sitting at the breakfast-table safe and sound? He grew more and more repugnant to her every day. How long--how long would she have to bear it? Had Heaven no understanding? So many husbands died and left wives to weep and mourn for them, and he--

he--she wouldn't shed a single tear for him, she was sure of that. She would laugh, laugh! Ha, and to-night she would dance, dance! She felt as though she must deaden all feeling.

* * * * * * * * * * * *

The Tirallas were anxiously awaited. The ball had no attraction as long as Mrs. Tiralla was not there.

As their carriage rumbled up to the market-place little Ziëntek, in evening dress and a tall hat on his fair hair, rushed to the hotel door to receive them. Thank goodness, there they were! He, as master of the ceremonies, had suffered agonies at their nonarrival. What should they have done with all those bouquets for the cotillon? Half of them would have been enough.

A good many of the guests had congregated on the dirty, straw-covered pavement, in order to watch, by the feeble light from the lantern that swung backwards and forwards in the wind, the fair Sophia get down. Many eager hands were stretched out to assist her, but she did not seem to notice them. She gave a neat jump, and next moment stood on the stone steps, over which a piece of old carpet had been laid, shaking out her skirts. She did not wait until her husband had got down, but, walking straight into the cloak-room, took off her things, gave a peep into the dingy glass, and was dancing the mazurka with Mr. Schmielke when Mr. Tiralla entered the ballroom.

He at once looked out for a seat for himself. Let her dance, he liked her to do so. He was not afraid of her virtue, for she was as cold as ice; you had to be thankful when she did not scratch your eyes out. She had been trying him very sorely lately. Since Röschen's illness she would have nothing to do with him.

Then he played a game with Count Jagodziúski, the cards for which (a pack soiled by much usage and many dirty fingers) the Count at once produced from the back-pocket of his coat. What did it matter to Mr. Tiralla if he lost three or four pounds? It amused him when the Count won them, for that was the only harvest the poor devil had nowadays.

The Count was not accustomed to have such an indulgent opponent; everybody else used to keep a strict eye on him except Mr. Tiralla. In his heart the gallant old Count pitied the latter's beautiful wife. Poor thing, to have such a fool of a husband.

Mrs. Tiralla was like a flame, in spite of her white dress and her cheeks that never got red--hot, but never red--for she set fire to the whole ballroom.

Crimson and white flags, that swayed incessantly backwards and forwards in the draught created by the dancers as they whirled past, had been fixed to the bare wooden partitions, through which the wind whistled straight from the plain. The withered garlands, that had been there since the Sokol's [A] last entertainment, rustled softly as they hung from one flagstaff to the other. The boards on the floor were only loosely laid down, and moved up and down under the hopping and gliding of many feet. If a foot happened to stamp a little more than usual, or a couple to fall down with a crash, then clouds of dust would whirl up and obscure the light from the swinging paraffin lamp, round which twelve candles, fixed in a metal disc, were flickering. A stove roared in the corner. The wall behind it had been scorched by the heat, and in front a large iron-plated screen had been placed, in order to protect the women's dresses from the sparks that flew out of the open door.

A A Polish gymnastic society.

The piano stood on a platform, which was now and then used as a stage; and there was a pianist from Gnesen, not at all a bad player, who was supported by a violin and a double-bass. The musicians played with a good deal of rhythm, a fiery rhythm that carried the dancers away. People danced well in Gradewitz. Schmielke's dancing was nothing special here, although it had been considered exceedingly good at home. The girls were as light as soap-bubbles; even stout Miss Trampel, the baker's daughter, and the stupid, snub-nosed Miss Musiëlak, the stationmaster's daughter, danced like feathers; still, they were not in very much request.

Little Jadwiga, the rich mill-owner's daughter, who was wearing a brand-new pale blue cashmere frock, cut square in front, which left her neck bare as far as the freckles went, did not meet with as much success as could be expected from her dress, which the Gradewitz dressmaker had declared to be her masterpiece. And even Mariechen Rózycki, whose very red arms and hands stuck out of a pink silk blouse, had to look on, while one man after another marched over to Mrs. Tiralla. It was a bitter blow.

The girls put their heads together in the intervals between the dances. All of them, whether fair or dark, brown or red, had had their hair done exactly in the same way. The Gradewitz hairdresser had waved their front hair and made it into an enormous roll over the forehead, with the help of some padding. And then she had made three puffs of the back hair, which she had placed at the top of the head. The only difference between them all was the greater or lesser quantity of hair they had, and the colour of the little bow placed coquettishly on the left side.

How awful these young girls looked. The one in bright pink, the other in bright blue, the third in almost orange, the fourth in the colour of arsenic. And then the women! Mrs. Rózycki, the butcher's wife, shone in a stiff silk-

-dark reddish brown, trimmed with yellow lace--not at all bad in itself, but how common her fat face looked over her tight silk bodice that seemed ready to burst. And then the others! Mrs. Jokisch, in black, trimmed with mauve and a white lace collar, looked exactly like her own grandmother. How a man's soul seems to show itself in his garments. Mr. Böhnke, the schoolmaster, stood in a corner of the ballroom criticizing the company. He had never laid so much weight on appearances before--his mother was a very unassuming woman, and his sisters, oh, dear!--but he had been spoiled since he had made Mrs. Tiralla's acquaintance. She was always beautiful, and especially so this evening. He almost devoured her with his eyes. How splendid she looked in that dainty white dress. She was harmony personified in this confused mass of gaudy colours. The only coloured thing about her was her smooth, silky dark hair, with the rosebuds in it, and the little bouquet at her bosom.

She was the only one who was wearing a low-necked dress. Such a thing had never been the fashion in Gradewitz, where it was only customary to expose the throat and shoulder-blades. It was really extremely indecent to be so uncovered; but none of the women would have dared say that aloud, and the young girls even less. Next time, however, that there was a ball in Gradewitz, all the dresses should be made like Mrs. Tiralla's. The men seemed to approve of it. Even the most innocent children noticed how their fathers' eyes glittered as they looked down at Mrs. Tiralla's shoulders.

Sophia Tiralla did not seem to notice all these looks. She gave herself up to the pleasures of the dance like a child--like a little innocent child. All her misery had been wiped away for this short hour. What did it matter to her that all these men stared at her in the same way as her husband always did? Her blood did not course more quickly on that account. Let them! She laughed at them, laughed! If they had known that she had almost killed a human being! Almost poisoned her! She was seized with a nervous inclination to laugh.

When Mr. Schmielke whispered to her, as he pressed her to his heart in the gliding waltz, "My beautiful one, the sweetest rose in Poland"--he thought that very fine, really poetical--"I'm dying of love for you," she laughed in his face.

"You're dancing very badly, Mr. Schmielke," she said, and next moment flew past him in little Zïentek's arms.

"*Psia krew!*" Mr. Schmielke had already accustomed himself to the Polish way of swearing. That hop o' my thumb, that little milksop of a post office clerk, had better try to come near him, he would soon take him in hand. He called himself master of the ceremonies, and his duty was obviously to provide for the entertainment of the guests. Why, he was thinking of nobody but himself--the perjurer, the liar! the vain little Pole!

Mr. Ziëntek danced much better than the Prussian tax-collector, but even he found no favour in Mrs. Tiralla's eyes. She finished the dance with him; but just as he, with laboured breath and beating pulse, was about to commence an intimate, low-toned conversation with her, she nodded an absent-minded "Thanks," without listening to what he was saying, and was immediately carried off by Mr. Rózycki, the butcher.

Rózycki was a capital dancer, in spite of his stoutness. He had dragged on a pair of white kid gloves, and was enjoying himself so much that the perspiration was streaming down his face and falling in big drops on to his partner's shoulder. But that was quite immaterial to Mrs. Tiralla at the present moment, and she did not mind either if it were butcher or baker or post office clerk with whom she was dancing, as long as she could dance. But not with Mr. Tiralla, she would not have liked to dance with him. As their eyes met, and he raised his glass and gave her a pleasant nod, she frowned gloomily and took no notice of him. She looked very worn at that moment; all her youthfulness seemed to have disappeared.

But that was only for a moment, and her face became quite smooth again as she whirled round the room with her skilful partner, against whose body she was constantly knocking. He remained in the middle of the room with her, just under the chandelier, so that everybody could see him and her. He felt as though he were the king of the ball. He would soon stop his wife's tongue if she should venture later on to reproach him for having danced so long with Sophia Tiralla. He had now danced three times round the room with her without stopping, he didn't seem to be able to tire her out. However, when he felt that he could not dance any longer, he drew a deep breath, gave an exultant cheer, and lifted his charming partner right up into the air.

Deafening cheers resounded through the ballroom. The men were like mad. They pushed and buffeted and pressed round the snow-white little lamb under the chandelier like rams that had been let loose.

Mrs. Tiralla did not utter a sound as her strong partner raised her from the ground. Her lips were scarlet, her little nostrils trembled, her eyes laughed.

A feeling of deep dejection came over her later on when she was sitting at the table with Mr. Schmielke, with Ziëntek on the other side, and her husband opposite to her. She did not want to eat anything; when she saw how Mr. Tiralla was devouring his food she lost her appetite. All at once she felt she had had enough of it all; the dance nauseated her as well as the food.

For to-morrow she would again be alone with her husband at Starydwór. The more court the men paid her that evening the more she abhorred him. There was nobody here who could have charmed her. This Mr. Schmielke at her side, bah! True, all the girls ran after him, and he was constantly whispering some amorous nonsense in her ear and secretly pressing his knee against her dress, and seeking her foot. But she could have lived a hundred years on a desert island with him, and he would never have been dangerous to her. And Ziëntek, that little fair-haired fellow, what did she care for such a stupid boy? Her lip curled with a disdainful smile. What did she care for all the others, those husbands who cooed round her like pigeons? On the whole, what did she care for all the men in the world? She felt herself infinitely superior to them all; her hand remained cool in spite of the most ardent pressure; no hot blood ever flew to her head. And still she would rather have given herself to any one of them than to her husband. It angered her that he should show so little jealousy. Was he so sure of her? What would he say if she chose somebody else?

Her eyes began to rove about--big, restless eyes, that wandered all over the table.

Mr. Schmielke intercepted such a glance, and took it as an encouragement. What, was he to conquer this little woman after all? He boldly pushed his chair still nearer to hers, for he knew that audacity had more effect upon women than anything else. He had drunk a considerable amount during the course of the evening, and he went on drinking during supper: a glass of Tokay with the salad, beer with the roast pork and duck, and now he ordered a bottle of Moselle with the vanilla ice.

Others followed his example. Count Jagodziúski would not be satisfied with anything less than champagne, for Mr. Tiralla's silver was burning a hole in his pocket.

They all grew very animated. The gentlemen in their black clothes showed they had fists, and now and then one of them banged on the table.

The tightly-laced Mrs. Rózycki gave a loud shriek--the man next to her had tickled her. Her daughter Mariechen dung languishingly to her neighbour, the forester's young pupil, with whom she was already very much in love. They had all been rather stiff and shy when they entered the ballroom a few hours before, but now they showed that they could eat, drink, and be merry. Enormous quantities of food disappeared; Mr. Tiralla alone had eaten a whole duck. The women especially liked the ice, for they were so very, very hot, and all that beer and sweet wine had made them still hotter. The men cast ardent glances at their neighbours; it was immaterial to them now if it happened to be Sophia Tiralla or anybody else, for they were all nice. And the glances were returned. The young girls were no longer so shy.

They threw themselves back in their chairs and laughed as they listened with glistening eyes and red ears to the young men's compliments. The married people told each other tales; Mr. Tiralla especially excelled in that. Mrs. Jokisch, the inspector's wife, who sat next to him, gave him a tap on his mouth; but you couldn't be angry with him, all the same, she said, however horrid he was. Thereupon he pressed a resounding kiss on her cheek. And then he kissed the baker's wife, who was sitting next to him on the other side--otherwise she would have been offended--and neither of them made any resistance. They evidently didn't find him so repugnant, thought Mrs. Tiralla, much surprised.

The schoolmaster sat stiff and silent amongst them all. Their mirth disgusted him. What a party! And he had thought he should meet people like himself there. Raising a pair of reproachful eyes, he caught a glance from Mrs. Tiralla. She looked at him for a second, and her face, that a moment before had been so bright, became more and more serious. Then she raised her glass a little, gave him a slight nod, and emptied it in one draught.

He felt so happy whilst she looked at him, so elated; but only for a few moments. For Mr. Tiralla, who had noticed his Sophia's nod, now also wanted to show some politeness to little Böhnke, who walked out so regularly to see them all, and brought his Sophia books and the latest news, and sat for hours with the child. It was really very kind of him. So Mr. Tiralla also raised his glass and bawled at the top of his voice, so that everybody could hear it, "Your health, little Böhnke. Have you nothing to drink? Come here, sonny, you can get something from me. *Dalej, dalej,* why aren't you coming?"

All eyes were fixed on the schoolmaster, who said "Thanks" in a curt voice and without looking at the farmer, but did not move.

Then all the others raised their glasses as well. "Your good health, Mr. Böhnke."

Had none of them noticed how rude that was of Mr. Tiralla? Böhnke's blood boiled. He, the schoolmaster, whose mission it was to train the young--he, the only one there who could lay claim to any education, he was to stand that?"*Dalej, dalej!*" the peasant had shouted at him, as if he were his stableboy or his farm horse. Was he to put up with that? Was he really obliged to put up with it? No, no, no! The slim-looking schoolmaster was on the point of jumping up from his seat, but he got no further. He had again caught a glance from Mrs. Tiralla, and he had understood what those black eyes were saying to him. His fury subsided as he remained quietly in his place, but deep down in his heart there was born a hatred for Mr. Tiralla.

The dancing recommenced after supper, but the feet did not trip as lightly as before, and they did not always agree; for when the man's foot went to the left, his partner's wanted to go to the right. The dancers also fell down more frequently. The boards shook, and the clouds of dust became thicker and thicker. The ballroom was gloomy and oppressive.

Mrs. Tiralla's dress no longer flew about as it had done during the first part of the evening. She was standing in the cloak-room with Mariechen Rózycki, who was sobbing bitterly, whilst old Piasecka, the attendant, whose business it was also to carry "In Memoriam" cards round, was busily rubbing her. "Oh, my pink blouse!" wailed the girl, "my beautiful blouse!"

The forester's pupil, the idiot, had poured a whole glass of beer down the front of it, when she was tenderly leaning against him just before they left the table. She was beside herself with grief.

"You can send it to Spindler in Berlin," said Mrs. Tiralla consolingly. "There is also a very good dry cleaner in Posen. Why, child!" she exclaimed, putting her finger under the girl's chin and raising her face, that was quite swollen with crying, "surely you aren't crying for the sake of a blouse?"

All at once it seemed so infinitely futile to cry on account of a spoilt blouse. Mrs. Tiralla had quite forgotten that she also had shed tears on account of her hair just before she had left home. She felt so much more unhappy now, really so miserable. She would have liked to stop up her ears so as not to hear that twanging music. The dancing disgusted her. She had never gone to a dance as a child. What would her priest have said if he had seen her that evening? Father Szypulski was not so strict; but she would be strict with herself. She wouldn't go into the ballroom again, she would drive home and sit by Rosa's bed and be her guardian angel. Perhaps she would then see some of those wonderful things that had been revealed to the child. She would pray for it, pray for happy dreams. She longed so ardently, so impatiently for happiness.

She called to a waiter who was running past in a short black jacket and a white apron spotted with gravy, and sent him back to her husband. Would Mr. Tiralla kindly tell them to bring the carriage round, it was time to be going? The cocks were already crowing in the little yards behind the labourers' cottages.

She remained standing in the cloak-room, gloomily gnawing her Up, with Mariechen, who was still sobbing on account of her blouse, as her companion. She had hidden herself behind the clothes-rack, nobody would discover her there. Vain hope! Scarcely had the waiter given the message than the whole flock of her partners came rushing in. Sophia Tiralla wanted to go--go away now? But they wouldn't let her go, even if they had to make a wall of their bodies before the door. Ziëntek wrung his hands in despair; if she went away the whole cotillon would be spoilt, that up-to-date cotillon with all those bouquets.

They discovered her and brought her out from behind the rack. They begged, flattered, teased, threatened, and swore loudly that they wouldn't let her go, she would have to remain and dance.

"Of course she'll stop and dance!" bawled Mr. Tiralla from the doorway leading into the ballroom.

What, he as well? No, she wouldn't stop, not even a quarter of an hour longer, hissed the woman like a serpent that has been trodden on. "Tell the carriage to come round," she said to the waiter in a curt, shrill voice. Then, without looking at her husband, she added, "I'm going. If you don't want to go, you can stop. I'm going."

Mr. Tiralla looked very discomfited; but then he grew angry. What, to be so horrid to him before all those people? A wife had to obey. He was the one who had to decide. He was very drunk, or it would never have occurred to him to oppose his wife's wishes in this way. And that was what made him now shout, "Confound you, woman! You shall not drive; for I intend stopping here as long as I choose--until six, seven, or eight o'clock, if I choose."

"Stop," she said icily, but her eyes glowed. "Then I'll walk."

No, she couldn't do that, surely she wouldn't do that. That would be quite impossible through *that* snow.

But she did not listen to her admirers' persuasions; she tore her fur cloak down from the peg and threw her shawl over her head. She felt that if they did not let her go she would burst into tears--into loud, hopeless tears. She stamped her foot defiantly; why did they all stare at her with such stupid, glassy eyes? And Mr. Tiralla, was he already asleep?"*Dalej!*" she said curtly, and her voice sounded like the cut of a whip, "*dalej!*"

He obeyed her. What else was there for him to do if his dear little wife was so anxious to get home? "Women are amorous little doves," he lisped, "they always want to be going home to their nests." Laying his arm heavily round her neck he stammered caressingly, "Yes, yes, I'm coming, my dove, only have patience." And then he gave such a sly wink with his glassy eyes that the men broke into a laugh, which resembled nothing so much as a horse whinnying.

Mrs. Tiralla had shrunk back. A wave of burning colour mounted to her pale face. Oh, if he treated her in that way, was it surprising that they all ran after her like that? But they should not imagine that she was ready to cast herself into the arms of the first man who came along--far from it.

Throwing her head back with a curt, scornful movement, and restraining her tears with the utmost strength of will, she said, forcibly jerking out every word, for she could hardly speak, her lips trembled so, "You can lie on the threshold, as you've done before, you braggart!"

Now the laugh was on her side. They were all delighted to think that Mr. Tiralla had been reprimanded in that way. Why did he brag like that? They also found favour with the ladies, but they didn't boast of it in that way. What did this vulgar peasant want with such a dainty little wife? A milkmaid would have been good enough for him. They all applauded the little woman, who seemed to have grown a head taller, she held herself so erect. But when Mr. Schmielke, who now hoped to win the prize, bent his knee and said jokingly, "*Padam da nog!*" and then, stroking his moustache in his usual challenging way, added, "Allow me to see you home," she stared at him for a moment. And when he smiled at her with all the impertinence which the wine and the advanced hour, the spectators' goading looks, and the conviction of his own irresistibility had given him, she administered such a violent, resounding box on his ears that he and all the others started back.

She rushed out of the cloak-room and across the passage to the front door, and, standing on the pavement which the downtrodden straw had made still dirtier, she shouted for her carriage. She was weeping.

The wind had veered round in the early morning, and was blowing from the west, as she stood in the deserted market-place. Large flakes of watery snow were being driven along before the wind, and clung to her cheeks and mingled with the hot drops from her eyes. Oh, how she would have liked to lie down there in the dirt and die! That beautiful ball! Alas, there would never be any more pleasure for her where her husband was. How he had made a laughing-stock of her before them all. And he had lied into the bargain.

The carriage had not come yet; she stood trembling with cold and grief. She clenched her hands; she would do it quite, quite alone now, if she couldn't find anybody to help her.

All at once she had a feeling that somebody was standing behind her; that somebody was breathing on her cheek. It was the schoolmaster.

He had quietly followed her. He was no less excited than she. She had been insulted by Mr. Tiralla, but Mr. Tiralla had also insulted him; he had insulted them both.

The schoolmaster looked upon the harmless man as a criminal. "He doesn't deserve the sun to shine on him," he whispered, in a voice that was hoarse with excitement. Then he snatched hold of the hand which she held out to him, and pressed it to his lips, to his eyes, and stammered wildly, "Pani, let me die on the spot--God punish me if ever I forget Mr. Tiralla's behaviour. I--I----" he suppressed something he was going to say. Then he once more pressed her willing hand to his burning lips and stood near her in silence, until they heard Mr. Tiralla's voice at the hotel door at the same moment as the carriage rattled out of the yard and round the corner.

She got in without help; the schoolmaster had disappeared, swallowed up by the darkness. Mr. Tiralla was hoisted up on the front seat with great difficulty by the boots. He was a heavy weight and the man's shoulders and arms ached, but he was pleased to help the gentleman. That good Mr. Tiralla--Heaven bless him--had given him a new two-shilling bit as a tip.

Not a word was spoken by the couple. Mrs. Tiralla sat motionless at the back with her cloak wrapped tightly round her, for she was icy cold. She had drawn her shawl far down over her forehead, but her burning eyes wandered in mute despair over the desolate, slushy fields in the early morning twilight. Oh, how uncomfortable she felt, how tired out. She couldn't understand now why she had wanted to go to the ball instead of lying in her warm bed and being lulled to sleep by Rosa's soft-toned prayers, and thus forgetting her miserable existence in the arms of the saints.

She was seized with an unutterable aversion for her present life. There, alas!--and her big eyes grew bigger and bigger and more desperate-looking--there was the first of the big pines on the Przykop, looking just like a flagstaff with a waving pennon on it, and near it, although not yet visible, lay Starydwór, the old, lonely farm where she had to go on living year after year with Mr. Tiralla. How much longer?

A ditch ran along the side of the road, a broad, deep ditch. The carriage jolted as they rumbled along. How would it be if they were to fall into the ditch with carriage and horses, and break their necks? Ha, wouldn't that be a good thing? She stood up in the carriage--how stiff she was after sitting so long--and, resting her left hand on the side-rail, carefully bent over her husband.

He was asleep. His head had fallen on his breast, his snores mingled with the rattle of the wheels. He was sleeping as deeply and soundly in the wet and cold and discomfort as though he were at home in his bed. The reins hung loosely between the enormous fingers of his fur gloves. All she had to do was to take them away from him, he wouldn't notice it. She did so. He was sleeping so soundly that he had no idea of what was going on behind him.

She was standing on the seat now, erect and with flashing eyes, holding the reins with both hands. Now a tug, a turn to the left--she could not reach the whip, but a *"Huj, het!"* was enough--then a sudden jerk with all her strength, and the terrified horses jumped to the left. One wheel was already hanging over the side of the ditch--farewell, Mr. Tiralla!--a grimace partly of horror at what she had done, partly of triumphant delight, distorted the woman's face--crash--they lay at the bottom.

But not the horses and not the carriage, only Mr. Tiralla and his wife. The clever animals had stopped short as though they recognized the danger, and were now standing quite close to the edge, their bits covered with foam.

"Psia krew!" Mr. Tiralla scrambled out of the ditch, all of a sudden quite sober. The soft snow had felt like a downy feather bed, and he hadn't hurt himself in the slightest. What a joke! How often he had been upset in that ditch. H'm, if the horses hadn't been so sensible. He patted their necks and praised them. And then he called to his wife, "Heigh, Sophia, where have you got to?"

She did not answer. She had not hurt herself either; she lay on her back in the ditch, snow under her, snow on both sides of her, and above her the early morning sky, clear and rosy. She closed her eyes again; let him call her, she would remain where she was for ever.

Then she suddenly remembered that her beautiful ball-dress from that good dressmaker in Posen might be spoiled. Her fur cloak could not keep the snow-water out very long; she already felt it penetrating into her shoes. Ugh, how wet and horrid it was! She would never be able to put the dress on again. She jumped up hastily, and called to her husband to help her. And when she had safely got out of the ditch, she shook her skirts and examined her dress, and was delighted to find that nothing had been spoiled.

They got into the carriage again. But now Mr. Tiralla kept his eyes open, although he felt fit to drop with fatigue. What would Sophia say if he were to upset her once more? "I'm sorry, my dear," he murmured, in a crestfallen voice. She said nothing.

As they reached the gate, they found it wide open just as they had left it. The front door was not locked either, the latch was, of course, down, but the door had not been bolted.

"Jendrek, Marianna," shouted Mr. Tiralla, at the top of his voice. Was nobody coming to take the horses? Where were those rascals sleeping? And the other men, the day labourers, hadn't come yet. The farmer scolded and groaned when he found that he would have to unharness the horses himself and take them to the stable.

Mrs. Tiralla went into the room and called the maid. But Marianna, who always came running so submissively when her mistress called her, did not appear either. The woman grew so angry, that she almost tore the ball-dress off her back, and then let it lie on the floor. Disgraceful, disloyal, shameless hussy! Where could she be sleeping so sweetly that she neither heard nor saw anything?

When Mr. Tiralla came into the room his wife snubbed him as angrily as if he had been Marianna.

He tried to appease her. "That'll do, that'll do, my love. We know all about it." He laughed good-naturedly. "They're young, we must excuse them."

Oh, so he condoned such things? Perhaps even considered them right? Well, then! There was a strange expression in Mrs. Tiralla's eyes as she stared straight in front of her. She let her husband press a kiss on her neck without feeling it, and then she ran in her petticoat and without anything over her shoulders through the cold house up to her bedroom.

There lay Rosa with the feather bed drawn up to her eyes. The woman fell on her knees beside the child's bed, and, burying her head in the bedclothes, she sobbed aloud.

Rosa awoke. "Mother, sweet mother?" There was a note of anxious inquiry in her exclamation; was her mother in a good humour again, was she no longer cross as the evening before?

"Do you love me?" stammered the sobbing woman. "Tell me that you love me."

"Oh, I do love you, I love you so dearly."

"Tell me that you'll pray for me. Swear that you'll pray for me--always."

"Oh, I'll pray for you. I always pray for you."

"Pray for me, pray for me," sobbed the excited woman. "I'll pray with you, perhaps that'll help me. Rosa, my angel"--she covered the child's face with kisses--"we'll pray."

"What shall we pray?" asked the child. "What do you want to pray now, mother dear? Shall I pray to the beautiful guardian angel, 'Holy angel, thou who standest before the throne of God,' or shall I repeat the litany to the sweet name of Jesus? Or shall I pray as I did at my confirmation, 'Come, thou Heavenly Physician, I need Thee. Heal my soul, oh Saviour. Come, save me'? Oh, you left me alone," cried the child, in a plaintive voice, as she broke off in the midst of her prayer. "You were at the ball, you were so beautiful, mother. Daddy was with you. Marianna went away as well. She said it would only be for half an hour; she wanted to see her little ones, who are living with an old woman in the village; but she stopped away. I was all by myself in the house. And something creaked in the big cupboard, and in the stove, and in all the furniture. And something moved in all the corners. Ugh, the room was so lonely, I ran out of it. And the candles--those two before the looking-glass--flickered so. Marianna says that if you look into a glass before which two candles are burning, as the clock strikes twelve, either Death or your future husband will be standing behind you. Oh, and I daren't cross the passage, it was so dark. Just think if anybody had been lurking there? I screamed aloud, but nobody answered--ugh, the passage was so icy cold--so I rushed into the kitchen; there was still a little fire there, and I crept behind the stove. Oh, mother, I was so frightened, I couldn't stop there either. I trembled so, my heart went like that the whole time"--she took hold of her mother's hand and moved it quickly up and down--"the whole time like that. Just think if that fiery man, that Marianna is always telling me about, had got out of the stove? I believe that fiery man is the devil; I've asked Marianna, but she didn't know. Do you think, mammie, that it's the devil?"

She sat up in bed. She was still completely dressed. "Is it the devil?"

Mrs. Tiralla nodded.

"So you also believe that it's the devil?" Rosa's voice expressed a certain satisfaction, a kind of childish pride; oh, yes, she knew all about such things. "I know him." she said triumphantly.

"What does he look like?" whispered her mother, with a shudder, as she hid her face in her hands. Oh, if that should have been he, that handsome young man who had suddenly appeared before her a short time before, as she stood half-dressed in the room downstairs and Mr. Tiralla was making excuses for the amorous maid?

"I saw him on the altar in the chapel," whispered Rosa. "Holy Michael was treading him underfoot. He's like a worm, but he has a face and horns on his head. Father Szypulski says he comes to tempt us. Pray, pray! He pokes the fire in Purgatory, in which the souls are burning. 'Pray for the peace of the poor souls in Purgatory,' says the priest, 'and for your own as well.' I commend all the souls in Purgatory to thee, oh, most holy Mother

Mary." Rosa's whispers became more and more agitated and her wild, restless eyes began to wander about the room. "He's red, mother, red with black horns. He dances in the flames wherever there's a fire; he sends out sparks, mother--he's fetching us all! Mother! Oh, he's burning us all!"

The child uttered a heartrending sigh, and pressing both hands to her breast reared herself up in bed. Throwing back her disordered hair, she shrieked in a loud voice, "Oh, it hurts me, it hurts me so here--it hurts, hurts, hurts!"

"It hurts, hurts, hurts!" shrieked her mother. She did not know that she was repeating the same words.

Rosa tore her dress open, her breast heaved and sank as she gasped for breath in her terror. Then she clung to her mother, and hiding her face in her neck she whimpered, "Carry me out of the kitchen again, carry me up the dark stairs, oh, Holy Mother, that I needn't fear. Put me down, keep me warm--hail, Mary, thou that art highly favoured"--(the child's voice had grown soft and low)--"how beautiful thou art--I love thee--hail, Mary, blessed art thou among women--blessed--the fruit--of thy womb----"

Her words grew more and more indistinct, until they at last became nothing but an incoherent murmur.

Ah, now Rosa saw the Holy Virgin. Seized with a superstitious terror, Mrs. Tiralla loosened the child's arms from about her neck. What did Rosa see? What did she hear? Did she really see something? If only Rosa could find out something which could be of use to her--her!

The child had fallen back on her bed heavy and stiff. Spurred on by an intense eagerness her mother leant over her and whispered:

"Ask the Holy Virgin--tell the Holy Virgin that I'll let ten candles burn before her on the altar--ten wax candles--she's to release me--Glisten, all she's to do is to release me."

Rosa was silent. She did not hear. Although her eyes were wide open, she did not seem to see her mother's terrified, excited mien, nor her burning, piercing looks, so full of entreaty.

"Listen!" Mrs. Tiralla's voice sounded almost fierce as she shouted to the child. "Listen, listen!" she repeated several times, in an impressive voice. "Tell the Holy Virgin she's to release me--I want to be released--I must be released--listen, listen!"

All at once a convulsive movement passed over Rosa's face. Her mother bent over her, lower and lower, full of trembling eagerness. The child's staring eyes began to move, and her mouth as well.

"You'll be released," she stammered, as though in her sleep. "The dear Virgin hears all prayers--she is smiling--ah, how she's smiling."

Bearing herself up once more, and stretching out her arms, the over-excited child burst into tears.

Her mother wiped the tears and beads of perspiration away from her face with her trembling hands. Oh, her little dress was quite wet through, and her bodice and chemise as well. She undressed the child and made her bed more comfortable. Poor little thing! Her mother felt very sorry for her, although she was full of joy and of an insuppressible exultation. She was to be released! The Holy Virgin had spoken. She was to be released from him, from Mr. Tiralla!

CHAPTER VI

Rosa was singing as she crossed the fields. She felt so well, so light-hearted. At last she had been to confession. The snow had melted, Eastertide was drawing near, now she could sing.

"Mary Magdalene weeping

Went to Jesu's tomb.

Her dear Lord, her sorrow knowing.

Came to light her gloom.

She saw His glorious countenance."

Her clear voice sounded jubilant as it rose into the blue sky. It was spring, spring. The fresh grass was sprouting near the broad ditch, the corn that had been kept warm under the snow was now green and thick. Christ was risen and therefore the earth rejoiced.

Rosa took out of her pocket the paper on which she, during the winter, had noted down all she had to confess. She had examined her conscience most carefully; it was a long, long piece of paper, with many sins written on it. But she had got rid of them all now, and that was why she felt so happy. Now she could tear it to pieces.

She stood still, and tearing the paper into shreds threw them high into the air. Off they flew. How the wind carried them away, higher and higher, as high as the lark which was hovering up there. They were flying to God.

Rosa mingled her song with the lark's trills, in joyous, jerky rhythm.

"The stone was rolled away
As to the grave they came.

At its right side in raiment bright
An angel sat and calmed their fright. Hallelujah."

It was no longer the same shrill, piping child's voice; it was a girl's voice now, full and pleasing. When there was any singing going on in the school, the master always told Rosa Tiralla to stand up first so as to lead the others. She liked doing that. Mr. Böhnke was altogether very good to her, and it would grieve her to leave school. She would soon be fourteen, and then she wouldn't do any more lessons; then--a strange, dreamy look came into her eyes--oh, no, she wasn't going to marry like other girls and have children--no. Her face, that had all at once clouded over, grew bright again; she was to be the Bride of the Church, her mother had said so. Mr. Böhnke said so as well, and the priest said so. And they praised her for it. And Marianna stared at her, "Oh, a nun! That's something very beautiful, something very grand, oh!" And Jendrek almost looked upon her as a saint already. Everybody looked at her in quite a different way now from what they used to do when she was nothing but little Rosa Tiralla. Only her daddy wouldn't hear of it--poor daddy. What a pity it was that he was so wicked. A look full of deep thought cast a sudden gloom over the young face that had just been so bright. Was her mother right? Would it have been better for him never to have been born?

Rosa used to cry bitterly when the thought came to her that her father might perhaps never go to heaven. Her dear father. He really was good; how could it be that her mother and Mr. Böhnke always said he was not?

Doubts had lately crept into Rosa's heart, her belief in her father had been shaken. Had her mother or the schoolmaster brought this about, or had she become alive to many things that did not please her? Why did her father always pinch Marianna's cheek, or even her leg when she was standing on the ladder? That wasn't nice of him. And he used to swear, and it's wicked to swear. Oh, how she would beg her dear father to leave off swearing--her dear father--yes, yes, he was still her dear father.

When Rosa now saw him come tramping across the field to meet her, she ran up to him and threw herself into his arms.

He had been looking out for his little daughter for a long time, and welcomed her with a loud laugh that could be heard far across the fields.

"Well, my darling, have you confessed all your sins? *Psia krew*, if a man had as few sins to confess as you, he wouldn't need to go to confession."

"I've fourteen rosaries to say over," said Rosa, looking very important. Then she added gravely, "Seven for myself and seven for you, father."

He gave a boisterous laugh. Then he kissed her. "You're my consolation, the key which is to open heaven's door for me. I've always said, pray, pray, my angel. If you're praying, the devil will bang the door and leave me outside."

Rosa shuddered. What horrid things her daddy always said. How could he joke about such matters?

"Ah, daddy," she said, in a low, insinuating voice, thrusting her narrow little hand into his big one, "I'm always praying that you may go to heaven."

"Really?" He was touched. "That's very nice of you."

"Mother also prays that you may go to heaven, father."

Mr. Tiralla was also very touched to hear that. Oh, yes, she was a splendid little woman was his Sophia, and loved him even if she didn't always show it, especially lately. Ugh, how cold and forbidding she was sometimes; she made you freeze. But she was a pious woman. Then knitting his brows together, as though something were tormenting him, he said to the child, "When you are married, my dear Rosa, always try to please your husband; he'll like that." He gave a little sigh, but then he laughed. "When Mikolai comes back from the army and marries, I'll rub it into him, too, 'Take a complaisant wife.' Ha, ha, his mother, my late wife, Hanusia, was complaisant enough, that's certain--ha, ha."

"Will Mikolai soon be coming back from the army?" inquired Rosa. She had been such a stupid little thing when he had gone away three years before. But now she was wiser, and she realized how nice it was to have a little brother. The only time he had come home on furlough during all those years she had been very ill with scarlet fever, and he hadn't been allowed to come to her on account of the infection. She was, therefore, doubly glad to see him now. How she would love him. "Will my little brother soon be coming back?" she repeated anxiously.

"H'm, a nice little brother!" laughed her father. "Do you really think they could do with a 'little brother' in the horse guards? He's a big brother, I can tell you, an enormous fellow. He was as tall as I when I went to see him last autumn. And what fists he has got. He won't want a team of oxen to pull the cart, he'll do it himself. But he'll be good to his little sister. Who wouldn't be good to you, my wee one?" He took hold of her little face with his big hand and stroked it tenderly and carefully.

Rosa smiled. "I'll love him," she cried enthusiastically, "and he'll love me. We're all to love each other, Jesus bids us do so."

"Yes, that's what I think, too," said her father, "we're all to love each other." He suddenly thought of his wife, from whom he had neither received kiss nor friendly look that day. So instead of inspecting his corn, as he had intended doing, he returned home with his daughter.

They walked hand in hand. Their figures--his thick-set, a massive tree-trunk, hers a delicate leaf blown about by the wind--could be seen afar off in the flat, treeless field.

Mrs. Tiralla was in the sitting-room with Böhnke, and saw them in the distance through the gateway. "There he is again," she said, with a look of disgust on her face.

Already? The schoolmaster sighed. He had been so delighted to find the woman he adored alone at home--he had seen little Rosa on her way to the village--and now they were so soon to be disturbed. What did that horrid fellow mean by always coming back? Böhnke quite forgot that this house to which he came regularly every Sunday and very often besides, belonged to Mr. Tiralla, and that the latter invariably received him with a loud welcome and ordered the best they had to be served up in his honour. But the farmer's presence always inconvenienced him, and especially to-day. Mrs. Tiralla had been about to pour out her heart to him, and the thought of the moment when at last he would be able to console the sad-looking woman made him tremble.

"I'm in trouble," she had said, when he had asked her if she had a headache. There were dark, heavy shadows under her eyes, and her pale mouth drooped so sadly that he had thought she was ill.

"Oh, how I'm suffering," she had cried, in a sudden outburst of grief and fury, and had run up and down the room with both hands flung high above her head. She had come to a standstill close in front of him, and her black eyes had blazed. "What would you say if I ran away from him? Away, anywhere, over the fields, only away."

The passion with which she had uttered those words had terrified him. Away, away over the fields, but where would she go?

"That's for you to tell me." Then she had given a loud, scornful laugh; in spite of all his cleverness he did not know where she was to go either. There really was nobody, nobody who could advise her. What would he say if she went into the Przykop into the deep morass, where the pool under the drooping birches was just now as deep as any lake on account of the rainy spring? If she went into it up to her mouth, or even a little further, and never more appeared, what would he say then? Would he shed a tear in memory of her, a little forget-me-not in his book of memories?

"God forbid!" he had exclaimed, seizing hold of her hand in sudden fear. How could she say such things, even have such thoughts? She was so good, so beautiful, there was still much happiness in store for her.

"Never, so long as Mr. Tiralla is alive!"

"But he won't go on living for ever."

Then she had flashed a glance at him, a swift and strangely scrutinizing glance. It was as though she had wanted to confide something to him, but dared not. Had he said that without thinking, or did he really mean it?

Mrs. Tiralla had shrunk back into herself again in a sudden fit of shyness. But she could not bear to keep silent, she simply longed to speak to somebody about it all. If only she could--dared--say to him, "In a secret chamber of the loft there stands an old chest, and in that old chest I've hidden something." But then if he should say, "Poison!" and should shudder with horror when he said it? She eyed him narrowly through her lowered lids, whilst her long lashes slowly fanned her pale cheeks like a pair of weary wings.

But the young man saw nothing but her beauty, his eyes were fixed on the mental vision of the charms which her enamoured husband had described to him. How he pitied this beautiful woman. What a misfortune to be chained to such a man. She wanted to run away, to take her own life? Oh, how dreadful for such a beautiful creature to be sick of life. That overbearing fellow, that scoundrel! *Psia krew*, why couldn't he die? Then she would be free.

He had not meant anything when he had said before, "But he won't go on living for ever." It had merely been a phrase, used in order to console the poor woman. But now those words seemed to express something desirable, something really necessary. Was there any reason why the man should go on living for ever? An all-wise Providence had no doubt seen what was happening and would probably remove this fellow, who would leave no vacant place behind him, and would be mourned for by no one. How easily he could be carried off by illness, brought on by a cold in the spring, or by excessive eating. No, Mr. Tiralla could not go on living for ever. Besides, he was much older than she. Only have patience, he would not go on living for ever. He must not, no, by all the saints--and this certainty impressed itself firmly on the schoolmaster's mind--Mr. Tiralla *should* not go on living for ever!

The man drew a deep, trembling breath of relief, after which he felt easier. Then he raised his eyes, which had been lowered in profound thought, and met those of the woman. They looked long and searchingly at each other.

"There he is again," sighed Mrs. Tiralla, who was standing near the window.

Böhnke noticed the disgust depicted on her face, that beautiful face, whose mouth was polluted every day by the word "beast." Had he not seen for himself how that monster had annoyed her with his kisses? The young man grew cold, then hot, whilst the flames of jealousy rushed to his head. Nobody, nobody should kiss her mouth, if he might not kiss it, too--no, only he, quite alone. He stretched out his hand gropingly and seized hers. The woman was weeping, and she allowed him to do so. Then he jerked out hurriedly--there was no time to lose, Mr. Tiralla could come in any moment--jerked out in a breathless voice and without reflection, but still as though he were swearing it solemnly:

"Don't cry. By God, Mr. Tiralla shall not go on living for ever!"

"Mammie," cried Röschen joyously, as she came into the room, and letting her father's hand go she ran up to her mother. "I'm to give you Father Szypulski's kind regards. Oh, it was so beautiful! I'm so happy! I could sing the whole time, I----" Then, catching sight of the schoolmaster, she curtseyed and held out her hand to him, blushing.

Böhnke bent over her more than was necessary, for she reached up to his shoulders, but he wished to hide his gleaming eyes and his cheeks that were burning with excitement. He could not have looked Mr. Tiralla in the face at that moment.

But the woman was perfectly calm. She had fully understood what it was the schoolmaster had said to her, and a feeling of profound relief filled her heart with joy. Ah, now the Holy Virgin was at last going to keep the promise she had given her through Rosa. She had sent her somebody who was on her side, and who would advise her and help her--for had he not clearly said, "I'll look after that"?--and who belonged to her alone.

She felt so happy and cheerful now, so different. She kissed Rosa and even held out her cheek of her own accord when her husband, with a smirk on his face, reproached her for not having given him a single kiss that day. But all the time she kept her eyes fixed on the schoolmaster, who was standing at the window biting his lip.

How could she be so calm, so bright, yes, really so bright? Böhnke couldn't understand it. He felt far from happy. He felt as though he had done a very stupid thing, as though he had allowed himself to be carried away by his emotions. He was seized with a sudden feeling of anger and indignation against Mrs. Tiralla; why had she complained to him, what had that disgusting tale of her marriage to do with him?

But then when she gazed at him with her beautiful, sparkling eyes in that familiar, friendly way, and smiled at him with the same sweet smile that little Rosa had inherited from her, then his anger melted as well as all his scruples. She had never seemed more lovely. Her white ball-dress had suited her well, but this short, plain, woollen skirt, which showed her neat feet and shiny leather slippers, the white apron, the check blouse and small white collar suited her a hundred times better. Oh, how beautiful, how beautiful she looked! His head was in a whirl.

The farmer invited him to have supper with them, and he gladly accepted. He even accepted an invitation for Easter.

Mr. Tiralla was basking in the light of his Sophia's smiles, and felt so happy that he would have liked to invite the whole world. He sat at the table and laughed as he satisfied his enormous appetite. It was still Lent, and the meal was frugal, "but at Easter, my little Böhnke," he cried, filling his mouth with fried potatoes, "at Easter you shall have a feast!"

Mrs. Tiralla and the schoolmaster exchanged a glance. What impertinence to say, "my little Böhnke!" But he was always so rough and vulgar.

Rosa sat near her father. She did not want anything to eat; she never ate much, and to-day her happiness had quite taken away her appetite. It had been such a beautiful, beautiful day. Was it because she had prayed so very fervently at the altar that her daddy was now so good? He didn't swear at all, he didn't even look at Marianna, although her short, white sleeves were fresh from the wash. They reached as far as her bare elbows, and she had a black bodice on and all her coloured beads round her neck. Now her mother would be kinder to her daddy. Oh, if only it could always be like this. How much nicer it was when her mother didn't cry or look angry. To-day was just like Easter, when the grave opened and Christ rose, hallelujah.

Her quiet happiness had brought a flush to her pale cheeks. She did not say much; Rosa was only eloquent in her prayers and when she spoke of what transformed her narrow, dark chamber into a Garden of Eden, and of what took place between heaven and earth. But she pressed her father's hand repeatedly, and when her mother happened to touch her in passing anything over the table, the child would furtively raise her sleeve to her lips and kiss it.

"Rosa looks better than she did last winter," remarked the schoolmaster, in order to say something. It was really quite immaterial to him if the anæmic child looked paler or not, but his own silence terrified him. Surely the old man must notice something?

"She is certainly much better," answered Mrs. Tiralla hastily. "She only complained of being ill for a short time. Our winters are so raw. But now she's always well and happy, aren't you, darling? How could she be anything but happy, she, the Holy Virgin's favourite? Tell Mr. Böhnke what she has revealed to you in your dreams, darling," and she nodded encouragingly to the child.

"I've not dreamt it." Rosa grew almost angry, and she flushed up to her hair-roots. "You're not to say that I dreamt it, mother. It was really true; I was just as wide awake as you are, and father, and Mr. Böhnke. If you dream you surely don't see the cupboard and the clothes rack and the washstand and the wall, and you don't hear the clock ticking and father snoring downstairs and the wind howling in the pines outside. It was all there as usual, and I was lying in my bed as usual. But the room was full of a bright light. That was because the Holy Virgin was there. She was standing in the middle of the room. She had her crown on her head, and she wore a blue mantle, which was wide and had lots of folds, oat of which little angels were peeping."

Rosa made a pause, as though she wished to note the effect of this wonderful communication on her hearers.

Mr. Tiralla did not say a word. He was sitting with his head buried in his hands.

"Dear, dear!" exclaimed the schoolmaster, in order to show that he was attending. What on earth was the child talking about? He had not been listening very carefully.

But the woman nodded again to her daughter, who continued with sparkling eyes.

"Rosa,' said the dear Virgin. 'Rosa Tiralla, be not afraid.' 'I'm not afraid,' I said. Then she went on, 'I've chosen you. You are to remain a virgin and to go to the Grey Sisters or to the Ladies of the Sacred Heart, and there you are to pray for the conversion of sinners, for the strengthening of the faith----'" Here Rosa broke off. "I told all this to Father Szypulski to-day, and he explained to me what she really meant by it. I'm to pray for the conversion of the heterodox (those who don't believe the same as we do) and for the strengthening and propagation of our faith, which is the only faith which can save. And I'm to pray for my dear parents, and especially for my dear father, that his soul and his hands may again become clean, so that he can leave Purgatory and go to the dear angels above. Oh, father, dear father," she cried, in a terrified voice, putting her curly head down on his shoulder as he sat next to her, "how awful it would be if you were to be lost for ever!"

"*Psia krew!*" So far Mr. Tiralla had not said a word, but now he started up from his seat and banged the table with his fist. "Stop that twaddle!" He raised his hand as though he were going to box the child's ears. She shrank back and grew deadly pale.

"But, Mr. Tiralla!" exclaimed the schoolmaster, seizing hold of his arm, "it's wonderful, perfectly wonderful!"

Mrs. Tiralla made the sign of the cross as she cried, "Holy Mother! What a sin he's committing! May God not lay it to our charge."

"Hold your tongue," shouted her husband furiously. "You're making the girl quite crazy. And I'll not have her made crazy. Holy Virgin--Grey Sisters--Ladies of the Sacred Heart--all twaddle. She's to sleep when she goes to bed and not invent such nonsense. After to-day her bed is to be brought down into my room. Then I'll see if the Holy Virgin will come to her again. I feel certain she won't."

"That wouldn't be at all suitable," said Mrs. Tiralla in an icy tone. "Rosa is already a big girl."

"Tut, tut! Whether it's suitable or not, it'll be better for her to see what a man is like than to have her head turned with such unnatural stuff." He cast a suspicious glance at his wife.

Mrs. Tiralla grew frightened. If there were any talk about Rosa she knew that her husband was quite a different man; then he was no longer a fool, or a bear that growled a little and then let her lead him. So she wisely said:

"Very well, as you like. Let Rosa sleep down here with you. But I tell you, you'll not be able to scare away what is coming to her. Nobody can scare away what is coming," she added impressively, and gazed at him with such a strange look in her black eyes that the superstitious man shuddered.

"Rosa is one of the chosen ones," she continued. "She sees what you'll never see, and hears what you'll never hear. Very well, let her come down to you. Take firm hold of her hands and of her feet, too, she'll still leave you." The woman grew more and more excited the longer she spoke, and she gazed at her husband with eyes full of rebuke. "It'll be bad for you that you resist in this way. The saints will bear it in mind, and will not forgive you, and when you cry out for them to deliver you from Purgatory, they will not deliver you. You're a wicked man, a scoffer and a blasphemer! Alas, alas, what will become of you?"

"Do you really think so, really?" Mr. Tiralla felt somewhat disconcerted, her great earnestness bewildered him, and he moved restlessly backwards and forwards on his chair. If she were right? No, it was nothing but romantic nonsense. He was still in possession of his senses, and he would never, no never, allow any one to persuade his little girl, his dear Röschen, who was to bring him so much happiness in this life--healthy grandchildren and all kinds of good things--to go into a convent. Yes, persuade her, that was the word. Sophia had always been too pious, he was sorry to say, and the priest, and the schoolmaster? "To the devil with you all!" he shouted, gaining courage at the sound of his own voice. "May he be struck with lightning who dares contradict me, when I say she's to be married as soon as possible. Nobody can be too young for that. And I'll procure her a nice husband. Then she'll grow happy and buxom, and when she gets a little boy on her lap--such a wee fellow who kicks about and wants nursing--then she'll not get any more of those stupid fancies. The Holy Virgin, the Holy Virgin! we pray to our Lady. But when Rosa is a mother herself, she'll have other things to think of." He laughed, his anger had almost disappeared again at the beautiful prospect which lay before him.

At that moment Mrs. Tiralla gave a shrill scream. "There, you see--there, you see what you've done."

Rosa had given a deep, plaintive sigh, her head had drooped forward like a withered flower, and she would have fallen from her chair if the schoolmaster had not caught her in his arms. She had fainted.

Mr. Tiralla was frightened to death. Alas, alas, what had he done? He would have liked to beat himself, to pull off his head. He struck his forehead with his clenched hand and called himself the most unflattering names he could think of, "fool, blockhead, idiot." He shouted for Marianna, roared for water, ordered Tokay--no, gin--wanted to pour it down the girl's throat, spilt it all over her, then called himself once more all kinds of names and almost wept.

They had pushed him away from his daughter. The schoolmaster still held her in his arms, whilst Marianna rubbed her cold feet and Mrs. Tiralla her temples, and breathed on her with the warm, vivifying breath from her powerful lungs. She did not feel so terrified, she knew what it was. Rosa used to faint very easily, it was on account of her age, the doctor had said, and there was nothing to be anxious about. But she pretended to be alarmed, for he deserved it. What if the child never recovered consciousness, never opened her eyes again? Alas, the Holy Virgin had sent it as a punishment.

The terrified man groaned aloud. Oh, God, he hadn't wanted to do that, not that! She should continue to sleep upstairs, he wouldn't say a word more about it, he would hide his own wishes deep down in his breast. Never again would he pollute her ears with such things, although he really couldn't understand in what way he had wounded her innocence to such a degree that she had fainted. Oh, he was a fool, he didn't understand any more what was going on in his own house. He remained sitting some time in silence, with his head buried in his hands. And then when the child began to stir and he heard her sigh and say in a feeble voice, "Ah, mammie," he got up hastily, took down his hat and coat from the rack and staggered out of the house.

He remained standing for a long time in the middle of the yard with his eyes fixed on the house. Wouldn't Rosa ask for him? Wouldn't she beg him to come to her?

But as nobody called him, and the light downstairs began to move about, then disappeared and finally shone in the little room upstairs--they were taking Rosa up to bed--he walked out of his gate with bent head.

* * * * * * * * * * * *

"He has really gone out," whispered Mrs. Tiralla, when she came back to the sitting-room. She had sat a long time with Mr. Böhnke at the child's bedside. Rosa had been very excited. When she had recovered from her faint she had wept bitterly and had wanted to see her father. He had gone out, they told her, his conscience had left him no peace. After that the child had wept for a long time. Then she had been so worn out that she had dozed a little, but it had been no peaceful slumber, although her mother had held one of her hands and the schoolmaster the other. She had given several loud, terrified shrieks, her brows had contracted with pain. And then she had begun to talk in her sleep, a confused medley of words.

"I suppose she's delirious?" said the schoolmaster. But the woman had whispered to him that Rosa was having her visions again, and that if he would listen quietly, he would soon make sense out of what she was saying.

Mrs. Tiralla knelt down by the bedside, and resting her head on her hands which she had folded round those of the child, she began to pray in a soft voice.

All the man could see in the twilight had been that bent head, the silky smoothness of which seemed even silkier than usual in the dim light from the shaded lamp. He was seized with a mad desire to press his lips to that bowed neck which was so near him, to thrust both his hands in that beautiful, black hair. He could scarcely bear it any longer, his heart throbbed so tumultuously that he trembled. What did it matter to him that the servant was crouching at the end of the bed with her face buried in her knees? And the delirious child would be no hinderance to him either. Who could prevent him from stretching out his arms and drawing the kneeling woman to his side and closing her mouth with his kisses? Mr. Tiralla was not there; it was as though he would never return. And around them was darkness. And still he dared not do it. This woman--he groaned--ah, this woman could do anything she liked with him.

"Sh!" Mrs. Tiralla raised her head. "Sh! now, now! Do you hear?"

"Oh, my poor father!" sighed Rosa. It sounded as though she were going to cry; there was something unspeakably touching in her plaintive voice. "My poor father, what are they doing to you? You can't escape, alas, alas!"

The child's low voice shook with fear, and she threw herself about on the bed with a convulsive movement.

From what couldn't he escape? The schoolmaster knitted his brows, her words made a strange impression on him.

But Mrs. Tiralla leant over the bed so that the man could feel her breath on his cheek, and whispered in his ear, "Sh! be quiet!" Now she sees him being tormented in hell. She often sees him like that. "Röschen, my darling," she whispered softly, bending over the child, "leave that wicked man in hell, don't be frightened. Don't you see the Holy Virgin this evening, and the dear Child Jesus on her lap? Oh, how sweetly she's smiling. Hark, doesn't she say something? Hail, Mary----"

"Thou Gracious Mother," the child struck in immediately, and her voice had lost its note of fear, "thou pure Mother, thou spotless Mother, thou wonderful Mother. Ah, I see her!" cried Rosa triumphantly, and her pale face flushed a rosy red. "Mother, Marianna, Mr. Böhnke, pray that she may not turn away from us. Come, come!" She stretched out her hands as though she wanted to draw the three people around her bed still nearer. "Kneel down," she called out in a loud voice. "Oh, thou Lamb of God that takest away the sins of the world, spare us, good Lord----"

"Hear us, good Lord," droned Marianna. She had dragged herself nearer the bed, and now she hit her breast and bowed every time as she repeated, "Spare us, good Lord! Hear us, good Lord! Have pity on us, good Lord!"

Mrs. Tiralla and the schoolmaster exchanged a glance.

"The spirit has come over her," whispered the woman, and made the sign of the cross. "She will soon reveal a great deal to us."

The schoolmaster hastily pulled out his notebook with trembling hands. He felt somewhat embarrassed and whispered uneasily, "Marvellous, very marvellous!" He would have given much to be away from it all, but he couldn't go, it was too wonderful. He would have to write it all down so as to repeat it to the priest. What would he say to having a clairvoyante among his congregation? Holy Mother, only not that!

A sudden terror gripped him. He felt cold and hot by turns, and his hands trembled as he held the book and pencil. If she really could see into the future? Pshaw, she was nothing but a sickly, romantic, delirious child. And still--he could not help shuddering in the semi-darkness of that lonely little room, near the woman he coveted--and still his excited fancy at once gave shape to what Rosa's dreamy babbling had stirred up within him. The child was enraptured with the dear Virgin who smiles at the innocent, but he adorned her with all the voluptuous charms which she--his eyes glittered as they hung on the woman he coveted--she possessed.

It was midnight before Mrs. Tiralla and the schoolmaster returned to the sitting-room. The favoured child was sleeping soundly, there were no more marvellous utterances to listen to. The trance was now over, which had filled them all with such delight and during which Marianna had buried her face in her hands and groaned:

"How beautiful, how beautiful! I don't understand it; but oh, how beautiful!"

But the man was still in a state of great excitement. What else was there for him to do, now that Mr. Tiralla had really gone away, but clasp this smiling woman, whose eyes shone like candles, to his breast?

He approached her full of fierce desire. Now that the so ardently longed-for moment had arrived all the scruples which had hitherto deterred him had disappeared. Now, now!

He went up to her with outstretched arms, but she escaped from him as she so often had escaped from her husband, and ran behind the table. This was now between him and her. Her husband had always tried to catch her on these occasions, and had run after her round the big table like a boy playing at tig, but the schoolmaster did not do that. He did not move; he had suddenly grown very pale and his outstretched arms had sunk down. So she didn't want him to? It was a very keen disappointment.

What on earth was the schoolmaster dreaming of? Mrs. Tiralla almost flew into a passion. But then she noticed how dejected he looked, how his eyes avoided hers, and a sudden fear befell her. What if he were to be so angry with her now that he turned away from her, and she were to be as lonely as she had been before? Oh, only not that, she must have one helping hand. Wasn't he the helper, the friend whom the Holy Virgin had sent her? She daren't let him go away like that, she would have to grant him one favour, but only one. And she came from behind her bulwark; she had no fear, for she felt that she had this man entirely in her power. She went up to him, put her arms round his neck and kissed him quickly on the cheek.

"Go now," she whispered, "go! It's late--midnight--what will Marianna think? I shouldn't like people to talk about me. Go!"

She urged him to be gone and he obeyed her, for he had got a kiss, a kiss from her. He thirsted for another one, but wasn't this a beginning?

When Marianna lighted him to the road, he embraced her with such force that she let the lantern fall, she was so startled.

The sober man was quite changed. He stumbled across the fields as though he were intoxicated, and everything seemed to swim before his eyes. Starydwór lay behind him, Starydwór lay in front of him, Starydwór lay to the right, Starydwór lay to the left. Starydwór was everywhere.

* * * * * * * * * * * *

The schoolmaster seemed almost as intoxicated as Mr. Tiralla was, as he crossed the fields on his way home from the village some hours later. But he did not see Starydwór everywhere, as the other man had done, for it was quite impossible for him to find his own farm. It was as though it had disappeared from the globe, or as though he had nothing more to do there.

It happened now and then that Mr. Tiralla indulged in too much drink--now and then on special occasions such as the Sokol's entertainment, or lately the Gradewitz ball--who wouldn't have done that? But as a rule Mr. Tiralla was what you might call a sober man. The fact was that he could stand a great deal. But this evening he had drunk nothing but gin. He had felt so sad, oh, so sad; he didn't know himself why he had felt so sad. He had known for a long time that his Sophia was very irritable, so that couldn't have caused it; he had also known that his Rosa was a very pious child; really too pious, a remarkably pious child. But to-day there was something else, something that weighed him down to such a degree, that it had almost broken his heart. He had to drink in order to get rid of the weight that was oppressing him; drink until he was intoxicated. And he could only arrive at that state with the help of gin.

The acquaintances he had met at the inn had been very much surprised at his behaviour. Mr. Tiralla was so quiet; he didn't brag at all about his Sophia. It was as though he had been put to silence. The priest had said a few kind words to him about his daughter, when he came to the inn for a short time after his supper; she was an excellent child, a pure soul with whom God was well pleased. But Mr. Tiralla had only smiled feebly.

He had sat staring into his glass with both elbows on the table, and his red head buried in his hands, without saying a word. He had sat like that for hours.

One man after the other had said good night, first the priest, then the gendarme, then the forester, then Mr. Schmielke. Jokisch, as a good neighbour, had stopped the longest with Mr. Tiralla. He had plucked at his sleeve when the others had departed and had said in a confidential tone, "Listen, old fellow, I must tell you that the others are saying that Böhnke, the schoolmaster, comes too often to see you--I mean to see your wife."

"He's been to see her this evening," said Mr. Tiralla, in a calm voice. And when the other man had stared at him in a disconcerted kind of way, he had continued in a voice that was still calmer, "You envious scoundrel, *psia krew!* Don't you know my Sophia? Do you think it's that what's oppressing me? Not that, oh God, not that!"

And he had given a loud sigh, and burying his head once more in his hands had said no more. Then Jokisch had said good night. They could very well have gone home together--their roads only parted at the Boża męka [A] just before you come to the Przykop --but Mr. Tiralla's company wasn't amusing enough. By Jove, the old man seemed quite stupid.

A *The wayside image of a saint.*

Mr. Tiralla had remained sitting all alone. The landlord would have liked to extinguish the lights and go to bed; his wife, servant, and children had been asleep for a long time, everybody was asleep except Mr. Tiralla, who did not seem to think of going to bed. At last the landlord had fallen asleep behind the bar, and was only awakened by a dull sound. Mr. Tiralla had thrown the big, empty gin bottle at him, after helping himself to the very last drop.

Was Mr. Tiralla going home alone? How would Mr. Tiralla get home? The landlord was very anxious about him.

It was a night in early spring as Mr. Tiralla staggered home. A long time would elapse before the lilac-bushes near the dilapidated railings in the weed-grown herb garden would bloom; there was still no sign of buds on the trees, the plain was still bare and wintry-looking. But something was already moving deep down in the earth. The furrows, through which Mr. Tiralla tramped as he crossed the fields, were thawed, and lumps of soft earth clung to his boot-soles. He had lost his way; he could not get any further.

"*Psia krew!*" He stumbled, cursed, and scolded, and then he laughed. He felt that he had drunk too much--oho, he would never be so drunk that he couldn't feel what he had been up to. But to be a little drunk was a very useful thing now and then. For then you didn't feel the oppression quite so much.

CHAPTER VII

The strawberries were ripening in the Przykop. The children from Starawieś would go there to look for them, and when they had all been gathered it would be the time for mushrooms. But the village children did not like the gloom that reigned in the Przykop, they were accustomed to let the rays of the burning sun scorch their brown bodies a still darker brown amid the flat turnip fields and immense plains covered with corn, where there were no shadows to arrest its full force.

The big pines commenced just at the back of Starydwór, and beyond those were the alders and willows, extending as far as the low-lying marshes, where the frogs croaked at night, the white water-lilies opened their golden calices at midday, and where towards evening the game from the royal forest in the blue distance beat a path through the rustling reeds on their way to quench their thirst at the pools. A long, long time ago the whole of the Przykop was said to have been an enormous lake, ten times as big as now. Now nothing remained of it but the basin in the centre, that deep depression which, so to speak, formed a hollow amid the yellow and green carpet of this fruitful corn-land. But at night, when the will-o'-the-wisps wandered about the marshes and danced on the duckweed, in which a man could be swallowed up if he did not take care where he put his foot, the pious people would make the sign of the cross when they were obliged to pass that way. For the will-o'-the-wisps were the souls of those who could not find peace in the grave.

Rosa Tiralla much preferred the Przykop to the bare fields. If she stood at the farm gate and looked across the fields she could see the whole way to Starawieś, the path she took to school every day, the wooden church tower and the cottage roofs covered with moss, that almost disappeared from view behind the pale, waving corn when it stood high. But from her bedroom window at the back of the house, she could look into the Przykop, where the dark trees rustled so strangely.

The white-faced child felt the mystery of the morass just as much as the brown-skinned children from Starawieś; but while it terrified them, it attracted her. How beautiful to be in the deep, cool shade when the sun was scorching outside. There was always a soft twilight under the trees, and when the light fell through the interlaced branches on the damp, green moss, it was no longer cruel, it was transfigured.

Even as a small child Rosa Tiralla had often been in the Przykop. Her nurse had always taken her there, for the wind, which swept across the plain endangering the life of the delicate child, was hardly felt there. The trees in the hollow were so well protected by the rising ground that only their tops rustled slightly in the wind. Rosa very often lifted the rusty latch of the gate that separated the morass from the little garden at the back of Starydwór. "How lovely the mountains and valleys of the Przykop were," thought the child of the plain. In her eyes the slight incline down which she used to glide was a deep, deep valley, and the hill she used to climb so laboriously, holding fast to the luxuriant moss, ferns, and projecting tree-roots, a big, big mountain.

The deer would approach Rosa without fear, and look at her with their limpid eyes. But she was full of fear; not of the deer, however, but of the other creatures which surrounded her in the Przykop. The older she grew, the more fearful she became. Marianna had told her too many tales about them. The deep, deep silence, in which the woodpecker's hammering on the bark used to sound like peals of thunder, made her shudder. And still she would not have liked to give up that sweet emotion, nor give up lying in the thick moss, gazing up into the tree-tops to find a bit of sky. She was always within call, and that reassured her. But if a sound found its way to her--her father's deep, bass voice, or her mother's treble, or the maid's "*Psia krew*, where have you got to?"--she would give a start as though she had been roughly handled or had been caught doing something wrong, and turn scarlet and sigh as she smoothed her thick, tousled hair.

* * * * * * * * * * * * *

Rosa Tiralla was very busy looking for mushrooms in the Przykop this summer. It was the time of the damp, sultry dog-days, in which they sprang up in a night. But not many were eaten in Starawieś or the neighbourhood, for the public had been warned against them. The schoolmaster had also warned the children in the school; they were neither to gather nor eat any they were not quite sure of. People grew alarmed.

"Many people have made themselves ill with eating mushrooms," said Marianna to her mistress, when the latter spoke of sending Rosa to fetch some.

Mrs. Tiralla laughed. "Nonsense, I know mushrooms very well."

"That makes no difference," exclaimed the maid, growing warm, "I won't eat them even if I do know them. Ugh!" she spat on the ground, "mushrooms are the devil's own vegetables."

"Why?" The woman looked at the maid with dull, wide-open eyes, in which a dawning light suddenly began to gleam. She turned red and pale by turns, blinked her eyes a little as though something were dazzling her, and then smiled. "What do you mean by 'the devil's own vegetables'? I don't understand you."

Marianna made the sign of the cross. "God bless it! But I don't know if even that always helps. Many a one has got his death from eating a dish of mushrooms. Who can say which are poisonous and which are not? Good and bad ones grow side by side; the devil passes his finger over them during the night, and in the morning they all look alike, you can't see any difference. You gather, you cook, you eat--oh!" Marianna stretched out her fingers and rolled her eyes. "Holy Mother. I know how awfully you suffer. I won't eat mushrooms, I know that." She shuddered.

"Well, you needn't eat any, nobody has asked you to," said the woman, soothingly, to the girl, who grew more and more vehement. "You hadn't eaten mushrooms that time you fell ill. Oh, we know all about it," she said jestingly, shaking her finger at her. But it was no real jest, for all merriment was wanting, and there was something forced in her laugh as she added, "Jendrek has let it out; you had drunk too much, and that was why you were ill."

"Oh, the rogue, the scoundrel," cried Marianna furiously, clenching her fist. "How can he say so? The liar! I hadn't drunk too much; I had drunk nothing, I remember it well. It was the day after the master had been to Gnesen to fetch the rat poison. I had drunk nothing that morning but a sip of coffee, a sip of the coffee I was taking to the master. I can swear to that."

The maid cast an inquisitive, scrutinizing glance at her mistress. Would she turn red, or pale? Now it was out; what had been the matter with that coffee? Would she be brazen-faced enough to scold her because she had drunk some of the master's coffee? Well, then, she would just give her a piece of her mind, she would let her know that there had been poison in it.

Mrs. Tiralla, however, took no notice of what had been said.

Marianna kept her eyes fixed on her mistress. Who could say what the Pani was thinking of now? But no deeper colour came into Mrs. Tiralla's face. The maid felt quite bewildered. What! the Pani remained so calm, she neither looked terrified nor changed colour? Why, she was even smiling like an angel from heaven. She would have to get to the bottom of this. So she quickly said in a bold, resolute voice:

"I had only drunk some of the coffee which the Pani herself had made; I can't imagine how that could have made me so ill." She shrugged her shoulders and put on her most stupid and innocent look, whilst her sly eyes roved about. "The Pani would surely not cook anything bad for the master."

"No, certainly not," answered Mrs. Tiralla, quite calmly, although her heart almost stood still with terror. No fear must be shown now, not an eyelid must quiver. Ah, she had learnt to dissemble more easily now. The woman was filled with an almost fierce, triumphant joy, which gave a natural cheerfulness to her voice as she added, "He's such a judge of good living, he'll have nothing but what's good." And then she said in a friendly tone, as though she had quite forgotten Marianna's pointed words and the coffee she had taken, "Jendrek must have told a lie, then. Here." She put her hand into the little bag that hung on her belt near her keys, and brought out a new shilling. "Here, Marianna. I'm sorry that I've wronged you so long in my thoughts."

The servant forgot to thank her mistress, but stared at her completely bewildered as she left the kitchen. Oh, she--she was really--she, she--had she really put nothing into the coffee? Marianna felt she was too stupid, her head ached with all the thinking; it would be better to leave it alone. The Pani had given her a new shilling bit, the Pani was good. She was happy now.

Mrs. Tiralla stood outside the door and called for her daughter, and when Rosa obediently came she gave her a basket and put on her broad-brimmed straw hat with her own hands, "There, my darling," and told her to go and look for mushrooms for her father's supper.

Many different kinds of mushrooms were to be found in the Przykop--yellow, red, brown, orange-coloured, and greenish. When Rosa had gone out the first time to find some she had felt very anxious. There was a dark brown one growing under a pine tree, big and firm, with a strong smell and very appetizing in appearance. But she had eyed it very uncertainly. Was that the devil's toadstool, which the schoolmaster had marked on the board at school as poisonous, or was it one of the dainty *boleti edules*, which her father liked so much? Oh, dear, she had not listened very attentively; Mr. Böhnke had given them all the characteristics, but she had been dreaming as usual. Her thoughts had flown away into infinite space, away over the board which Mr. Böhnke was holding before them. He used to be very annoyed with the other children if they were not attending, but he was never annoyed with her, for she was Rosa Tiralla. Oh, if only he had been.

She did not know what to do. She hesitated doubtfully; should she take the mushroom or not? There were many of the same kind growing in the moss; they seemed to smile at her.

A wood-pigeon was cooing over the lonely girl's head. It had fluttered down from the high pine treetop and was now sitting on one of the thick bottom branches watching her. It cooed and cooed. Then Rosa at last felt certain that the bird wanted to warn her. It was a messenger from the Holy Virgin; these mushrooms were all poisonous. And the girl lifted up her dress, so that not even the hem of it should touch them, and stepped over them with anxious haste.

So Rosa came home the first time without any mushrooms. "Mother, I didn't know which were poisonous and which were not. I was afraid, so I left them all." Then Mrs. Tiralla had been more angry with her daughter than she had ever been before, and had pulled her plaits and called her a stupid goose. All the mushrooms growing in the Przykop were fit to eat; there was not a single poisonous one among them.

"But Mr. Böhnke says, and Marianna says--oh, mammie, I'm so afraid of poisonous mushrooms. How awful it would be if anybody ate one."

"You're very stupid," said her mother, but in a gentler tone. "Next time I'll go with you and show you those you are to gather. Don't cry." And she stroked the hair which she had pulled a short time before.

Then Rosa felt pleased that her mother was no longer angry with her, and would teach her to find the right mushrooms.

The golden sun was smiling down on the moss, and everything was bright and cheerful even in the Przykop when Mrs. Tiralla went with Rosa to gather mushrooms.

"Look here, Röschen, this one. And here, this one." She pointed to different places in the moss with her foot and told the child to gather.

"But aren't those poisonous, mammie? Marianna says----"

"Fiddle-de-dee. What does Marianna know about it? She's more stupid than I took her to be; she a country girl and doesn't even know mushrooms? Pick them, pick them. They're good. They're your father's favourite dish when they're fried in butter and then stewed in cream."

So Rosa knelt down quickly and was soon busy gathering the red mushrooms that had an orange tinge and little white knobs on their caps as though they had been embroidered; such bright looking mushrooms they were, the prettiest of them all. And then she gathered some of the brown ones as well, which she had avoided so carefully the first time, and her basket was soon full.

"Now we've got enough," said Mrs. Tiralla. "Now you can't make a mistake, and you'll know where to find them. Next time you can go alone."

"Oh, yes, of course I know now. But it's nice to go to the wood with you," said the child ingratiatingly, hanging on her mother's arm.

She was almost as tall as her mother now, their shoulders were on the same level; they could have been taken for sisters. The black-haired woman with her velvety, sparkling eyes was certainly more beautiful, but there was such a gentle, happy expression on the girl's face that made one forgetful of her freckles and her pale blue eyes.

"How father will feast," said Rosa, and pressed her mother's arm. "Shall you prepare them for him this evening?"

"I shall prepare them for him this evening," repeated the woman absent-mindedly. Her thoughts were already far ahead. Would he suffer when he had eaten them, as Marianna had said? She trembled. But there must be no compassion. Had she not suffered, suffered agonies from the very first hour he had come to her mother's sewing-room and had stretched out his coarse fingers to take her? She did not like him, no, she had never liked him. And she disliked him more than ever since he had begun to drink, since he had returned one evening from the inn dead drunk; and now he often came home so intoxicated that Marianna and Jendrek had to take him under the arms and drag him into the house. If he ate some of the mushrooms, and the Holy Virgin would stand by him, he would close his eyes immediately afterwards. That would be the best thing for him. Had he not said the last time he was drunk and was crying so bitterly, "I don't suit this place. When my Sophia is a widow, will she love me more than she does now?" Yes, she would. He was quite right, and he had felt it dully in his intoxication. A monument should be erected to his memory, as beautiful a cross as could be ordered in Gradewitz, or even in Gnesen. If only he would depart, it only he would depart and leave her in peace.

The woman's feelings towards her husband became almost tender. She would make the mushrooms very nice, and neither spare the butter nor the cream.

They should taste very, very good.

＊＊＊＊＊＊＊＊＊＊＊＊

As mother and daughter left the Przykop they saw Mr. Tiralla standing at the garden gate looking out for them. He was longing for his supper, for which he felt an aching void. But there was another kind of void which tortured him still more. Now Sophia had even taken the child away with her. It was fortunate that Mikolai was coming home in the autumn, then he would have more company. Mr. Tiralla had never liked being alone, and now he liked it less than ever. There was an indefinite something that frightened him; he could not have said what it was, but it seemed to be lying in wait for him at every corner.

He called out to the two in a joyful voice. He was holding up his hand to his eyes in order to protect them from the sun that was setting blood-red behind the pines, and the two figures in their light-coloured dresses looked like angels of light. "*Psia krew*, why so late? Come, my dears, come along."

Rosa let her mother's arm go. Swinging her basket in the air she ran up to her father, "Mushrooms, mushrooms." She was glowing with happiness.

He stroked her flying hair away from her face and patted her cheeks. "My darling, my consolation."

Why did her father look so serious? He was low-spirited. Rosa gazed at him with womanly, anxious eyes that love had sharpened. Her daddy was growing old. What a lot of lines he had in his face, lots of crooked lines like those the crows made in the snow with their feet. And still he was so stout, and had such a good appetite. "Do you love me?" she asked affectionately, raising her face for him to kiss. "I love you."

He did not kiss her; he was looking at his wife, who was coming on more slowly.

It seemed to Mrs. Tiralla as though her foot faltered, as though a leaden weight were almost paralyzing her. There he stood waiting impatiently. Well, he should have them. She ran past him with a muttered "God be with me!"

Nobody was in the kitchen. What had become of that slow hussy Marianna? But never mind, she could not have done with her to-day. She put wood and peat on the fire with her own hands, so that the embers were soon ablaze, placed a pan on the fire, and fetched butter and cream from the larder. She was very busy.

At that moment Rosa came running in. "Mother, daddy asks if the mushrooms are really good?"

"Why, of course," said Mrs. Tiralla, and pushed her daughter impatiently out of the kitchen. She could not have her looking on. Then she cut the mushrooms to pieces and threw them into the pan and poured boiling water on them; they were to boil for some time, bad and good all together, so that they might lose their shape and colour and all resemble each other so much that they could not be distinguished. Nobody should say of her that she had set poisonous mushrooms before her husband; besides, he would not have eaten them.

The water bubbled and hissed on the stove; it was boiling fiercely, as she had made a huge fire. The food must be cooked quickly, Mr. Tiralla was longing for his supper.

Just then he stuck his head into the kitchen. "Will there soon be something to eat, Sophia?"

"There'll soon be something to eat." She put some more wood on the fire; the mushrooms were already getting tender. The pan was filled with a slimy sauce that had a very powerful smell. She bent over it and sniffed. Good gracious, the smell was so pungent that it would betray her! Away with it! She quickly poured the sauce and scum off to the very last drop, took another pan, melted some more butter in it, and then put the mushrooms into it. The horrid odour had disappeared, now they smelt delicious.

While the mushrooms were frying in the butter, Mrs. Tiralla stood by with folded hands. "Holy Mother, I call on thee, do not forsake me, pray for me." (Oh, if--it only these mushrooms were cooked, he would eat them, and then?) "Jesus Christ, hear us, now and in the hour of our death." (If--if he ate some, then--then?) "Son of God, we commend this soul to thee, have mercy on it." (Oh, when he had eaten?) No, she could not pray any longer, all she could do was to whisper just above her breath, "Jesus, Mary, Joseph, assist this soul in its death-agony."

Marianna came into the kitchen. Dear, dear, was the mistress already cooking? Bustling about in her haste to get on, the girl knocked the plates together. Oh, how the Pani would scold. She ducked her head involuntarily.

But the Pani was looking straight into the glowing fire. Then suddenly awaking as from a dream she seized the pan containing the cream, poured its contents over the dish of mushrooms, shook it, and told the maid to carry it into the room.

As Marianna placed the dish on the table at which the man, woman, and child were already seated, Mrs. Tiralla turned deadly pale. She gave a start as her husband began at once to help himself; it seemed as though she were about to grip his arm.

"God bless it!" said the maid, in a loud voice, and then, turning round, she furtively made the sign of the cross and spat three times. Ugh, mushrooms! She shuddered. And how strange the mistress was; she must also be afraid, her face was so pale. Marianna ran out of the room, she felt all at once so frightened. How could anybody eat mushrooms? Ugh! She again felt the horrible, choking sensation which had oppressed her heart and numbed her limbs the time she was so ill. She could not fight against it. She crouched near the fire and folded her hands, she was so terribly frightened. But one thing she did know, and that was as soon as she could she would go to the priest--no, rather to the gendarme. But then she rejected the idea of the gendarme, for would he believe her? But if she could swear to it by all the saints? But she could not swear to it, not exactly swear to it. However, she would tell the priest about it. What a house this was! How dreadful it was for a poor servant girl like her to have to serve in such a place. She wept bitterly.

However, when Jendrek knocked at the kitchen door a moment later for her to come out, she ran behind the stable to him and forgot her master and the mushrooms.

Mrs. Tiralla noted with horror with what relish her husband was eating the mushrooms. She felt quite numbed, she could not move. But when Rosa asked for some, too--they smelt so good, she had taken a fancy to them--she screamed, "They're too indigestible for you. I shall not eat any either. We can't touch them."

So Mr. Tiralla finished them all. "I've not tasted anything I liked do well for a long time," he said with a fat smile as he stroked his paunch. "That's because my little daughter has gathered them for me and my dear wife has cooked them. Thanks, both of you." He nodded to his daughter and took hold of his wife's hand and kissed it.

He was remarkably gentle, so strangely tender. His wife felt startled, his voice already sounded quite different. She watched him with anxious eyes--he had asked for a glass of gin after the rich food--did he feel ill already? She could scarcely keep her feet quiet under the table. Away, away, oh, how she would have liked to run away; she did not want to look on any longer.

"Give me a kiss, Sophia darling," begged her husband.

She humoured him. It would be the last, why should she refuse him the last kiss?

He drew her on his knee. Then he sent Rosa out of the room; she was to go to bed so that she could get up next morning and fetch lots of mushrooms. "Go, go, I say," he urged, as she clung to him tenderly. However much he loved her, he had only thoughts for his Sophia at present. She was so good, so affectionate to-day; oh, God, were the good times returning?

* * * * * * * * * * * *

Marianna was in her first deep sleep that night when she heard her master's door creak. Suddenly everything came back to her. Holy Mother, the mushrooms. Did he feel very bad? The poor master! She jumped out of bed as quick as lightning and rushed to the door. But when she tore it open, she saw that it was only her mistress who had just carefully closed the master's door opposite and was standing outside. What had she been up to in that room? The maid almost screamed, she was so surprised.

Mrs. Tiralla looked frightened when she caught sight of the maid, and they stared at each other for some moments. Then the woman put her finger to her lips, "Sh! I--I--couldn't sleep upstairs--I heard something--and I thought of thieves--yes, thieves--and then I ran down."

"Oh, there are no thieves here." The maid gave a loud laugh, it sounded too ridiculous that the Pani, who had never been afraid of thieves, should suddenly speak of them. Surely she had not come down on account of them? But why? It had never occurred to her to creep down to Mr. Tiralla before? Marianna's eyes grew very big. But then she suddenly thought, she has wanted to see how he feels after the food, for he ate every bit of it, the poor man. Marianna sighed. Then she cast an insolent glance at her mistress and said:

"Well, and how's the master? I suppose he's not very well, eh?"

"Why, why?" asked the woman, trembling. But then she grew calm, the girl's impertinent glances helped her to regain her composure. "I don't know what you mean," she said in a lofty tone. "Mr. Tiralla is sleeping quietly." With a slight nod she turned away and crept so softly up to her room that not a stair creaked.

Driven by curiosity Marianna put her head into her master's room. All was dark; she could see nothing, but she heard him breathing regularly and deeply. He did not even groan, he was sleeping so quietly. Was he still alive? She groped her way to the bed. Thank God, there he lay warm and comfortable.

As she bent over him he stretched out his arms and stammered, half asleep, "Heigh, darling!"

* * * * * * * * * * * *

Mrs. Tiralla was standing before her glass upstairs looking at her pale, disfigured face. She felt overcome with shame, a shame that was even greater than her terror. What must the maid have thought of her? Dark lines under her eyes, her hair dishevelled, her face all mottled. Oh, God! She had submitted to it all--and he was still alive. She was seized with a violent fit of fury, she would have liked to destroy everything, smash everything to pieces. Pressing her clenched fists against her forehead she uttered a deep groan. She was the one who had been deceived, she always was. Böhnke, too, had deceived her. Had he not told her that fly agarics--the orange-red mushrooms with white warts--were very poisonous, and that the devil's toadstool--the brown, squat one which so strongly resembled the *boletus edulis*--was even more so? He had brought a book with him, and had read it to her secretly in the little garden with the palings all round, where they had stolen like a pair of lovers who want to be as far away from everybody as possible. He had also shown her the illustrations, and she had watched most carefully as he pointed out what the poisonous mushrooms looked like. She had impressed it firmly on her memory. Four fly agarics were enough to bring death, people said, but he--he lived. But had she not also read in the schoolmaster's book that "death can either occur in the course of an hour or two, or after two or three days"? H'm, Mr. Tiralla was very strong, what would kill any other man scarcely affected him. She would have to wait then, wait.

She threw herself on her knees. If only he had died at once, this waiting was so awful. She dreaded the thought of what the morrow might bring forth. She had been calm enough while cooking the mushrooms, but now she was the reverse. She could hardly bear to wait any longer. But now it was no longer a great longing for his death, which was to bring her release, it was only a fervent desire to be free from this great fear which oppressed her heart and confused her senses. She sprang up from her knees as though she were out of her mind, then threw herself down again, the next moment to jump up once more and raise her clasped hands to heaven. "Mary, Holy Virgin, pray for me!" What was the Holy Virgin to pray for? Oh, she knew what for; knew better than she did herself, for *she* did not know any longer. Life? Death? Alas, alas, now she would have preferred him to live; only not to see him lying there distorted with convulsions, and with the hue of death already on his face.

The woman crept into the darkest corner of the room like a frightened animal, and bit her hands, which she had pressed against her mouth, and wept and trembled. How slowly the night crept on, would it never, never be day? How quietly Rosa was breathing. She was sleeping so well. Oh, to be a child once more, an innocent child who knows nothing of Life's wickedness.

Mrs. Tiralla was filled with an intense longing for innocence and purity, for a blameless, peaceful life. She would go to confession as soon as possible next morning. She would confess everything, so that she could breathe once more as quietly as her child. Even at the last examination of conscience she had not been able to find the right expression for what was stirring in her heart. But now, when the sins against the fifth commandment were being enumerated: "Have you by means of blows, curses, and such-like injured yourself or others, are you angry, envious, revengeful, have you lived in hatred and enmity with others, have you grieved others by bitter words, have you hurt them intentionally?" now she would strike her breast and cry, "Yes, yes," so that she might say later on, "I thank Thee, Divine Redeemer, that Thou hast given me absolution and forgiveness for my sins in the Sacrament of Penance."

Then she grew more composed; the mere thought of confession calmed and relieved her immeasurably. She recovered so far as to creep out of her corner and go to Rosa's bed, although she was still trembling, and wake her. "Let us pray, dear," she said, clasping her hands round those of the child.

"What shall we pray?" inquired Rosa, who was always ready to pray and was instantly wide awake.

"Repeat the Act of Desire used at the preparation for Holy Communion."

"Oh, mother, I don't know it." Rosa bent her head in deep shame.

"But I do," said Mrs. Tiralla. "Lord, my soul is longing for Thee. Let me again to-day partake of Thy saving grace. Thou knowest my misery, come. Thou who hast redeemed me by Thy blood, O Son of God. When Thy holy body, O most sweet Jesus, unites itself with my body, and Thy holy soul has poured itself into my soul, oh, what a new, happy life I shall lead. Be gracious to us. Hear us."

She repeated it in a loud voice, and the child raised her hands devoutly and with a pious shudder murmured it after her mother.

* * * * * * * * * * * *

When Mrs. Tiralla came down next morning it was late. She had at last fallen asleep whilst kneeling by Rosa's bedside, so that she did not see the sunbeam dancing on the wall, nor hear the cock crowing, the clatter of the milk pails, the squeaking of the chain in the old well, nor the lowing of the cattle. She had fallen into a dead sleep. And when she at last started up in confusion, awakened by Rosa's caressing touch, she did not venture to go downstairs. She sent the child. "Look if he's up."

But Rosa did not return. Why did she not come? Mrs. Tiralla waited and waited; the minutes seemed to lengthen themselves into hours. Holy Mother, what had happened downstairs, as the child did not return? Courage, courage, courage! She pressed both hands to her heart that was throbbing furiously. If only she had never come to Starydwór, if only she had remained the poorest among the poor, the most wretched among the wretched.

She listened involuntarily. Hark, was that not his voice? No, neither scream nor groan reached her ear. There was no help for it, she would have to go downstairs. It would seem so strange if she were to remain in her room any longer; she would have to go down at once.

She drew a deep breath, tore the door open, took a run and rushed downstairs. Where was he lying? Where should she find him?

"Good morning," said Mr. Tiralla. He was in a good humour and was just coming out of his room. His eyes were still full of sleep and he was rubbing them.

But his eyes were quite clear, they still saw the light of day. The woman started back as though she had seen a ghost.

"Why are you so frightened, eh?" he cried, laughing. "You've slept too long, I suppose? Ha, ha."

She did not answer. Even if her life had depended upon it, she could not have uttered a single word. It was too terrible, too terrible!

He did not pay any attention to her silence nor to her disturbed looks. He was in a very happy frame of mind and was waving a letter in his hand, a letter from his soldier son.

Mikolai had not written for a long time, he did not care for writing. But now he wrote:

"Dear Parents,--Your son, Mikolai, sends you his love, and he is very well. I can tell you I am pleased to get away from the army. It is not the work for me, I prefer to till the ground. And my friend, Martin Becker, who is a miller by profession, but has not got a mill at present, because, although he has some money, it is not enough to buy a big mill, and he won't have a small one, will come home with me. He will help to manage the farm. Dear father, you will not want so many hands then; we will do everything, and you will like Martin. He has no parents, and hails from Klein-Hauland, near Opalenitza. I will let you know the day we are coming. Dear mother, if you will be kind to Becker I shall be grateful to you, for he is a good fellow. Dear sister, I kiss you in my thoughts; our Rosa has, no doubt, grown into a pretty girl. We shall come, all being well, in seven weeks' time. With a kiss to you all,

"Your affectionate Son."

That was his son, just as he was in reality, his dear, good son. A sudden affection for the boy who had been away from home so long awoke in Mr. Tiralla's heart. It was such a long time since he had seen anything of him. He had been away almost three years, and although he had twice driven to Breslau during that time and had looked him up at the barracks, still it was very different from having him at home. It was a good thing that the boy was coming.

It seemed to Mr. Tiralla as though he had been thinking of his Mikolai the whole time he had been away; but that had not been the case. How could he have had leisure to think of him? All, all his thoughts had been taken up with his Sophia. But now he was filled with an impatient longing for his son; he could hardly await the time when the reserves would be dismissed. If only he were at home. The evenings were already growing long; there were no more beautiful summer evenings, for the weather had turned cool and dreary unusually early. Such evenings were very dismal in Starydwór if you had nobody to sit and talk to.

Mrs. Tiralla was ill, and her strange behaviour had made her husband quite ill, too. His Sophia! What was the matter with her? Was she angry with him? He ransacked his brain to find out what he had done to her, but he found nothing. He had done his utmost to put her into a good humour. He had driven to Rosenthal's in Gnesen and bought her a smart black-and-white check coat and skirt. It suited her admirably, and when she had it on she looked like a fine lady going on her travels. But all he could get from her was a feeble, "I should have preferred a black costume." Then he had driven to Gnesen and ordered her a black costume, and as that had not turned out satisfactory, he had even gone to Posen about it. But when he had brought it home--it had been nice and dear--she had only said, "But I can't wear it after all." The deuce, why not? The truth was, he never could do anything to please her. That made him very low-spirited. Why was she so perverse? Why did she look at him so strangely?

He had caught one of those rare glances she vouchsafed him, and it had bewildered him. He had asked Marianna if she knew why her mistress was in such a bad humour, and why she frowned so.

"Let the wicked look fall on the dog," whispered Marianna, and spat on the ground whilst she made the sign of the cross. She would take good care not to mention her suspicions to her master. If she said to him, "That woman is up to something," he would turn her out of the house as a reward. He was still so wrapped up in the woman. And she really did not know herself what the Pani was up to. The mushrooms had agreed with the master all right; he had not been ill after them. She had had nothing to confide to the priest. And even if she had had something to tell him about the Pani, he would never have believed a particle of it, he was so attached to her. She, Marianna, had even had to acknowledge her own sinful thoughts when she had gone to confession. When the priest had asked her, "Do you nourish wicked or suspicious thoughts against anybody in your heart?" she had had to confess that she did, and he had seriously exhorted her not to transgress against the eighth commandment.

So Marianna shrugged her shoulders when Mr. Tiralla stood before her with a perplexed look on his face, and gave him an evasive answer. How horrid his Sophia had been to him again, he complained. He had hardly been into her room--she had established herself in the little room upstairs now and rarely came down--and then merely to ask how she was. He had only ventured to take hold of her hand and ask her if she were feverish, as her eyes burned so, and she had flung his hand away as if he were some unclean animal, and had wept, and wept, until he had grown quite uneasy.

"I don't know," said Marianna. "Pani must be ill, I suppose; you had better ask the doctor." She really felt very grieved about the poor master. And who knows, if he were to die now, perhaps he would bequeath her something, so that she and her little children could have enough to live on, or at least give her such a good dowry that Jendrek or another would make her his kobieta [A] ? So she was very obliging, and was always finding something to do for her master. She would come at least ten times into the room, when he sat alone with his bottle--poor master to have to sit quite alone and drink like that!

[A] *Wife.*

Mr. Tiralla did not go to the inn any more, he shunned all those inquisitive eyes. Everybody used to ask him about his wife when he went there, and he confessed to the maid with a sigh that he could no longer boast about her, for when he did he felt as if he were going to choke, and he could not utter a single word.

Mrs. Tiralla often heard her husband and the maid laughing together as she sat in her room upstairs; and drinking as well, for she could hear them draw four or five corks every evening. Ugh! how he could drink! The woman shuddered with disgust. There was that monster sitting with the vulgar hussy, cracking jokes that were anything but refined, and drinking hard. How could he forget himself like that! How could he intoxicate himself to that degree! Beer alone could not do it, it must be Tokay as well. But wait, was it not a good thing that he drank so much? What would otherwise have happened to her? He would have worried her continually. If she could not be released from him altogether, in this way she could at least reckon on some hours' freedom. And after such nights he used to sleep until morning without waking. Oh, if only he were always, always drunk!

Mrs. Tiralla lay in bed listening to the sounds downstairs, with her nerves on edge. Now the jokes must have become very practical, for the girl was screaming with laughter, and it sounded as if he were choking. And now--she heard it quite plainly, although not a single word reached her ears--now he was babbling some absurd nonsense, at which the girl was almost suffocated with laughter, until he at last grew silent, and letting his head sink on the table fell asleep.

Now he was happy; he was dreaming blissfully. Oh, it could not be so bad when you got to the stage of neither knowing nor feeling anything of it all. She really did not wish him ill--Mrs. Tiralla was almost praising herself--when she wished for his sake that he were always so drunk. What good did he get out of life? He had no sense for higher things, and he did not derive any pleasure from her. He really did not, she must be just. But how could she give others any pleasure if she were not happy herself?--for he was there, still there.

She clenched her fists and bit her lips so as not to lament aloud. Nothing, nothing had helped her, neither the mushrooms, nor throwing him into the ditch, nor the rat poison. She had not cooked any more mushrooms for him, although he had often asked for some. "Gather them yourself," she had answered curtly, and had not allowed Rosa to fetch any more. There was no object in doing so. And throwing him into the ditch? Bah! Her upper lip curled contemptuously at the thought of her own childish stupidity. A ditch was nothing to Mr. Tiralla; he was able to get out of a much deeper pit. But rat poison! What about that poison still lying in her chest in the lumber-room? A great longing for it took possession of her. There was release, it lay in her hands, and still she did not venture to make use of it. Would he also be guarded against that poison, which was said to be strong? Or was it after all not strong enough to kill people? If only she could find out exactly. Who could give her the most reliable information? Böhnke? Oh, that liar! Her whole body shook, she sobbed so tempestuously. He had deceived her. He had pretended to teach her which were poisonous mushrooms, and he had not done so. The wretch! Let him never appear before her eyes again.

Mrs. Tiralla felt furious when she thought of her slave. Had he not sworn that he was devoted to her, first mutely and then in words? On Easter Sunday after their festive meal, when Mr. Tiralla had fallen asleep, surfeited with all the usual rich dishes, and Rosa had gone to the village church with Marianna, he had besought her on his knees, and she, with a look at the sleeper, had hastily whispered to him, "If I were free." Then he had sworn to her with the most solemn oaths that she should be free, that she must be free. And now? Oh, the coward! The whole summer had passed by; the swallows had departed long ago, but the son was flying back to the paternal nest and was bringing somebody else with him; four more eyes to pry on her.

She was tormented with a great fear when she thought of Mikolai's return. He had keen eyes, he was not stupid. He was certainly not like Rosa, who had only one foot on earth, and who used to dream with open eyes, and believed implicitly what was told her. If anything were to happen, it must happen before Mikolai returned to his father.

Mrs. Tiralla made up her mind to get out of bed; nobody would see or hear her now. She had sent Rosa to another room, she could not bear to have anybody with her. Now the child slept in a room on the other side of the passage that had stood empty; and Marianna would sleep with her when the room downstairs was to be used for the two men; that is, if Mr. Tiralla's were not at liberty by that time.

She hastily stuck her feet out of bed. She would slip over to the lumber-room now and fetch it out of the chest. She would not let Marianna take it to him any more, she would give it to him herself tomorrow, either in his coffee or wine.

She put her feet on the floor with a jerk. But all at once she felt she could not walk; her limbs refused to move. She felt as weak as the first time she got up after Rosa's birth. She began to tremble and perspire, to sigh and pray, but no angel restored her strength.

Then at last she perceived that the saints did not will it at present, that the right hour had not yet come. So she crept back into bed and drew the feather bed over her head. She lay under all the feathers, and still she felt icy cold, and unutterably miserable and wretched. Downstairs her husband was carousing with the woman, but she was as though tied hand and foot. She thought she was dying. She gnashed her teeth and clenched her hands; she could not move a limb, but her thoughts flew with lightning rapidity. It was fury, pain, and disappointed hopes that made her feel so ill, that were consuming her life. She was going to die; alas, die, before she had lived, before she had even lived one year in the way she wanted to live.

CHAPTER VIII

When Marianna was sent to the grocer's in the village, she used to talk to everybody about the lively time they would soon be having at Starydwór. The young master was coming home, and was bringing somebody with him. "Nice young gentlemen, two at once," holding up two fingers. And then she would laugh so merrily, so incorrigibly, so shamelessly, with dancing eyes and big white teeth, that the listeners had to laugh too.

Jendrek was the only one who did not laugh. He was not at all glad to hear that two more were coming. He had no fault to find with the old man, who had given him many a cigar and penny for a drink, but he did not approve of those young fellows. He would prefer to seek another place and another sweetheart.

Mr. Tiralla was rather pleased that Jendrek wanted to leave, although he would never have had the heart to give him notice. For when Mikolai was at home, his dear Mikolai, he would help him.

And Marianna did not mind much either. Let him go. Two handsome young gentlemen were coming now. True, she had not seen the young master yet, as she had not been very long at Starydwór, but according to Rosa's enthusiastic accounts her little brother must be something wonderful, splendid, the like of which had never been seen before. And the other one, his friend?

"Oh, I love those my brother loves," Rosa had replied.

* * * * * * * * * * * *

"God be with you," said Marianna, in a calm voice, as she shook hands with Jendrek, and put up her mouth for him to kiss. He was going to Mr. Jokisch, so it was not as though he were going far away. "If ever you care to see me, you need only whistle under my window, and I'll come out," she added.

Mrs. Tiralla, however, seemed to take Jendrek's departure to heart. "I'm sorry you're going," she said to him, pressing a two-shilling piece into his hand, as she shook hands with him. "Think kindly of us." She looked so long and earnestly at him as she said this that he felt quite touched. The Pani had grown much thinner lately, what could be the matter with her? And she was as pale as she had been when she was so anxious about Marianna's illness.

H'm, that girl did not deserve that the Pani should feel anxious about her. The Pani was much too good for her and also for the master; she was much too good for the whole confounded place.

If Mrs. Tiralla had been able to read Jendrek's thoughts, she would not have fretted so much about what he did, or did not, know, and about what he would tell when he was no longer in their service. She felt very uneasy when she saw him going to somebody else. She always had that feeling of terror and uneasiness now. The doctor put it down to nerves. A doctor had been sent for; Mr. Tiralla would not hear of anything else, and she had even asked for one herself in the hope that he might be able to help her.

Now she was constantly taking medicine to soothe and strengthen her nerves, and still she found no peace by day or by night. Her eyes were dilated from want of sleep, from staring into the dark. Her hands had become thin, nearly as thin as Rosa's, and she had grown as slender as a young girl; she could almost have worn her child's dresses. She was too slender. The woman looked at herself in the glass with a feeling of dismay. Was that really her face, the "beautiful Sophia Tiralla's" face? Her skin, which had been as smooth as satin, had begun to fade. Was her beauty disappearing? Was she to lose that as well, and at her age? A deep sigh full of the most grievous impotence filled the lonely room.

Mr. Tiralla was whistling in the yard. Rosa and he were feeding the poultry, and the birds were pecking and scraping and cackling and quarrelling, as they greedily looked for the yellow corn that had been scattered to them.

The woman stared at the two from her window with burning eyes. There they stood, Mr. Tiralla so broad and beaming. He had grown quite cheerful lately, for the day after to-morrow, perhaps even to-morrow, Mikolai was coming. Everybody in the house was delighted except her. When Mikolai was there, there would never be another chance.

That was Mrs. Tiralla's fixed idea. In a transport of despair and fervour, hatred and devotion, all strangely mingled, she flung herself on her knees before the picture where she had prayed for so many years, and which reminded her so strongly of her best and only friend's delicate, beautiful face. "Help, help!" After praying and weeping for a long time, weeping so bitterly and so copiously that her face and hands and even her bosom were quite wet with tears, she rose. She had made up her mind. Mikolai was coming to-morrow, therefore quick, at the eleventh hour.

She went to the lumber-room and fetched the poison. The yellow grains looked exactly like those her husband had just been scattering. She would throw some of them to the poultry that very evening when they were hungry. And if they died--what a pity it would be about them--then Mr. Tiralla should get some of the powder in his wine or coffee.

Rosa had gone to the Przykop with Marianna to fetch some branches and moss. She had made up her mind to place a wreath over the front door in honour of her brother's return; he should see at once how happy she was that he was coming back to her. And the stranger's first impression of the old house, with its dark, yawning passage, would thus be made a pleasant one also. Rosa had never had any fault to find with her home; still, she felt in a dull kind of way that Marianna was right when she used to say, "Ugh! how uncomfortable this place is!"

So the two gathered some of the green, damp moss, with small, delicate, feathery leaves on short stalks, that covered the ground in the morass like a carpet. Rosa was going to wind it round a rope; she had made many wreaths like that for the Holy Virgin's altar at Starawieś and for the Boża męka, which stood on the outskirts of her father's field, and they used to look lovely when she stuck a few flowers among the moss. True, she had no more flowers, for the few that she once had in the little garden behind the palings had lived only a very short time; they had soon been choked by the weeds that flourished so luxuriantly there. But if she put some of the bird-cherries which grew on the roadside into it, or some of the cranberries that shone like drops of blood in the moss, the wreath would look very bright.

Rosa was very happy and excited to-day. The sedate girl was completely changed; she tore up handfuls of moss and, standing behind Marianna, threw them gleefully on her cap and down her neck, as she bent forward. And when the latter, scolding and panting, loosened her frill and picked the earth and bits of moss off her neck, she jumped upon her like a wild cat, put both arms round her, and imprinted numerous boisterous kisses on her brown throat.

"Just look at little Rosa, she's like a lover," cried Marianna. Throwing her arms round the girl she wrestled with her and kissed her merrily, so that Rosa's delicate little face glowed and she was quite breathless.

What a beautiful day it was! At last the two let go of each other, and falling on the grass lay there and laughed. There was only a little bit of sky to be seen between the interlaced branches; they were quite alone. Then Rosa, summoning up her courage, said to the maid:

"Do tell me, Marianna, I should so like to know what happens when a man says to a woman, 'I love you.' Does he kiss her then as I kissed you? And then does she kiss him as you kissed me? I should like to know it; please tell me." She folded her hands as she always did when she was praying.

Marianna laughed.

Why did Marianna laugh so? Rosa felt annoyed; the girl had no right to make fun of her. "Don't laugh," she said angrily, stamping her foot.

"You'll find out what it's like when somebody says to you, 'I love you,'" said Marianna, hardly able to contain herself. How stupid the girl was still.

"Nobody will ever say to me, 'I love you,'" whispered Rosa, bending her head, suddenly saddened. "I'm going into a convent. But, of course"-- she jumped up, and opening her eyes wide spread out her arms--"of course, He'll love me as I love Him." Passing from sudden sadness to brightness, she sang in a loud voice:

"Pray to God for us, then shall it be,
Rejoice, O Mary--
That we with Jesus heaven shall see."

Marianna joined in, she knew the hymn. The maid's deeper voice mingled with Rosa's treble; they sang with great fervour:

"Pray to God for us, O Mary."

It sounded beautiful. The tree-tops ceased their rustling, the autumn wind stopped blowing; the Przykop had grown perfectly calm and was listening.

Then the two went home hand-in-hand with their aprons full of moss. They had not spoken much more, for Rosa had grown quiet. When Marianna, who could not stand the silence any longer, had begun to tell a gruesome story about a servant girl who had once lived at Starydwór and had buried her child in the Przykop, Rosa had given her such a look that the talkative woman had held her tongue as though she had received a blow on her mouth.

The late afternoon sun was shining on the roofs of the old farm when they reached home. Marianna had also brought a quantity of mountain ash with her, and Rosa at once sat down on the doorstep and began to make the wreath. First a bunch of green moss, then red berries, then green moss again; it grew rapidly under her practised fingers. Putting her head on one side and raising the wreath she eyed her handiwork with complacence.

Just then her mother came past; her dress touched the girl as she sat on the doorstep.

"Good evening, mummy."

Mrs. Tiralla did not hear; she was like a woman walking in her sleep, and had not noticed her child. She was enticing the poultry to come and eat. "Chuck, chuck, chuck, chuck, chuck."

The birds came running, and in front of them all was a white hen, a very good layer.

Mrs. Tiralla hesitated for one moment--that was her favourite hen--should she not shoo it away? But then she decided to scatter the corn after all. There must be a victim.

And the beautiful white hen flew at the other greedy hens with open beak, and ate almost all the corn herself. The cock, her lord, was the only one she did not venture to chase away, so he got a little as well, and the chickens furtively pecked a few grains too as they stood behind their mother.

Now all the corn had been devoured. The woman, who had been crouching on the ground, got up with a sigh; now she would soon see the result. She went back into the house without noticing Rosa.

But the latter caught hold of her dress, "Mother, do look. To welcome Mikolai." She held out the green wreath joyfully.

"For Mikolai?" The woman stared at the wreath. For Mikolai! She had to restrain herself from screaming. It would not only be of use to welcome the living, such wreaths are made for the dead too. She shivered and rubbed her cold hands together, as she cried, "I feel chilled," and then, running past Rosa, who was grieved that her mother took so little notice of her beautiful wreath, she hurried upstairs and locked herself into her room. She would not see nor hearken to anybody. And still she listened to every sound downstairs, and would have liked to see what the poultry were doing. Had the beautiful white hen fallen down already, stiff, with outstretched legs?

Her longing drew her to the window, from whence she cast a covert glance from behind the curtain. But she saw neither hen nor cock. Had they been able to run away? Where were they now?

The shades of evening grew heavier and heavier; soon the farm lay in complete darkness, and the woman could distinguish nothing. Her eyes smarted as she stepped back from the window. She felt tired to death.

Then she heard her husband call to Marianna, as he came in from the fields, to bring him something to eat and drink. That drove her on. Yes, he should have something to eat and drink--but from her hand.

"Hi, where are you all? Sophia, Rosa, there's a postcard," shouted Mr. Tiralla.

Doors banged. Then a jubilant cry was heard from Rosa. "He's coming, he's coming. Mikolai is coming to-morrow afternoon."

To-morrow? Already? The listening woman shuddered with terror; it must be done then. Putting her trembling hands into her pocket, she got hold of a little box, and in the little box was----

Clenching her teeth together she went downstairs. She wanted to go into the yard, but whilst flitting through the passage she heard her husband and Rosa talking together in the sitting-room.

"Where's your mother?" Mr. Tiralla was asking. Call her; she's to come. I'm so happy."

"She won't come," answered Rosa timidly.

"Why not?"

"Because she has locked herself into her room. Oh, father, I believe she's not well."

"Well or not well," shouted Mr. Tiralla--he banged the table, and Rosa began crying--"to the devil with her if she doesn't come down. I've had enough of it now She's to come down at once. *Psia krew!*"

H'm, his son's arrival had evidently given him courage; how would he otherwise have dared behave like that? So rough, so brutal. Good!--she put her fingers once more into her pocket and gripped the little box--she would soon come.

First of all, however, she went into the yard to look for her white hen. Where was it lying? Where had it crept to? She sought for it in every corner; she trembled whenever she saw something white gleaming, a piece of paper, a rag, or a little chalk that had crumbled off the wall--could this be it, or that? She felt so miserable that she at last did not know if she wanted to find it or not.

She wept as she sought her beautiful white hen. But as she could neither find it nor the cock nor any of the chickens in the corners or on the dunghill, she at length crept back into the house. But she dared not go into the room; she feared her child's eyes. She would bring Mr. Tiralla something to drink when Rosa had gone to bed. "Your health. Much good may it do you!"

But it seemed as though Rosa would never leave her father, and the listening woman neither heard her husband's drunken jokes, nor the maid's ribald laughter that evening. What could the two be doing? She crept downstairs in her stockings; the kitchen door was ajar and Marianna was asleep by the fire, and perfect peace and calm reigned in the sitting-room. It was as though an angel were sitting at table with Mr. Tiralla.

Then Mrs. Tiralla perceived that she could do nothing that evening. Besides, would it not really be better to wait until the early morning? At daybreak she would find the poultry dead, and before the sun stood high in the heavens Mr. Tiralla would have received his coffee.

Mrs. Tiralla watched and prayed quietly the whole night through. When she crept downstairs next morning there was nobody up. The eastern sky was only faintly streaked with red, the morning light was still very wan and pale, but she could see a little, nevertheless. She groped her way across the yard, holding up her dress so as to prevent it from getting wet. There was not a sound to be heard. But hark, what was that cry that sounded so shrill and penetrating in her ear? She gave a sudden start and let her dress fall on the wet grass. Why, it was the cock! The crowing came from the hen-house. She ran there. Was he really alive? She tore the door open, and out walked the cock, stretching his gleaming neck to its utmost extent and crowing shrilly. The cock was alive. But what about the hen, her beautiful white hen? She had eaten much more--was she alive too?

The woman's eyes almost started out of her head, and she stretched out a trembling finger. There, there came the hen out of the house, shook herself, put her claws first through one of her outspread wings and then through the other, smoothed her white feathers with her beak, and cackled long and proudly. She had already laid her egg that morning.

And the others? Mrs. Tiralla hastily stuck her head into the hen-house. There they were, all sitting on the perch; not one of them was missing, not one dead.

Suddenly a heavy load fell from the woman's heart. There was nothing the matter with her beautiful white hen. She caught hold of the bird, and, pressing it in her arms, caressed and stroked it in spite of its struggles.

But her joy was followed by the most violent fear, a fear that was mingled with disappointment and relief. Now Mr. Tiralla would not die either. The poison was no good, they had been imposed upon. Or--she put her hands to her head, and then she felt as though she ought to fall on her knees--the saints had not willed it. Yes, they had prevented it. It was poison after all, that, she had in the box. She felt it burning her skin through all her skirts. "Jesus, Mary, Joseph!" She heaved a sigh as she tore the box out of her pocket. The saints were not on her side, so it was still not the right thing; away with it. She wanted to hurl it away, into the pool, or there on the dunghill. But then she let her outstretched arm sink--not there. Innocent people might find it, the animals might eat it. But what should she do with it? All at once she dreaded it; she would not have it in her chest any more.

Besides, she had no use for it now; if the saints were on her side, she would not be obliged to give him the poison.

She returned to the house like one who had been saved. There she found everybody astir. Mr. Tiralla had also got up early, and was already busy helping Rosa to fix the wreath over the door. He was standing on a stool and she was handing him the nails, and at every dull stroke from the hammer he gave a laugh, and the child clapped her hands. "Now it's fast. It looks pretty like that."

Mrs. Tiralla beckoned to her husband as she passed by. "Come here a moment."

She was beckoning to him? He felt much surprised, but followed her at once into his room.

As he entered she was standing in the middle of the room near the table, holding out a little box. There it was, she did not want to keep it any longer, not a day, not an hour, not a moment longer. She urged him to take it.

What was it, eh? He took the box from her and turned it round, eyeing it curiously. Well, what was he to do with it? He was about to open it, but she held his hand fast. No, he must not open it nor look at it. She might perhaps have regretted it then. "Put it away, put it away," she cried hastily, turning her head aside. "It's the poison! Holy Mother, the poison!"

"What poison?" He felt very astonished; where did this poison come from all at once?

"From Gnesen--from the chemist's--you know, the rat poison," she cried irately.

"Yes, I know." Now he remembered it.

"But----" he started. She had brought it to him to-day? And, *psia krew!* how strange she was. He stared at her with open mouth.

His stupid expression irritated her. Why did he stare at her like that? Oh, yes, he could still look at her, but little was wanting and he would never have been able to look at her again. And she would not have been obliged to look at him either. "Alas, alas!" She buried her face in her hands and groaned aloud. Now she had given it back, now she was powerless, helpless, hopeless. "Give it back to me," she cried, and tried to tear it out of his hand.

But this time he held it fast; he put his big fist, in which the little box lay quite hidden, behind his back. "What am I to do with it?" he asked, all at once suspicious. "I thought the rats had eaten it all, and you've got some still?"

"No--yes, yes, they have--no, no, I didn't give it all." Her voice was unsteady, hesitating. She felt that he suspected something, and it terrified her.

"Oh, I don't know, leave me," she said suddenly, in a faint voice, and broke into a hopeless fit of sobbing, terrified and completely confused.

"*Psia krew!*" Mr. Tiralla raised his brows, and his eyes wandered restlessly from his wife to the little box in his hand, and then from the poison to his wife. He opened the box. H'm, there were still five whole powders left in it, and he had only brought six in the first case. Yes, there had been six. And now? "There are still five powders in it," he murmured.

He was only thinking aloud, but she immediately took it as an accusation. Her pallor changed into burning red, she trembled and swayed so much that she had to rest her hand on the table in order to support herself. It was as though she were standing at the bar. But her present danger helped her to regain her self-command; all at once she was no longer at a loss for a lie.

"There were twelve powders in it," she asserted boldly. "I've used the half--more than the half."

"Really?" He shook his head doubtfully. "Twelve powders, really?"

How strangely he said that. She cast a hasty glance at his face in the hope of being able to read his thoughts. But it was as red and fat as always, perhaps even a little redder. It told her nothing.

She turned to go, full of desperate defiance. Let him think what he liked then; it was all the same to her. She saw him go to the old bureau that stood close to the bed-curtains, in which he kept his money and papers, and then she closed the door with a bang.

Mr. Tiralla remained alone in the room. He was standing near his bureau; he had let the box fall, and it was lying on the dusty flap that he had just drawn out. He looked down at it, and there was a peculiar, uneasy expression on his face, which had never been there before. He passed his hand over his forehead; it was damp. Had that been caused by fear? What absurd nonsense it was to think such things. His Sophia, his dear Sophia! The poor thing was ill, that was all. Who can understand women who suffer from nerves? Nerves are very bad things, very bad. You never know what to expect.

"Nerves, ah, nerves," he murmured, and stared in front of him. Then he took hold of the box once more, but he did not open it. His dread of the poisonous powders was even greater now than when he had brought them into the house. He turned the box round and round, and then shook it. Would it not be best to throw the horrid things on the fire? Let them burn.

But he did not take the box into the kitchen after all, where Marianna was keeping up a flaring wood fire in order to make the coffee. Later on--to-morrow--when Mikolai had come home--then--then he would burn them. They would be well hidden here in the little drawer where he kept his most important papers, his deeds of mortgage from Posen and other securities, the testimonial he had received on leaving the Agricultural College, his first wife's "In Memoriam" card, and his second wife's marriage certificate. So he pushed the box under them all, locked the drawer, tried carefully to see whether the lock were secure, and put the key on the same bunch with the others which he always carried in his trouser pocket.

There, now that was done, now he would get on with the wreath, which was not yet up. He would also tell them to have the yard thoroughly swept, the stables and sheds tidied up, as well as the coachhouse, thrashing-floor, and harness-room. Everything was to be bright and clean when the young master came home.

But the man no longer felt happy. Why not? Mr. Tiralla sighed and cast a timorous look round the room. His Sophia's black eyes, which were so beautiful that they could steal a man's heart out of his body, could look very terrible--ugh! very terrible. They gazed at him from every corner; their glances seemed to pierce his body. What was it that Marianna used to say? "Let that wicked look fall on the dog," and then she would make the sign of the cross. He did the same now, but he felt that it was of no avail at the present moment. It did not exorcize the restlessness that made him walk up and down the room, the strange feeling of terror that took possession of him and seemed to encircle him in such an incomprehensible way. What did those eyes betray? Thank God, Rosa had not such eyes, that looked like black, poisonous berries, like the deadly nightshade that intoxicates you and then kills you.

Mr. Tiralla stood pondering gloomily, his brows contracted. He did not think much as a rule, but to-day he had fallen into a reverie.

He could not recover his good humour, even after he had put the last nail into the wreath with Rosa, and when she went to a sewing class in the village--she no longer went to school--he felt quite forlorn. Nothing was to be seen of Mrs. Tiralla; nobody knew what had become of her. So he sat down in the kitchen with the maid--he could not stand being alone--and told her to fetch him something to drink.

She had not got the key of the wine cellar, as the Pani kept it, and there was no wine out. But Mr. Tiralla put his back firmly against the lattice door.

It yielded to his strength and flew open, and in the future it was to remain so.

Marianna triumphantly dragged one bottle after the other upstairs.

It was not yet ten o'clock in the morning when Mr. Tiralla had finished the first bottle of Tokay. But even that did not improve his temper. By eleven o'clock the second bottle had been emptied; but his temper was no better, his head was only heavier. It would have to be gin if he wanted to be in a good humour--real Geneva, which looked as clear as water in the glass.

When they sat down to dinner Mr. Tiralla ate nothing, his appetite had vanished, but he told them to bring him some beer. Rosa did not eat anything either, she was too happy to eat. She jumped up every moment from her chair to see what time it was. Was it not yet time to fetch her dear brother?

Mrs. Tiralla also came to dinner, but only for a moment. Her eyes were very red, like those of a person who has wept very much, or who feels worn-out. She said she had a great deal to do still, and had no time whatever for dinner, and ran into the kitchen again almost immediately, where she began to mix flour and lard, break eggs, grate sugar, pound spices, and stone raisins. She intended welcoming her son with a fresh cake, warm from the oven, his favourite cake. That touched Mr. Tiralla.

When he got into the carriage with Rosa--she jumped up like a bird, but he found difficulty in getting to his seat--his face looked brighter. His lip, which was blue and swollen, no longer drooped so much that it almost touched his chin.

Rosa had swung herself on to the front seat next to her father, and now and then she would take hold of his arm and press it, or poll his ear or stroke his fat, bristly cheek, so that he could not drive. But even if she had not played all these pranks in her great happiness his driving would not have been up to much, for he began to feel the effects of the wine and beer on an empty stomach. He would have liked to sleep; his head fell first to the one side and then to the other, and his eye was no longer steady. He, who generally drove as straight as anybody, could not keep a bee-line to-day.

Röschen chattered incessantly, even when her father did not answer her. She spoke to the wind, as though it could understand her, and only fanned her so merrily because it was just as happy as she.

The white gossamer threads blew over the big plain, where the fields full of stubble were already being prepared again for the new seed, and hung around the young girl's face. Rosa had put her prettiest dress on, a light blue summer dress. It suited her well, and she did not feel at all cold to-day, although she was very chilly as a rule. Her thin blood coursed warmly through her veins and painted roses on her cheeks, that were usually so pale. How happy she was!

"Mikolai, Mikolai," she sang to the wind. What did he look like? Handsome and smart, of course, much handsomer and smarter than she remembered him. Her eyes gleamed, her lips burned; she would give him a hearty kiss, many, many hearty kisses. It was nice to be able to kiss somebody whom you were very fond of.

Marianna had washed her head the night before with soft soap, and rubbed pomade well into the hair, so that it should shine brightly and be smooth when Mikolai came. As Rosa did not wish to be outdone by her, she had put her head into a basin of water. But she could not make up her mind to use the greasy pomade, so her dry hair--brittle like that of all anæmic people--was twice as dry as usual, and stood out like a reddish, curly mane round her head. Her blue ribbon could hardly keep the plait together, and the dry, curly mass emitted hundreds of sparks as soon as a sunbeam fell on it.

As they drove through Starawieś they saw Mr. Böhnke coming out of the rectory. They were stopping for a moment at the inn, as Mr. Tiralla felt so chilly that he wanted a glass of gin. They called to him, that is, Mr. Tiralla shouted with a loud voice, "Little Böhnke, heigh, little Böhnke. *Psia krew!* where are your ears?"

The schoolmaster gave a start. He hesitated for a moment; there was the corner, should he not get out of the way quickly, as though he had not heard the call? However, he crossed the street.

There sat Mr. Tiralla in the carriage, fat and red as usual, and there was nothing in his face, neither pallor nor lines of suffering round his mouth, to betray that he had eaten mushrooms, poisonous mushrooms. Or had she not given him any? If only she had not--oh, if only she had not!

Böhnke came slowly across the broad village street, as though something were holding him back. He had a shrinking feeling when he looked at Mr. Tiralla. The man had received him hospitably, had been delighted to see him, had put food and drink before him, and he had---- No, he was a rough customer, a hog, a bully, quite a vulgar fellow, for whom he had no pity. Had she not set the mushrooms before him? She intended doing so.

Böhnke had not heard anything of Mrs. Tiralla for a long time, as Rosa no longer came to school. He could have gone to Starydwór, as he had so often done before, but he had not ventured to do so. She would be sure to give him a sign. However, she had not given him one, and in spite of his great longing to see her, he was glad she had not. He did not want again to see Mr. Tiralla alive.

But there he was, sitting in his carriage in high spirits, tipping his glass up and laughing to him. Had he the constitution of a giant, or had nothing happened? The schoolmaster stood in front of the carriage with downcast eyes, full of uncertainty and embarrassment.

"Why haven't you been to see us, little Böhnke?" asked Mr. Tiralla upbraidingly. "It's wrong of you; I've had to sit a great deal alone and drink." He gave a loud laugh, but then he added in a gentle voice, "If my Röschen hadn't been there. I suppose, little Böhnke"--he bent down from the box, gave the other man a dig in the ribs, and whispered with a grin--"I suppose there's a woman behind it in your case as well, eh?"

The schoolmaster recoiled; he felt disgusted. Mr. Tiralla's breath smelt of nothing but gin and alcohol. "Oh, I'll come," he answered coldly, and was about to turn away.

But Mr. Tiralla did not let him off so easily. "We're driving to Gradewitz, will you come with us? We're going to fetch my son from the station; he's coming home. He's bringing somebody with him, a nice young fellow. Get up, little Böhnke, get up. This'll be jolly."

But the schoolmaster refused with thanks. He had something to do, he would have to stop at home, he could not get away--no, on no account.

However, when he had seen the carriage drive down the village street as quickly as the uneven road and deep ruts permitted, he turned into the fields and walked towards Starydwór instead of going home. She was now alone. It would be a long time before they came back; he would be able to question her without being disturbed, talk to her and hear why her husband had not had any mushrooms. He ran as fast as he could.

His coat-tails flapped in the wind like raven's wings. A sudden jealousy gripped him; Mr. Tiralla had spoken of a nice young fellow. And Mikolai was also a young fellow. Two young fellows, and with her day and night under the same roof. Stepmother? Pooh! She was still young and so beautiful.

His eyes wandered about restlessly; there was nothing to be seen but a desolate field over which black birds were flying, but in his mind's eye he already saw her. How she smiled! Always beautiful, either merry or sad; always seductive, either good or bad. The same fever was raging within him that had always driven him along this road. He ran until he was breathless; every minute longer that he could be with her before the others returned seemed of the utmost importance. He had hardly any breath left when he reached the farm, and he rushed into the room without knocking. There she stood, she for whom he was longing.

Hardly had Mr. Tiralla driven away with Rosa than Mrs. Tiralla left the maid to bake the cakes alone. There was no need to keep up appearances any longer. What did she care about the stepson who was coming home to-day? She had never liked nor disliked him; still, she felt that he played a more important part in her life now. She must, she would please him. He must like her so well that he would turn and listen to her rather than to his father. She must win his ear and his eyes, and thereby his heart. She, therefore, went up to her room, combed her beautiful thick hair, so that it looked silkier than ever, and put on a pretty dress; not too grand a one, but still, not her everyday one. If he had eyes, he must be able to see that she had put on her Sunday dress for his sake. She rubbed her cheeks; did they still look pale? She endeavoured to put on a pleasant smile; did she look beautiful now, as beautiful as formerly? She examined herself attentively in the glass upstairs in her bedroom, and then downstairs in the big room; she was wrapped up in her own thoughts.

Thus Böhnke found her.

His noisy entrance had startled her, and she flew at him. Böhnke--what did he want? Why did he come to-day and disturb her?

"So you've really shown yourself again?" she said. "Why have you come to-day? What do you want?"

"Mr. Tiralla--was in the carriage--I met him," he said with difficulty. He stood before her with bent head, as though he were a miserable sinner.

She was half beside herself with anger when she saw him standing like that. Such a wretched coward, and a liar to boot. "Why have you deceived me?" she cried furiously.

"I--I've never deceived you." He understood at once to what she was referring. So that was why she was so angry with him. He raised two fingers as though he were taking an oath, and said eagerly, "By God, I've not deceived you. If you had the right mushrooms, then"--he shrugged his shoulders--"then I don't understand it. I'm blameless."

"They were the right ones," she answered tersely. "He ate them."

"Ate them? Ate them?"

"Ate them all."

He stared at her as though he could not comprehend it. "And he--he is--well?"

"He's well."

The schoolmaster put his hand to his head. He could hardly credit that anybody could have eaten those mushrooms--the devil's toadstool and the fly agaric--and remain alive and well. There was something wrong about it. Or there had been some mistake. But *he* had made no mistake--no, most certainly not, he protested, grasping her hands.

It was as though a stream of longing and love, of despairing, impotent, all-yielding, all forgetting passion were flowing from him to her.

But she remained cool. "My stepson is coming to-day," she remarked.

Then he burst into tears, and falling on his knees before her he pressed her hands, which she had to give up to him, against his face, and kissed them as though he were mad. It was so long since he had enjoyed the sight of her. But now her nearness overpowered him entirely, and he had no longer the strength to struggle against anything. He stammered words full of frantic, jealous passion and sobbed.

"Let my hands go," she said impatiently, endeavouring to free them. "Let them go, I tell you. How can you kiss these hands"--she laughed strangely--"hands that wanted to give Mr. Tiralla rat poison this morning. If the poultry had died from eating the corn this morning, he would by now have lain dead from taking the same poison."

He was not listening to what she was saying. Let her accuse herself, let others accuse her, she was still his sun, his heaven, his highest aim. And he would never, never, never leave her in the lurch. If she wished it, he would swear it by all the saints. If only she had asked his advice about this too. The poultry had not died from eating the poisoned wheat she had scattered, because--he had once read it somewhere--because strychnine, that fearful poison which kills rats at once, does not harm chickens.

"And human beings?" she interrupted him passionately. She seized hold of the man's shoulders as he knelt before her and stared at his face, which he had raised to hers with a look full of fervour. "What about human beings?"

"Human beings die of it."

Then she let go of his shoulders and with a loud cry put her hands before her face and ran frantically up and down the room like an imprisoned, impotent animal, that would like to dash through the walls.

The man stared at her in astonishment; why was she so beside herself? She knew that rat poison also killed human beings?

She did not answer him. But when he put his arms round her she feebly let her head sink on his shoulder. But only for a few moments, and when he wanted to kiss her she pushed him away. "Go, go--come soon again--but go now. What do I look like?" She smoothed her hair with her hands. "I mustn't look like that--the others can soon be here--go, go." She pushed him to the door almost by force.

He would not have minded, he would have stopped even if the others had come--what did he care for other people and their thoughts? What did it matter that he had told Mr. Tiralla he had something to do and would have to stop at home?

But she begged him pathetically, "Go, for my sake. If you love me, go."

So he crept out of the room. But when he came to the front door, over which Rosa's pretty green wreath was hanging, he stood still once more. There was nobody to disturb them, not a human being in sight. He besought her hesitatingly not to send him away without at least one kiss.

Then she gave him one.

It was high time the schoolmaster went, for hardly had Mrs. Tiralla cooled her cheeks with water and smoothed her hair once more when the carriage drove into the yard with cracking of whips, rattling of wheels, and much hallooing.

Mikolai was standing erect in front--or was it not Mikolai who was driving so smartly, and who now drew up before the front door, whilst the horses were going at full trot, and jumped off? No, it was not Mikolai, for he was sitting behind with his father, and had his little sister between his knees. But now he also jumped down, went up to his stepmother, who was standing in the doorway, and held out his hand.

She kissed him on both cheeks and smiled at him. He also smiled, and she felt that the reception had pleased him.

"Here we are," shouted Mr. Tiralla. "Mikolai, my son, help me down from this confounded conveyance." They all helped him.

"Oh, mummy, how dreadful!" whispered Rosa to her mother as she clung to her. "I believe daddy has been drinking too much. He stopped everywhere."

"That doesn't matter," answered Mrs. Tiralla, pushing her daughter aside. Then she bade her son's friend, Martin Becker, who had driven so smartly, a smiling welcome.

Mr. Tiralla had indeed overdone it. He felt very unwell. As they all sat drinking coffee round the festive-looking table, on which a coloured cloth had been spread, he looked at them with doll eyes. "So now we're all together again." Then he nodded to his son and got up. "I'll lie down a little on my bed. Send Marianna to help me. *Psia krew!*" He yawned, and staggered to the door.

His son jumped up and wanted to help him, but he sent him back. "No, it's not necessary, go back." And then he added in a furtive whisper, and it seemed as though there were a note of fear in his voice, "Go and talk to her, you must talk to her."

"Father has drunk a little too much," said the man, with a laugh, as he sat down at the table again. How good the coffee tasted; it had neither been so strong nor so pure in the army. And the cakes had turned out a great success. He nodded brightly to his stepmother, as she sat opposite him and his friend. He felt something like gratitude rising in his heart; it was really very nice of her to bake his favourite cakes, and to receive Martin into the house. She was gazing at his friend the whole time. Heigh, was she not going to cast a glance at him too? He cleared his throat and tried to attract her attention by looking her up and down in the same way the soldiers used to look at the girls as they strolled past them, arm-in-arm. She was certainly a good-looking woman, even if she were his stepmother.

But she paid no attention to her stepson, and when he at last addressed some indifferent question to her, she started, turned crimson, and then smiled absentmindedly. Where were her thoughts? Perhaps she felt disheartened because his father was drunk. It could certainly not be very agreeable for a wife. When Mikolai came to think of it, he did not take it amiss that she seemed to have neither eyes nor ears for anything. But if she did not want to talk, and only sat with her eyes fixed on vacancy, stirring her coffee without drinking it, he would talk to his little sister. Let Röschen come with him and show him the cattle in the sheds. Had the old sow, which he had purchased from Jokisch, farrowed? And how many cows were there now?

Rosa was in a state of bliss at the thought of having her brother all to herself. She would show him everything, and she had so much to tell him. There was a foal, too, in the enclosure, such a pretty one. It was the brown mare's child, and was as brown as its mother, but it had a white star on its forehead like Mr. Jokisch's horse. She put her hand into her brother's and drew him tenderly out of the room.

Martin Becker and Mrs. Tiralla remained alone in the room. Martin would have liked to go out with them and look at the cattle--he took great interest in such things--but he had remained behind on account of shyness. The girl had not invited him, and the woman's eyes fixed him to the spot. He was not shy as a rule; anywhere else he would have said, "I want to go to the stables too." But he did not feel at home here. Why did Mikolai's stepmother look at him so penetratingly? Was she not pleased that he had come? He dared not look up, he felt her eyes resting on him the whole time. He felt hot and cold in turns. What black eyes the woman had. How stupid that the old man should get drunk now. He simply longed for Mr. Tiralla; he was quite different, he had welcomed him with such a loud laugh and given him a resounding kiss on both cheeks, just as he had done to his son.

The man shuffled his feet restlessly. If it did not suit the woman that he had come with Mikolai, then he could pack up his belongings and be off again, rather to-day than to-morrow. He felt uncomfortable. If only she would talk; but she never opened her mouth except to say, "Finish what you've got in your cup." So he finished his coffee and let her pour out some more, and when he had finished that he let her fill the cup again. He was trying to make up his mind to get up, make her a bow, and go after Mikolai, whom that nice girl was showing about.

The daylight began to wane. The big, low room was only lighted by two small windows, and in the twilight that filled the room he saw--now that he had made up his mind to rise--that the white face opposite him was smiling. He felt quite embarrassed; was that meant for him? Yes, certainly, she was smiling at him in a friendly way--at least, her mouth was smiling, but her eyes still retained their strange, fixed look. Was the woman sad? It seemed so. True, Mr. Tiralla was no longer a young husband, and he was not a handsome one, but had not the woman a daughter who was so tall and so nearly grown-up that she could soon be a grandmother?

Rosa had pleased the young man. When the girl had returned Mikolai's kiss at the station, shyly and reservedly, but still warmly and heartily, he had almost envied his friend. It must be nice to have a sister like that, and--and to teach such a young girl how to kiss. Where would the two be now? In the cowshed? Or in the enclosure, where the mare was grazing with the foal that Rosa had spoken about? How prettily the little one had spoken about the mare and her child; it had sounded very sweet. Becker sighed involuntarily; oh, what a bore it was to have to sit here in this room, whilst those two were enjoying themselves outside.

"Why are you sighing?" inquired the woman at that moment. Her voice sounded soft and veiled in the twilight. The tone frightened him. "What are you thinking of? Don't you like being here?"

He grew still more frightened. Did she know what he had been thinking of? The woman was a witch who could look at you inside and out. He grew red and then vexed; what was it to her what he was thinking of? Well, as she already knew it, yes, he wanted to go away. But he said nothing of that to her, he stammered something, hesitated, and grew quite confused. By gad! how beautiful the woman was!

Mrs. Tiralla bent a little forward over the table, so that her face was nearer to him. In spite of the increasing obscurity the young man saw her eyes gleam. Her voice sounded very ingratiating as she said:

"I'm so pleased that you've both come, you and Mikolai. Mr. Tiralla is old. Now there are some young people in the house." She gave a slight sigh. "And he has got into the way of drinking, I'm sorry to say. It's so lonely for Rosa and me. Such a young girl wants a change too."

Oh, certainly. The young man understood that perfectly, he agreed with her mother that it could not be very amusing for a young girl there. Conquering his shyness, he asked if Miss Rosa had no friends whatever in the neighbourhood, and if she did not take part in any of the amusements in Gradewitz, or whatever the nearest town was called.

"What are you thinking of?" Mrs. Tiralla gave a soft little laugh. "Rosa isn't fifteen yet, she's still a child. Don't say 'Miss,' Mr. Becker. Besides"--she sighed again and became very serious--"my daughter will never care for what you, what people call amusements. Rosa has chosen another path for herself; she's going to the Grey Sisters, or to the Ladies of the Sacred Heart, who have that large hospital on the Wilda in Posen."

"To the Ladies of the Sacred Heart in Posen?" The young fellow looked quite horrified. Was it possible that that little thing with her curly hair and bright face wanted to be a nun? To be pious was all well and good--Martin liked to go to Mass every Sunday, and regularly went to confession as an orthodox Christian is expected to do--but in a convent! ugh! He shuddered. "*Psia krew!*" he burst out, "such a young girl doesn't know what she's doing. You shouldn't let her, Mrs. Tiralla," he said, almost upbraidingly. Why did the beautiful woman blink at him so with her black eyes? And she was going to put her young daughter into a convent? He would tell Mikolai, he ought certainly not to allow it. He struck the table a slight blow with his clenched fist that was so full of nervous strength. "That would almost be like murder," he said vehemently, and then added, quite shaken, "Foolish little girl, foolish little girl."

The woman answered nothing. Not a sound was heard in the darkening room during the next few minutes. She sat blinking at the man with her burning eyes. What did he think of her? Did he perhaps believe that she had persuaded the girl to become a nun? Oh, no; he must not believe that. She felt called upon to convince him that she had had nothing whatever to do with Rosa's decision. Had she ever persuaded the child to go into a convent? No, she could not remember having done so--no, certainly not, she had never done such a thing. She was quite innocent of it. But at the same moment her blood rose. Why did the young fellow trouble himself so much about Rosa? Why did he take such an interest in her? She was about to fire up--ah, now he was even reproaching her for it in words.

"Others who are older should be wiser," said Becker.

But she controlled herself; she must not be angry, it was better to win him with kindness. So she said in a low, dreamy whisper, as though she were speaking to herself:

"I was still a child when I wanted to go into a convent. I was forced to marry Mr. Tiralla. Oh!" She raised her hands with a deep sigh, and clasped them together and pressed them to her pale cheek as though in pain. "I've been married almost sixteen years, sixteen long years, and I still long for the convent. If I might be within those sacred walls, I should be hidden and happy. How can I oppose my daughter if she doesn't wish to become as unhappy as her mother? I can't help it, it's not my fault. You must blame Mr. Tiralla; my child has seen too much." She wiped a few tears away and then held her hand before her eyes, but she was watching the young man through her fingers. Would her fate excite his pity? It made her weep herself when she described it. She longed for his sympathy; she did not know why she especially wanted his sympathy, she merely felt in a dull kind of way that this man must take a much, much greater interest in her than in Rosa.

But Martin Becker answered calmly, "If the Pani has not been happy in her marriage that is no reason why her daughter should not be. She has a gentle disposition, she seems to be very pliable. My father--God give him everlasting peace--always used to say to me, 'Take a gentle wife.' My opinion is that a gentle wife will always have a good husband, because----"

He stopped. Mrs. Tiralla had suddenly jumped up; what a namby-pamby the fellow was, to be sure, in spite of his eyes that were shining with mirth and his fresh lips under his small black moustache, and his four-and-twenty years. His way of speaking angered her. He spoke like an old man with the mouth of a youth. Her fingers twitched, she felt so irritated she would have liked to have given him a blow on those fresh lips. What did he know of marriage, or what it was like to have a coarse, hateful, rough, vulgar, ugly old drunkard as your husband? She was raging. She felt she must convince this man, just this man, that it was terrible, and then----

She closed her eyes for a moment as though she felt dizzy.

An intense joy took possession of her. She was still "the beautiful Mrs. Tiralla." Whatever he might think at the present moment, he would learn to think differently. Her irritation disappeared, and she begged him in a voice that was almost humble not to be surprised that she had poured her heart out to him. She was surprised at it herself, but it must have been because she had lived such an isolated life for so long, and had had to be silent for so many, many years.

Then he grew milder too; he was never angry long. The woman certainly had a very touching voice. He also felt flattered that she had shown him such confidence. But he was not able to tell her so, as his former shyness had returned as soon as his anger disappeared. He let her carry on the conversation, whilst he sat silent in the dark room, and as he listened to her he thought how sweetly she was speaking.

They were still sitting thus when the maid burst into the room with the lamp. She started back, half terrified, half bewildered. Had the Pani been sitting the whole time alone with him in the twilight? H'm! Her eyes flashed, and she could not resist winking at her mistress as much as to say, Do you care for him? She could well understand that the Pani preferred this one to Mr. Tiralla, or to pale, lean Pan Böhnke. The schoolmaster would turn green with envy when he saw this strong, handsome fellow. What a capital joke it would be when those two met.

Marianna could scarcely restrain her chuckling. She was pleased to think that Böhnke was to have this vexation, for was he treating the master as he should? No, he did not wish him well, she felt that. The woman was the Pani, she could do what she liked; but strangers were not to hurt her master, she would not stand that. The maid grinned like a gnome; it served the schoolmaster right. If the Pani had chosen this man, then she, Marianna, would take Mr. Mikolai; he was not at all bad. He was certainly not so well-built as this one, he was a little more thick-set, but he too had a nice face with a little moustache; and when she came to think of it, he was even kinder. He had clapped her on her neck when he had come into the cow-shed with Rosa, where she was just milking a cow. And he had said "Good evening" to her, and had asked her with a merry laugh, "Who's your sweetheart, my girl?" Then she had had to laugh too, laugh so that the cow had grown restive and had knocked the pail, which she was holding between her knees, with its hind legs, so that the milk had been upset, the stool had fallen, and she with it.

CHAPTER IX

Mrs. Tiralla was kneeling in the confessional.

When the turn came for the sins against the sixth and ninth commandments, she trembled in all her limbs. How quickly and easily she had hitherto been able to answer in the negative when the question, "Have you had any unclean thoughts or desires?" had been put to her. But what was she to say now? How Father Szypulski, who knew her so well and whom she would probably meet again to-morrow or the day after, would stare at her when she confessed to him what had tortured her day and night for weeks and months, ever since Martin Becker had been at Starydwór. Especially at night when she tossed about so restlessly. If she were to whisper in a trembling voice that she longed for this man as she longed for her eternal salvation? And if the priest then questioned her further, if he went into particulars? If she had to describe every thought, every wish that filled her soul and her body, reveal them in such a way that her penitent confession might be followed by absolution in the Sacrament of Penance?

She felt overwhelmed with shame; she bent her head so low and whispered so softly that the confessor was not able to hear anything.

And Father Szypulski did not ask any questions; it was not necessary to go any further into the matter with this woman. Every country girl under sixteen had more to confess than she.

After resigning her seat in the confessional to a young peasant woman who looked contrite and anxious, Mrs. Tiralla repeated the prescribed prayers before the high altar, and then hastened home.

She hurried along as much as possible; she had even hurried over her prayers. What had they been doing at home during her absence? Was he sitting with Rosa again? It was not at all proper, the child was too old for that. Yes, the time was approaching when she would have to be taken to Posen, for it was better for her that she should not become acquainted with what could never be her lot--must never be her lot--never, never.

The woman's eyes blazed as she hurried along. She pressed her Prayer-book to her beating heart, and threw her head back with a proud movement. She had been to confession, and she, the beautiful Mrs. Tiralla, was now returning home with her sins forgiven.

As she approached the farm she met the schoolmaster coming away from it. She gave him a nod and wanted to hurry past him. Her uneasiness drove her on--what were they doing at home; what were they up to? But he barred her way, so that she was obliged to stop.

"Ah, Böhnke, I've no time now, I'm in a great hurry. Good-bye, let me go--let me go, I say." With a stamp of her foot she pulled away the hand which he had seized.

But she did not get rid of him so easily. "One moment. Surely you've got a moment to spare for me?"

As she did not listen, but continued to hasten on, he ran beside her. How troublesome he was, if only she could get rid of him. What did he want with her? Why did he force himself upon her in this way? Heaven forfend that he should return to the farm with her. She was furious; the spring evening was already drawing to a close, Martin would have returned from the fields, and now he belonged to her. And this fellow took upon himself to hinder her.

"I've not seen you for ages," stammered Böhnke. "It's so difficult to catch a glimpse of you."

"That's your fault, Mr. Böhnke," she answered lightly, and shrugged her shoulders. "You could have come more frequently, you know."

"You used to invite me formerly."

"Well, I do invite you." She gave a mocking laugh. "Do you, perhaps, expect me to write you a note every day saying, 'Come'? Come, for goodness sake. You can come whenever you feel inclined."

"I don't feel inclined," he answered bitterly. "How could I feel any inclination to come to Starydwór? But something drags me there all the same. I *must* come, and that's what is so awful, so awful!"

He shouted the last word in a loud voice, and his eyes, that were generally so dull, glittered as he looked at her.

Ah, so now he was going to reproach her. She slackened her pace involuntarily; there was no necessity for anybody else to hear it. But if he thought that she feared him--pooh! he made a great mistake. What on earth could frighten her now? Nothing whatever, and nobody, if only she could see Martin every day.

She boldly returned the man's upbraiding look, and they gazed at each other, until Böhnke had to cast down his eyes. He knew what kind of woman she was; oh, she was much more guilty than he, for he was only the one who had been tempted, but she was the temptress. What if he were to tell what he knew? She was entirely in his power. And still he lowered his eyes. He loved her, oh God, how he loved her!

He trembled at the thought that she might belong to somebody else, to that other one perhaps, who was so young and handsome and strong, and who had lived under the same roof with her since last autumn, during the whole winter, the short days, the long nights. What was it Mr. Tiralla had told him? Even he was full of Martin Becker's praises when they sat together in the evening at the inn. Mr. Tiralla had lately come more frequently to Starawieś; he said he felt ashamed of getting drunk in his own house. The truth was, however--the schoolmaster felt sure he was right--that he also was jealous of the young fellow, and that he did not like to see his wife smile at Becker any more than he, Böhnke, did. But she should not smile at him, no, she must not do so. And if Mr. Tiralla did not forbid it, then he--yes, he would do so.

"You're good friends with Becker," he hissed, and he seized the woman's wrists so firmly, in spite of his trembling hands, that she could not get loose.

She struggled, she would have liked to run away; no, she would hear nothing, nothing at all.

But he whispered in her ear in a hoarse voice that was half choked with grief and fury, "You're deceiving Mr. Tiralla and me. But if that fool stands it, I won't. Take care. I know everything--I know you well--I will speak--yes, yes, by God I will if you don't----"

"You're threatening me?" she cried, interrupting him with a shrill laugh. She jerked her hand free and flung his away. "You don't intimidate me. Go, inform against me, I'm not afraid. I"--she spread out her arms and an enthusiastic expression transfigured her face--"I should love to suffer. Jesus Christ also suffered on the cross. It would be no suffering for me, it would be a joy." Humbly bending her head she made the sign of the cross.

What did she mean? Why did she say that with such fervour? Böhnke did not understand her to-day, although he had hitherto understood her so well. He did not guess that she was seized with an ardent desire to suffer for her love, if necessary.

What could affect her if she only had Martin, only him? And he would soon be hers, she felt it. The woman looked down on the man from a triumphant height.

Böhnke eyed her in perplexity. He tried to endure her gaze, but he felt so confused that he once more had to lower his eyes.

What a poor wretch he was, a real coward. Her voice was full of deep contempt as she said icily, "Let me go on now, Mr. Böhnke."

"No, no," he cried, seizing hold of her dress. No, she must not leave him in anger. He would--he did--recall everything; he had said nothing, he knew nothing, guessed nothing. Only she must not look at him like that, he could not bear it, it broke his heart. He almost whined as he implored her pardon; surely she must know that he was mad, irresponsible, that it made him furious to know that she was always with the other man, whilst he, alas, had to remain so far away from her.

"You needn't stay away, Mr. Böhnke."

"But I can't bear to see you with the other man," he cried. "Can't you understand?"

Yes, she understood very well. She almost felt sorry for him now. Jealousy is a terrible torment. Would Martin have returned from the fields by now? Would he be sitting with Rosa, or perhaps standing about with Marianna? She grew hot and cold by turns. Both things were dreadful, she could not permit either of them. She, who a moment ago had been so triumphant, felt disheartened and cast down with fear and torment and uncertainty. Oh, this uncertainty was something dreadful; did he not care for her a thousand times more than for that little girl? Yes, it must be true, Böhnke must be suffering too.

Her glance was full of compassion as she looked at him. How he shuffled along; he looked like an old man, and he was so pale and emaciated, there seemed to be no youth left in him. She laid her hand on his sleeve. "Surely we are not going to be enemies, Böhnke?" she said gently.

"No, certainly not," he jerked out. He bent his head, and, hastily pressing his dry lips to the beautiful, white hand which formed such a contrast to the dark sleeve on which it was resting, said:

"Forgive me, for God's sake, forgive me."

"I forgive you," she answered. She stooped and picked up his hat which had fallen off his head without his noticing it. "Here, put it on."

And then she held out her hand, and allowed him to grasp both her wrists and stand thus for a few moments taking leave of her.

He felt a little calmer now; she was not angry with him, thank God, not angry. He stood a long time after she had left him, following her with his eyes. How daintily she tripped along in spite of her haste. Her dress did not knock against her like a heavy sail against a clumsy mast, but the wind played with it wantonly, so that you could see her ankles, her striped stockings, and smart white petticoat even at a distance. Böhnke felt his heart stand still with delight. There she went to meet somebody else, leaving him behind; but his thoughts hurried after her all the same and clung to her like a chain. She would never be able to get rid of him entirely. And even though she might curse the chain, it would always clatter behind her and warn her that he and she--yes, that they were forged together for time and eternity. That consoled him. And a hope arose within him that the chain might become still stronger and tighter. Then might the angels hide their faces and weep when God cursed them--if only he and she might go to hell together.

* * * * * * * * * * * *

Mrs. Tiralla rejoiced to think that she had so easily got rid of the schoolmaster. It would have been so tiresome if he had returned with her. She ran through the gate with a light heart.

The stillness of evening lay over the farm. The pigeons that had their cot on the high pole near the pond were already sitting huddled together on the perch in front of their door, cooing softly. How tender it sounded; it seemed to Mrs. Tiralla as though it had never sounded so tender before. And the cock was strutting about among his hens; the woman thought she could see that he particularly wished to please the white hen. A couple of early white butterflies, the first heralds of approaching spring, were fluttering about, exhausted by their amorous dalliance. Mother stork was standing on her nest on the old barn; the couple had returned the day before in renewed love to the home they had left last autumn. Marianna was crouching on the doorstep peeling potatoes for supper, and quite close to her stood Mikolai with his back against the wall and his hands in his trouser pockets, looking down with a smile at the girl's firm brown neck that showed above her white frill.

How beautiful everything was! Mrs. Tiralla closed her eyes as though dazzled, then opened them wide with a dreamy expression and gave a deep sigh full of longing. Everything spoke of love. What did it matter if the butterflies were dead by to-morrow morning, if they were found lying on the ground like small, withered leaves, killed by the night that was still so raw? Had they not spent a merry hour, disporting themselves at love's fair game? She looked round; where was Martin Becker? Had he not returned from the fields with Mikolai?

"Heigh!" Her voice sounded shrill as she called to her stepson. "Where are the others? Your friend and Rosa?"

Absolution | 137

"I don't know," answered the young man in a calm voice, and went on philandering with the maid, in spite of his stepmother's arrival. He had got hold of a long straw, with which he was tickling her neck, and which he quickly hid behind his back whenever she let the potato-knife fall and laughingly tried to seize it.

Where could Martin and Rosa be? They were not in the room downstairs, for she had looked in at the low window. She gazed around with burning, impatient eyes; where had they hidden themselves? All at once she felt disgusted with the two flirting on the doorstep. Were they not ashamed of themselves? She tore the straw angrily out of her stepson's hand and pulled it to pieces. "Stop that nonsense," she said sharply, frowning. "Go in, Marianna, *dalej*, don't lounge there any longer. When Mr. Tiralla comes home we are to have supper, *dalej*."

Disturbed in her amusement, the maid, who was still quite hot from laughing, murmured sullenly, "The master hasn't been out at all; he's in the house. That man was here"--she turned up her nose--"the schoolmaster from Starawieś. I had to bring some bottles up from the cellar, and they've been drinking beer and gin. Now the master has gone to bed and is asleep." She shrugged her shoulders and shook her head as she tripped away.

"Father drinks," said Mikolai, his laughing face all at once overcast. "He never drank before, why does he do so now?"

He looked at his stepmother inquiringly; he felt as though he must demand an explanation of her. How could she allow him to drink so much? And it was not only beer and wine, for a short time before, when he had gone to the pig-market in Gnesen, he had brought gin back with him, a whole keg of clear gin, some bad stuff made of potatoes, like that given to reapers at harvest-time. And he drank it off as if it were small beer. "Tell me how it is that father has so changed," he continued, in a voice that sounded quite rough. "He used to be so lively formerly. He has always been fond of a drink--who wouldn't be?--but still he never took more than he could stand. But now!" He shook his head, and his glance seemed to Mrs. Tiralla to have suddenly grown suspicious. "I don't know how it's happened."

"I don't know either," said she, as she cast her eyes around. Where had those two crept to? They had both gone, and probably together. Nothing else was of any consequence to her at the present moment. Let Mikolai think what he liked, it was perfectly immaterial to her. "Where can Becker be?" she asked impatiently.

Mikolai's thoughts were still with his father, and he kept staring at the pavement with a heavy frown, which was not at all in keeping with his round, innocent face. It grieved him very much to think that his old father, of whom he was so fond, should drink like that. It was fortunate that his mother had not lived to see it. It seemed to be quite immaterial to his stepmother. Or was he wrong? She was looking quite pale all at once, positively distraught. He must be wrong, she took it, no doubt, just as much to heart as he did. He felt sorry that he had wronged her if only in thought, and held out his hand to her with a good-natured laugh. "Well, what do you say to breaking the old man of this bad habit in good time? Anyhow, it won't kill him yet."

"Anyhow, it won't kill him yet," she repeated absent-mindedly. But she could not stand it any longer, she must know where the two were. "Where can Rosa be? *Psia krew!*" she cried in a furious voice.

Her stepson stared at her in amazement. How mad she was; it amused him to see her. She had always been so very refined, but now she could never make a wry face again when his father rapped out an oath or two. Besides, he never meant any harm by it, but she was furious to-day--ugh! He put his arm round her waist and said jokingly, "H'm, the Pani is in a bad temper to-day."

She could not control her feelings any longer, and burst into tears in her despair at not being able to find out where the two had gone. She laid her head on her stepson's arm and sobbed.

Mikolai felt dismayed and then overcome; he resembled his father in that particular, and could not bear to see a woman cry. And especially this woman, who really was good. He had never known that his stepmother was so tender-hearted. How she fretted about his father.

Mrs. Tiralla wept a long time on his shoulder.

* * * * * * * * * * * *

Martin Becker remained longer in the fields than Mikolai. He had still to sow some clover seed in a piece of fallow-land, when the latter led the horse home with which he had been harrowing.

The young sower whistled as he walked up and down the furrows. A mild breeze was blowing across the fields which had nothing in common with the raw March winds they had been having lately. Was spring really coming? Why, there was Rosa!

He put his hand up to his eyes that the last rays of the setting sun should not hinder him from watching her. The farm was not far from the field they were tilling, and the young girl had just come out of the gate and was walking towards him without hat or shawl, her hands hanging idly by her sides.

As Rosa saw that he was smiling at her, she smiled too; her radiant happiness made her look prettier than usual. "You must leave off working now, Mr. Becker," she cried gaily. "I've come to fetch you. You've been so busy. Aren't you tired?"

"No." As he smiled at her he showed his strong teeth, which looked whiter and more shining than ever under his black moustache.

"Jendrek has never done so much," she remarked knowingly, "and the other labourers haven't either."

"But I'm not a labourer."

"Oh, I didn't mean that"--she turned crimson--"oh, no." She held out her hand artlessly. "Please don't be angry with me. Mother has told me that you've some money and that you really need not work here. I know it very well."

"I like working here," he said quickly. "I like it very much"--he hesitated for a moment and cast a quick glance at the delicate face that was half averted--"very much indeed."

"That's very nice of you," she said innocently, looking at him with a friendly smile.

He cast a complacent glance at her; how blooming she looked now, much more so than when he came. She would soon be old enough to get married. Many a wooer would come forward; her curly hair that shone like gold was very conspicuous among all the smooth, dark-haired women of the country. She would also have a good dowry; Mr. Tiralla had hinted at that pretty broadly. And Mikolai was a good fellow and an affectionate brother; he would be pleased to let his sister have her portion. And she would be a patient, good wife. Martin felt as though he ought to make hay while the sun was shining.

"I'll stop now," he said, suddenly making up his mind, and throwing the last seeds he had in his bag at random; he put on his coat, which he had hung over the plough. "Shall we go for a little walk, Miss Tiralla?"

Yes, Rosa would like that very much. Had he ever been in the Przykop? Perhaps there would be some violets there now. But he must not say "Miss," she was not grown up, her mother had said that repeatedly, she was only a child.

"Well, then, Rosa--Röschen, let's go." He held out his hand and she put hers into it, and thus they strolled into the Przykop. There was not a shoot to be seen yet on the alders or willows, or on the few oaks that were scattered about, but the old pines were as green as ever and smelt fresh and alive. The woodpecker was hammering at their bark, and the wood-pigeons were cooing up in their big branches that shone so red.

Everything was very quiet in the hollow, and the air was so mild that you could have sat down. Martin felt a wish to do so, but the girl began to look about busily for the bushes in whose red sprigs the sap was already coursing, and to turn the big heaps of brown leaves over with her hands and feet. Would she not be able to find the first violet under one of them? Oh, now she had found one! She shouted with joy.

Who would have thought that this gentle girl could be so jubilant? The young fellow was delighted to hear her, and stood quite still and smiled down on her as she with nimble fingers stuck a violet and a leaf into the top button-hole of his coat. He very nearly gave her a kiss--nobody was looking on, and her shining parting was so near his mouth.

"The stars are twinkling, the night is cold,
Open the window for thy lover bold."

he began to sing.

"I don't know that song," she said innocently.

He felt ashamed of continuing it. It was a song that the soldiers used to sing, and also the couples as they walked through the corn in the evenings, but it was not suitable for her ear.

Then they strolled about hand-in-hand. How beautiful everything was. The man had never been accustomed to forest and shade, and the big trees in the Przykop inspired him with awe and reverence. He would never venture to take any liberties here; besides, it would be very wrong of him if he were to disturb this child's innocent mind.

He walked beside the girl as though he had been her brother. "Why are you so silent?" she asked. "Tell me something, but please no stories like those Marianna tells me, something nice. Do you always go to Mass as frequently as you do here? Shall you go to confession when I go? Is there a nice church at Opalenitza? Have you also a Holy Virgin on the altar who performs as many miracles as ours does?"

Then he spoke to her of his mother. She had been a happy woman, for she had had a good husband. And she had had many children, and they were good and honest, and happy too. Two daughters were married, the eldest son had the farm at Opalenitza, the second was an engineer in the Rhine province, the third had re-enlisted with the chasseurs in Liegnitz, and he, the miller, was the fourth and youngest. If everything went well, and he got a wife who had enough money, with the sum he had, to buy a good mill, then he, the youngest, would be the happiest of them all.

"If only my mother had lived to see it," he said softly, looking at the girl. And then he went on to speak of his parents, who had always been so united, who had almost died together--his father six years ago and his mother only a few months later--and there was so much love in his voice that Rosa began to cry. He did not understand her tears. Why was she crying? He put his arm tenderly round her shoulders and drew her towards him in the quiet Przykop. "Why are you crying, Röschen, my little girl?"

She said nothing, but continued to cry bitterly. Oh, how happy they had been. Husband and wife always united; many children; and almost dying together. She shivered; that must be even more glorious than in Paradise. She clung to him more closely in her longing and sadness.

* * * * * * * * * * * *

It was late when they came out of the hollow. A grey, rising mist covered the ploughed field as they crossed it hand-in-hand. They did not let go of each other until they passed through the gateway leading into Starydwór.

Now they were back at the farm again. Marianna was singing as she rattled the pots and pans, Mikolai stood laughing by the kitchen fire, but Rosa's face continued to wear a dreamy, radiant expression. Although she was always such an obedient, conscientious child, it did not affect her in the slightest when her brother shouted to her from the kitchen, "Your mother has been looking for you for such a long time; she's very cross. Where have you been?" She did not notice her mother's eyes resting on her with a piercing expression; she did not feel the oppressive silence that reigned at supper that evening.

Mrs. Tiralla kept an obstinate silence; she seemed so low-spirited that the men involuntarily became low-spirited, too--that is, Mr. Tiralla and Mikolai. Becker's eyes were fixed on his plate; he was quiet and happy, and ate with a good appetite. What did he care if the woman was in a bad humour? Let the old man and Mikolai dance to her piping, he would not. And then the thought came to him that a girl like Rosa would never want to order about, and that a man would fare well with a wife like her: always united, and many children, and, and--he did not get any further. He felt a glance resting on him that weighed him down, so that he could no longer think of all those pleasant things.

Mrs. Tiralla kept her eyes fixed on the young man; her brows were contracted, her lips pouting. She felt so scornful, so angry. So he preferred that chit to her! But then her scorn melted and a world of love, grief, longing, and even humility lay in her glance. If only he would look at her, only for one short moment. Ah, now he was looking up--her glance had drawn him--he had to look at her, was obliged to.

At that moment, when she was glowing with happiness, she became a most dangerous temptress. A seductive smile parted her lips, her eyes shone in radiant splendour. She had never been so beautiful, never so amiable.

Even Mr. Tiralla profited by her radiant smiles; he simply basked in them. She was looking at him so kindly; ah, there was not another woman who could be compared with his Sophia. Her smile intoxicated him. What did it matter that she had often been very horrid to him? Pooh! that was all forgotten now, it was some nonsense that he must have dreamt. She had certainly been very strange at times--h'm, very strange, but to-day she was an angel. He even forgot to drink when he looked at her. He kissed the tips of his fingers, threw her the kiss, and stared at her with watery eyes.

Martin Becker gazed at her too, as though there were something quite new about her. He had never known that she was so beautiful; by Jove, there was nobody like her. The girl certainly resembled her very little. No wonder that everybody ran after her, as Mr. Tiralla had told him the first day they met; he could easily believe it. He stroked his dark moustache and looked her full in the face with his fine eyes. Then she smiled still more seductively, and he smiled at her again. He liked her very much.

As they said good night to each other her hand nestled in his; he felt its warm softness, and pressed it more firmly than he had ever done before. How thin Rosa's little hands were compared with hers.

* * * * * * * * * * * * *

Mrs. Tiralla was standing in her room upstairs in front of the looking-glass, undressing. She was doing it very slowly; she felt the whole time as though she must go downstairs once more and walk down the long passage past the young men's door. Was he already asleep?

Mikolai and Becker had gone early to bed, as they had to rise with the lark next morning and go to their work. Rosa had likewise gone to her room after supper. But Mrs. Tiralla had talked some time to Marianna in the kitchen, whilst her husband remained sitting at the table with his head resting in his hands, dozing. He had made no attempt to keep his wife when she left the room.

Did he know by now that he was repugnant to her? Mrs. Tiralla almost thought he did; he often looked askance at her now, whilst his purple lip would droop sullenly. She was glad to think it; good, let him know it; it had taken her long enough to make him understand that she hated and despised him too. Thanks be to God and all His saints, praise be to them a thousand times, Mr. Tiralla had left her in peace for months, from the day his son had returned home, the day she had failed in her attempt with the poisonous corn. The saints had not permitted it at the time, and it was a good thing, for since he had taken such a liking to the bottle, she had got rid of him in that way. She had had nothing to confess to Father Szypulski.

"Thanks be to the holy saints." The woman devoutly made the sign of the cross as she stood before the glass. Then she thrust her hands through her hair and pulled her long, thick tresses down, so that they hung around her like a smooth, silky mantle. She shook them and drew a deep breath. How heavy, oppressive, and disquieting the room felt.

She went to the window, opened it with an impatient movement, and leant out as far as she could. It was like spring outside. The night was dark and mild, there was a smell of the earth in the air and the stars were twinkling. Just over the farm there was such a golden light, that she could see a couple walking up and down near the pond with their arms thrown round each other.

It was Marianna. But with whom? The man was tall, taller than Mikolai. A deadly fear overpowered her; she would not stand that, she had better run downstairs. But it was not Becker, he had not that clumsy, rolling gait, he was much more erect. But even if it were not he, how she envied the girl down there.

She pressed both hands to her face; she would not look at them, she would not listen to their whispers. But a shiver ran through her similar to what she had only felt once before in her life, and of which she now no longer knew if it had been sweet or terrible. She felt as she had done that time in the quiet room in early, long-gone-by days, when she had lain on her knees before her best friend and had implored, demanded his help. In those days that shiver full of presage and bliss had almost bereft her of her senses; she could have shouted with joy and still have died of weeping. Now, so long afterwards, she once more felt the same kind of shiver.

She turned away. She staggered from the window to the glass as though she were about to faint, and stared into it with half-closed, swimming eyes. The balmy air blew in through the open window and fanned her bare shoulders, neck, and arms. It felt like a soft hand, and she held her breath as it caressed her. She kept her eyes fixed on the glass; was she not too old, was she really young enough? Oh, yes. She had to laugh. A voice within her seemed to say, "You still look like a girl and you are still like a girl." And when she came to think of it, was she Mr. Tiralla's wife in the eyes of God?

No. He had forced her, but she was not his wife in spite of that. God alone makes husband and wife.

If only he would come now, if only he were here. "Holy Mary, all ye angels and archangels, ye fourteen helpers in need, lend me your aid."

The woman stretched out her arms as though she were intoxicated. Suddenly she thought she heard somebody coming cautiously upstairs. The floor outside her room creaked.

She rushed to the door and unbolted it with a jubilant cry like one who has been saved. There stood Mr. Tiralla.

* * * * * * * * * * * * *

The night grew dark, the stars hid themselves behind clouds, as though they were afraid of looking down on Starydwór. The balmy wind, which seemed to carry spring on its wings, had brought rain. All at once there came a heavy shower, which turned into a slow drizzle as soon as the warm air had grown cool, and which continued until the misty, grey dawn broke.

The young men buttoned up their coats before starting for the fields. What a change in the weather! They felt chilled to the bone. Somebody might at least have made them a cup of hot coffee. But nobody appeared, and there came no answer to their soft call of "Heigh, Marianna, heigh!" The whole house was as silent as death; it was as though all life were extinct. There was nothing for it; Mikolai had to make the fire and boil the coffee himself, or they would have to leave the house on that wet, sullen-looking morning without something warm to drink.

Mrs. Tiralla had heard their call. She was lying on her bed with open eyes, but was unable to rise. She felt worn-out, bruised in body and mind; she had only sufficient strength left to bite her pillow, so as to suppress her sobs. "Holy Mary, wert thou asleep?" Had the angels and archangels not heard her when she called to them? He, he had come--but not the one she had prayed for.

The woman clenched her fists in impotent fury, whilst her glowing cheeks burned with shame. All the aversion, all the hatred she had ever felt for her husband was nothing compared with this intense, blazing passion that raged within her. How was she to avenge herself? If only she had the poison which she, like a fool, had given back to him. Then she would have rushed downstairs and calmly, quite calmly, poured some of the white powder into his half-open mouth whilst he was lying in his bed snoring. It would have acted, she felt sure of that. The saints would not let innocent animals die, but they would look on with a smile when the devils carried Mi. Tiralla's soul off to hell.

The woman uttered wild curses as she reproached herself for her stupidity. How foolish, how unutterably foolish she had been to give up those powders that could have released her. If she had had them now, she would have given ten years of her life, nay more, her hope of everlasting bliss. "Yes, take it," she groaned, starting up in bed and stretching her clenched fists towards heaven, "take it in exchange for them."

Then she prayed. It was a meaningless jumble of words, for she was beside herself, but still she felt somewhat calmed as she moved her lips and made the sign of the cross and hit her breast. Her thoughts dwelt on the powders as she mechanically repeated the usual prayers. Perhaps she could get them again, after all? He had put them into his writing-desk that day, she had seen him do it. True, it was always locked, but--"Blessed be the Holy Virgin and all the saints," she cried, drawing a breath of relief--but the key was on the ring in his trouser pocket.

She sat down on the side of the bed, and pushing her dishevelled hair away from her distraught-looking face she groped for her slippers. It was still early; he would still be fast asleep and Rosa and Marianna, too, and Martin and Mikolai had already gone to the fields. There would be nobody to frustrate her plans this time.

She could not wait to dress herself properly, but throwing a petticoat on, she thrust her bare feet into her slippers and glided downstairs. She opened the door into Mr. Tiralla's room almost noisily; she was right, there he lay snoring, his eyes closed, his mouth wide open. Quick, quick!

She looked round the room; there stood the old bureau. But, alas, he had got the trousers on in which he always kept the bunch of keys. He had thrown himself on his bed half-dressed; a sock and a trouser-leg were sticking out from under the feather bed which he had drawn around him.

A feeling of intense disappointment took possession of her for a moment. But then a look of contempt crossed her face; he was snoring, he would not notice anything. She conquered the feeling of disgust at having to touch him, drew the feather bed away from his massive body that lay there like a felled log, and put her nimble fingers into his pocket. He was as lifeless as a stone; she hardly considered it necessary to suppress a cry of joy when she held the coveted key in her hand.

She ran to the bureau and stuck it into the lock; the desk creaked loudly as she opened it. There were the drawers. Heedless of danger she turned her back on the bed and began to search for the powders. She opened and closed one drawer after the other with an angry bang at not finding what she sought. Where were they, where could they be? Stop! In this drawer, quick, what was that that gleamed so white and new under all those papers yellow with age? It was the box, the box! She stretched out her hand to seize it--but the hand remained poised in mid-air.

"*Psia krew*, what are you doing there?" cried Mr. Tiralla. He had awaked.

She wheeled round and they gazed at each other with pale faces. She stood there like a delicate, feathery leaf that a breath of wind has caused to tremble; but he was trembling too. Neither of them was capable of saying a word. Mr. Tiralla had not uttered a sound since his first cry; he was like a man who is being choked, and his face grew purple as he struggled for air. What was she doing there, what did she want, what was she looking for? Why did she come so furtively when he was asleep? Did she want to rob him? He had never refused her any money, it could not be that she was looking for. Perhaps it was for the----? He grew rigid with horror, his tongue hung out of his mouth and he gasped and gasped. "Let, let----" He could not say anything more, but fury, fear, and the horror of it all, extorted from him an inarticulate cry like that of an animal.

Then she, too, gave a shrill cry and ran out of the room with hair flying, leaving the drawers and the desk open.

He remained lying on his bed as though paralyzed; only his eyes wandered timidly from corner to corner. He was so terrified; the strong, stout man felt all at once quite helpless. Had she gone--had she really gone? He listened to every sound. But there was nobody creeping outside in the passage, and everything remained perfectly quiet until Marianna's noisy tread was heard. Then her loud singing in the kitchen and her rattling with the rings on the stove gave him courage, and he stood up and tottered to the bureau with shaking knees, took the box with the powders out of the drawer which she had left open, and hid it inside his shirt. If only she did not find it--if only she did not find it!

Then he staggered to the washstand and stuck his head, which felt dizzy, deep down into the basin. How his face smarted. He was cooling it as the maid came in.

Marianna clasped her hands in dismay. "What is it, Panje?" Oh, dear, what a sight Pan Tiralla was. It was awful, his face was scratched all over. Where had he got it? Had he fallen amongst thorns? She ran into the kitchen lamenting and fetched a little lard to put on it.

Mr. Tiralla sat as quiet as a lamb and let the servant smear his scratches with it, but he never said a word, in spite of Marianna's inquiries. Fallen amongst thorns, fallen amongst thorns, yes, that he had! He continued to nod in a stupid kind of way. Then he groaned and moaned like a man who has been heavily wounded, and laid his head on the table. It was all up, all up. And he had believed, when she was so kind to him the night before, kinder than she had been for a long time--oh, what a fool he had been, what an idiot! He began to cry in a resigned kind of way. He could not think any more; besides, he did not want to think about it any more--what was the good? He could not alter what was coming.

He sent for gin. Ah, that made him feel easier, that did him good. He sat banging the table with his fist, and now and then he would give a hiccoughing sob, "So-phia--So-phia!" He had always loved her so.

CHAPTER X

If Mrs. Tiralla believed that she would have reason to fear her husband now, she was mistaken. There was no necessity for her to steal away so that he should not see her, for he kept out of her way as well as everybody else's. They were all so fond of her, they hung on her words; she was a witch, and if he were to tell what he knew about her, who knows, perhaps she might do something worse to him? He was terrified of her in secret. When he heard her steps he would cower involuntarily; he preferred her not to come where he happened to be. He scarcely ate anything at meal time; even if he had been hungry he would not have ventured to partake of anything. The drink he took nourished him; he grew stouter and stouter, and his eyes were embedded in fat. He would only eat what the maid brought him, but he ordered her not to say anything to her mistress about it. "Very good, very good," she would answer, with a nod, but when she spoke to others about her master, she would point to her forehead and say in a sad voice, "Poor master! I think he drinks too much."

Everybody said that Mr. Tiralla had become a drunkard. True, he hardly ever came to the inn now when the gentry were there, but he would drink in secret either at home or at the inn at a different time to the others. He avoided his former companions; they had not seen him for weeks.

Loud were the exclamations, therefore, when they caught him early one afternoon sitting all alone at the inn. They had made up their minds to take him by surprise some time, and now they had found him.

"*Psia krew*, old fellow," cried Jokisch, "where have you been? You and I are neighbours, and still I never see you."

The forester, who had been obliged to complain of Mr. Tiralla formerly, said to him in a friendly, reproachful voice, "I never meet you in the Przykop now." Schmielke and the gendarme also gave vent to their astonishment-- why did Mr. Tiralla no more appear at the usual table? The priest, too, had been very much surprised that he never came to church either. That was not right, he really must go. He ought to pray twice as much as others, he the husband of such a pious and--there was a momentary pause and Mr. Schmielke gave a waggish laugh--beautiful wife.

They poked each other in the ribs and laughed. Had he really not noticed anything?

But he glanced at them all in turn with a stupid, dull look, and then went on drinking as if they were not there. He did not want to have anything to do with them; he wanted to be left in peace. Why should it be such a pleasure to them to gloat over him? He had not grown so stupid but that he could feel they wanted to get some fun out of him. He gazed about him with a restless look; now this place was embittered as well. Where could he drink a glass in peace? At home he feared his wife. She was quite friendly to him now, and would often say to him, "Have something to drink, do." And when he had complained of the blood rising to his head, she had told Marianna to bring him a cooling drink from the cellar. "Why do you want to go into the fields?" she had even said; "let the young folks work there. Stop at home. It's so hot out of doors, you'll get a stroke." She was right, and still he did not believe in her any more. Why did she advise him in such a kind way to remain at home? He would have liked to know--yet he dreaded the knowledge. Is not everybody fond of life? It would be better to pretend that he had not noticed anything.

But inwardly the man was consumed with a terror that burnt him to such a degree that his mouth and throat and chest and lungs were as dry as a parched field that never can get enough moisture. He was obliged to drink to conquer the fear that always gripped him anew, that took possession of him day after day, whether he was in the room or in the passage, in the yard either when the sun shone, or on a moonlit night, in the barn, in the stables, in the house, round about the house, everywhere where his wife happened to be. Hitherto he had only felt safe in the inn, and then only when he was quite alone with his glass and the buzzing bluebottles that flew up and down the dull window-pane.

And now they were spoiling that for him too. He gazed at the laughing men as though they were his enemies. Then, finishing his glass, he turned away without saying good-bye or casting a glance at the numerous strokes which the landlord had chalked on the board, and trotted out of the door with his shoulders drawn up and his big head on one side, as though he were ducking down for some reason or other.

The men felt ready to laugh once more as they followed him with their eyes. "Mad!" exclaimed Schmielke, as he struck his thigh. But they did not laugh after all.

"If he makes himself so drunk every day, he'll not know soon what his wife is up to," remarked Jokisch, rubbing his nose thoughtfully.

"Who can blame her for it?" said Schmielke, in a tone of excuse. "She must be twenty years younger than he, and Mr. Tiralla has never been an Adonis. Between ourselves I can quite understand that a woman like the fair Sophia favours somebody else. You are still very narrow-minded in this part of the world, gentlemen. I'm only sorry that I'm not the favoured one."

"An idiot, nothing but a stupid boy," cried Jokisch angrily, full of envy.

They were all envious. But Schmielke, the man of the world, consoled himself and the others by saying, "Who knows whose turn it may be next, now that she has begun?"

So they all pinned their faith to that.

* * * * * * * * * * * * *

Mr. Tiralla tottered slowly down the village street. The sun was glowing so that the dust which flew up in clouds as he shuffled along glistened before his lowered face as though it were mingled with gold. He neither heard nor saw anything, and he was not thinking, either. After passing the last cottage in Starawieś, he mechanically took the parched track across the fields in the direction of home.

The early summer sun was shining down on the immense plains; the fine-looking ears of corn that swayed to and fro were already about as high as a man. The clover lay cut in the meadows, and emitted a powerful smell as it dried quickly in the sun. The air was full of a continuous buzzing of insects that glistened like gold, and of the trills of invisible larks. The blessing of a promising harvest lay spread over the broad fields as far as Starydwór, and everywhere as far as the eye could see. But Mr. Tiralla's heart did not rejoice as a farmer's should have done. He did not look about him, nor care whether the oats and wheat were getting on, and whether the rye was beginning to turn pale. He pressed his hat further down on his forehead and shuffled along a little more rapidly. Marianna should bring him something at once to his room. He would lock himself in; he had not had his daily quantity yet, those confounded fellows had disturbed him. He still felt very out of sorts.

"Mr. Tiralla! Mr. Tiralla!" shouted somebody behind him.

He did not hear. Then somebody seized him by the coat as he reached the Boża męka which stands at the cross-roads.

Mr. Tiralla turned round in terror--was it she? Ah, it was only the schoolmaster. He gave a sigh of relief.

"Why do you hurry so, Mr. Tiralla?" said Böhnke in a breathless voice. "You were almost running. I saw you in the distance when you left the village, and I've been racing behind you the whole way."

"Why did you do that?" asked Mr. Tiralla. "I want to be alone, I must be alone, I'm safest when I'm quite alone." Then he sighed again, and his swollen eyes glimmered as he cast a restless look around.

The schoolmaster sighed too; dear, dear, the man was quite out of his mind. It must be true what they were saying in Starawieś, that Becker had become Mrs. Tiralla's lover. Confound it! "May I offer you my arm, Mr. Tiralla?" he said, going close up to him. "You're walking badly."

"No, no--no, no!" cried the stout man, keeping the schoolmaster off as though he were afraid of him. And then he added in a gruff voice, as he saw that he would not be repulsed, "*Psia krew*, what do you want? Go to the devil, little Böhnke."

But the words "little Böhnke" did not have the usual effect on the schoolmaster, for he felt sorry for the man. Besides, he wanted to know, he must know, how far it had gone with Mrs. Tiralla and Becker. You could not believe all the gossip of the inn, but he would get at the truth from the man himself, the husband who had been insulted and deceived.

So after Mr. Tiralla had stumbled several times, Böhnke took hold of his arm. "Do let me accompany you," he said in an anxious, friendly voice.

"All right then," he growled. The man's solicitude did him good after all. Besides, what had he to fear from little Böhnke? He was pale and humble, pleased when you left him in peace, and did nobody any harm.

So Mr. Tiralla put up with the schoolmaster's company and they walked together like father and son. And when they came to the farm gate he did not even object to his going still further with him. "Come along, little Böhnke," he said, "come into my room. Marianna shall fetch us something out of the cellar; I've got the key. Then we two will have a drink by ourselves."

* * * * * * * * * * * *

It was a long sitting. It had been early in the afternoon when they came from Starawieś, now it was almost evening. During all those hours the house had been as quiet as though not a single soul, as though not even a mouse were there. And still every time a glass was put on the table with more noise than usual Mr. Tiralla had hastily put his finger to his lips, "Sh!" He had drawn nearer and nearer to his friend as he whispered to him. For the schoolmaster was his friend, and it did him good to have such a friend. Did little Böhnke know what a mouse felt like when it was being enticed into a trap with bacon? Oh, his wife was kind to him now, she was so bright, and smiled the whole day long. She would even have brought him something to drink with her own hands if he had asked for it, she who had formerly turned up her nose and said, "Pooh! you stink!" if he had only drunk one small glass. But who could trust her? "For listen, little Böhnke"--Mr. Tiralla put his arm round the other man's neck and breathed into his ear with trembling voice--"listen! she's laying a trap for me. And when I'm dead, my friend--sh!"--he clapped his hand over the other man's mouth as he was about to jump up--"be quiet. You mustn't betray me, hold your tongue. And when I'm dead, then, oh then----"

Mr. Tiralla could not speak any more. He hiccoughed and sobbed, for he had already drunk a great deal, and then, putting his head on the table, he began to weep.

The schoolmaster sat motionless. He scarcely heard what the man had been saying, for he was listening the whole time for a sound in the house. Would he not soon hear her steps, her voice? How he longed for them. But nothing moved. Everybody was in the fields bringing in the clover, Marianna had said when she brought the last bottle in, and then they had watched her through the window, as she, too, went off with her red skirt up to her knees and her rake over her shoulder. Bringing in the clover! Mrs. Tiralla had never helped to do that before. But this year--the man's face was distorted with jealousy--this year there were two young men there, her stepson and Becker. Which of the two was it? Perhaps both. The man gave a dull groan. Two lovers. And still he could not learn anything for certain. This man was so awfully stupid, such an idiot.

The compassion which Böhnke had at first felt for Mr. Tiralla was changed into anger. It was the man's own fault, it served him right; why did he not take better care of her? He gave the weeping man a rough push, "Your wife has got some good friends; I suppose you know it?"

Mr. Tiralla did not fire up, but let his head remain where it was. "Leave her. Oh, little Böhnke, the only friend I possess, if you knew, if you knew."

He gave several heartrending sighs, but when the schoolmaster was imprudent enough to ply him with questions in an eager, inquisitive voice, he suddenly grew silent. The other's eagerness had made him suspicious, and he obstinately closed his mouth; he would not be pumped.

So they sat in silence until it was evening, and still the schoolmaster delayed his departure. He must wait, she must be coming. The table and glasses were already swaying backwards and forwards before his eyes, and still he let Mr. Tiralla refill his glass, whilst he did the same to his. What else could he do, so as to beguile the awful time of waiting?

Böhnke had no idea how much he had drunk; if he had known it, he would have been terrified. He had always despised those who drank more than they could stand, and he had always known that he himself could not stand much, but he knew it no longer. She must come some time.

"Your health, Mr. Tiralla!"

"Much good may it do you, little Böhnke!"

They clinked their glasses once more without any sign of mirth or enjoyment, only for the sake of drinking; the one consumed by the pangs of jealousy, the other pursued by the fear of death.

Then the crack of a whip was heard. At last! There she was--but with the others. The schoolmaster had staggered to the window, and in his haste had upset his chair with such a loud noise that Mr. Tiralla, terrified at what might betray them, screwed up his eyes, put his hands to his ears, and would have liked to creep under the table.

They drove into the yard. The oxen in front of the wagon came slowly along with wreaths of red clover and blue cornflowers round their horns, quite conscious of their finery. On either side a young man was walking with a rake thrown over his shoulder; a dark one on the one side, a fair one on the other; the one slender, the other more thick-set, but both nice-looking and both happy.

Böhnke looked on with envious eyes. And there--he pressed still closer to the window--on the top of the sweet-smelling hay, handsomer and happier-looking than he had ever seen her before, there she sat enthroned. Her light-coloured dress was fresh and clean, her broad-brimmed hat hung down her back, her clear forehead was unprotected; she looked younger and more light-hearted than her daughter, who was crouching behind her. Brown-skinned Marianna was hurrying behind the wagon, laughing. She had fallen off the piled-up clover, and had now to run behind.

It was as though gaiety personified had entered Starydwór. The schoolmaster clenched his fist and shook it at the wagon, and still he would have given his life to have been in the procession and have taken part in Mrs. Tiralla's joy. "How happy she is," he murmured, turning away. He hated her at that moment on account of her happiness, but then he felt he could not begrudge her it, after all.

He walked past Mr. Tiralla with a gesture of loathing, and without saying good-bye.

"Come again, my friend, my brother, come soon," he said thickly.

154 | Absolution

Böhnke did not answer. He must go out, out to that deceitful, despicable woman.

He met her in the passage.

Did she know that the schoolmaster was there? Had Marianna prepared her? Anyhow, she looked neither surprised nor terrified. Her blooming face turned neither redder nor paler, it kept the same rosy tint, and there was a kind expression in her eyes as she looked at him. She held out her hand.

"It was so beautiful," she said, smiling, as she drew a deep breath of pleasure.

"So beautiful," he repeated softly, devouring her with his eyes. He drew her away from the light almost by force. When they had reached the darkest corner, he said to her accusingly, "You're deceiving Mr. Tiralla."

"Whose business is that?"

"Mine, mine, mine!" He shook her at every word, he was beside himself. He felt he was intoxicated, and still he could not control himself. He raised his hand as though to strike her.

She caught hold of his arm, "Oh, don't hit me."

The gentleness with which she said it disarmed him. How dared he strike her? How dared he, who was intoxicated, strike this woman? All at once he lost his courage and his anger disappeared.

"Oh, why do you disturb me?" she wailed, in a low voice, and closed her eyes. "Please leave me, oh, do leave me. I was so happy."

Her voice touched him. Yes, he could well believe it, it does one good to be happy.

She had slowly retreated; now she was again standing in the light. He saw that she was escaping from him, and still he could not hold her.

At that moment Mikolai approached. "Where are you, mother?" The others now also appeared; the schoolmaster saw her surrounded by figures in light garments as through a mist. Rosa had taken the garlands off the oxen and now asked, "What are we to do with them?"

"Come, let's adorn the saints with them," answered the woman. "It's the first harvest of summer; may they be gracious to us." Then turning to the schoolmaster she said, "Come more frequently, Mr. Böhnke. I should be pleased if you would often come to see Mr. Tiralla."

All the man could do was to bend over her hand and whisper in a hoarse voice:

"Certainly, if you wish it, Mrs. Tiralla."

* * * * * * * * * * * *

They had adorned all the saints in the house, as well as the image of the Holy Virgin in the niche over the gateway, with the clover and cornflowers. The wagon with its huge load of clover was standing in the shed; to-morrow early it was to be put into sacks, this evening they were to have a rest. It was quite like Sunday at Starydwór; even the Sundays were not so beautiful formerly as the workdays were now. Marianna was singing in the kitchen whilst making pancakes, and Mikolai was strolling about the yard smoking, with his arm round Rosa's shoulder. She was blushing and smiling at something he was saying to her.

"I tell you, you'll be sorry for it when you're once in the convent," he was saying in a persuasive voice. "It's a dreadful thing to have to nurse the sick, or pray the whole day. The Ladies of the Sacred Heart are all elderly, I've seen them once. And the Grey Sisters--oh, don't tell me anything," he said, putting her off as she was about to interrupt him, "I know what I'm saying. They're all old and ugly. What do you want to do there? Stop at home; we two get on so well together." He drew her more closely to him, and then said very seriously, although two dimples began to show themselves in his round cheeks, "As I'm your brother, I'm going to give you some good advice. See that you marry Martin. I like him just as much as a brother already, so what will it be then? Let him stop here and put his money into the farm, so that we can buy some more land, or perhaps build a distillery, or a brick-kiln. Or let him buy a mill here in the neighbourhood with the money that you'll bring him. It's all the same to me. All I want is that you don't go into a convent." He gave her a friendly push, so that she reeled a few steps away from him, and then catching her again he drew her to his side, laughing. "Won't that be nice, sister mine, eh? What do you say to it?"

"But does he like me?" she inquired, in a soft, timid voice. Her heart throbbed--husband and wife, and always united during many years, and many children. Her face flamed. If only he liked me, she thought, and it was as though she were praying.

"Why shouldn't he?" asked her brother, looking at her tenderly. He was really fond of his good, gentle little Rosa. But then his glance grew criticizing and appraising as he added, "You're certainly not half so pretty as your mother. *Psia krew!*"--he smacked his lips and his eyes grew ardent--"what a fine woman she is! What a pity--and the old man drinks. But people must not compare you two, that's all. Martin will understand that; besides, he isn't one of those who look at beauty alone."

Suddenly a violent pain pierced Rosa's heart, and she involuntarily pressed her hand to her side; it was as though her heart were broken and she must hold it together. Oh, yes, her mother was beautiful, and how she had laughed when they were turning the clover; just like the wood-pigeons in the Przykop. She could not be compared with her mother, she knew that. Her head drooped in painful humility.

"But you've got something too," said Mikolai consolingly. "Becker has to look out for a wife with money. Although he has some himself, he hasn't enough. Besides, I think he's very fond of you. Tell me"--he put his hand under the girl's chin and looked into her face--"do you like him too? Shall I tell him so?"

The tears welled into Rosa's eyes and rolled down her cheeks. She shook her head without saying a word, and as he urged her, "But why not? Don't be so stupid!" she said quite softly, "I don't want to; no, I would rather not," and then tore herself away from him and ran into the house, and up to the room she shared with Marianna. There she threw herself on her knees beside her narrow bed and began to cry and pray. She had to cry; she would have liked to check the tears that flowed, she did not know why, but she could not. Was that jealousy that was stabbing her heart like a knife? Oh, no, nobody in the world could admire her mother as she did. She would gladly have given her everything--only not Becker. How those two had gazed at each other. They had kept together the whole time in a remote part of the field, always side by side as though they belonged to each other. And her mother had laughed as though she were a young, happy girl, much younger and much happier than she, Rosa, had ever been. Was it not disgraceful to laugh like that when one is so old?

Rosa's lip curled, but then she felt very much ashamed of herself. How horrid it was of her to envy her mother because she had laughed. If only she might always laugh and be happy! Her lot would be to pray, pray always. She would go to the Grey Sisters and nurse the sick, or to the Ladies of the Sacred Heart. That was the only thing she wanted to do, nothing else was worth longing for.

Husband and wife, and always united during many years, and many children--it sounded like distant music. Rosa moved her lips more rapidly; she would have liked to stop her ears, she fought with all her strength against the distant music. "Jesus, my only Friend, I love Thee above everything. Sweetest Jesus, Saviour!" she whispered fervently; her eager eyes were full of longing as she raised them.

Rosa had never had a picture of the Saviour over her bed, nothing but a vessel containing holy water and some consecrated palm branches, but at that moment a picture shone on the bare wall which had never been there before. She stared at it in a transport of joy, and her eyes grew bigger and bigger; her lips faltered as she prayed, and she heaved a deep sigh--there--there--Jesus Christ! How Martin Becker resembled Him in every feature, and how He smiled at her.

The expression in the girl's face grew more and more ecstatic; it was as though all the blood in her body had suddenly become active, as it coursed down into the tips of her toes and then up into her hot cheeks. Rosa glowed with delight--there He was, there He was. It was no longer the Christ Child, whom she had got leave to nurse, it was He, He, so big and so beautiful.

"Jesus, O my Saviour!" She uttered a cry of joy and stretched out her arms.

It had grown dusk outside and the low room was already in darkness, but the picture shone with a wondrous splendour before Rosa's eyes. She writhed on the floor, her delicate body trembled with pain and ecstatic happiness.

When Marianna came upstairs to dress--for Mr. Mikolai had promised faithfully to take a short walk in the fields with her after supper--she found the Paninka lying on the floor, pale and almost fainting, as though all the blood had left her body. Poor little thing! The maid lifted the light body on to the bed and began to undress her.

But Rosa resisted with a wail and kept firm hold of her clothes. She would not come down to supper either, she wanted to be alone, quite alone with Him.

"With whom?" asked Marianna inquisitively. But she received no answer.

The young girl lay on her bed, pale and with a faraway look in her eyes. Marianna cast a glance at her in which there lay both fear and reverence--dear, dear, was that to begin again? She made the sign of the cross and then, as no sound came from Rosa and she seemed to be sleeping, hastily made herself smart, put on a dean cap and her beads with all the long, gay-coloured ribbons round her neck--Mr. Mikolai would approve of her now--and hurried downstairs, humming a song.

Nobody missed Rosa at supper. The evening was so warm, so mild and alluring that it had turned all their heads.

Even Mr. Tiralla, who otherwise would have asked for his little daughter, did not give her a thought. True, he was sitting at the table, but his eyes were fixed on vacancy, and he neither saw nor heard anybody. It appeared as if he might fall off his chair at any moment.

Martin Becker was filled with aversion as he looked at him; it was a shame, a disgrace to drink like that. He turned his eyes away. Then he flashed a tender glance at Mrs. Tiralla; poor, dear woman, if only he could carry her away in his arms, away from him, away from all this foulness! Would to God he could get away from it all! But they could not run away together, and so he, too, must stay to please her. It was not easy; it was no honour to serve such a fellow, as he had done now for well-nigh three-quarters of a year. But he was doing it to please Mikolai and her--yes, her. He had to stop.

The woman now cast a look at him as though she had guessed his thoughts. She did not thank him in words, but the thanks lay in her eyes. Mrs. Tiralla's eyes had always been beautiful, velvety, deep, speaking eyes, but now there was a soft gleam in them, instead of the restless flickering that had so often been there--the gleam of love.

She gazed at Martin Becker with a deep, warm look. When they went to the Przykop together, as they had arranged to do as soon as Mr. Tiralla was asleep, she would say to him, "I thank you." How she longed to say to him, "I thank you for coming to Starydwór, I thank you for coming as a deliverer. Look, I've become cleansed through you. Oh, how I love you, how I thank you!" But would he understand her? No, how could he, for what did he know? If she were to say to him, "I've become cleansed through you," he would look at her with big, astonished eyes, for he did not know of any guilt. But was she really guilty? No, she was not--the woman raised her head with a confident air--no, she knew of no guilt either. The memory of all those years with all those bad days and bad thoughts had disappeared as though they had never existed. She was once more as young and as innocent as she had been when she sat in her priest's study. It had been quite a different woman who had sighed at Starydwór for so many years, who had wept and had again and again endeavoured to free herself from this hateful husband. Poison? She had to smile; how kind the saints had been to her; they had preserved her from the poison. Now Mr. Tiralla drank. And if he continued to drink as he was doing, so much Tokay and beer and gin, then he would soon drink himself into the grave. God be gracious to his poor soul!

The look that the woman cast at her husband was almost compassionate; he never disturbed her now. She nodded with a smile to her lover and then pushed the bottle, which was not yet empty, nearer to her husband. "Won't you finish it?"

He mumbled something unintelligible as he gazed into his glass, but did not look at her. Then she filled his glass to the brim, and as he still did not drink and did not even stretch his hand out to take it, she took hold of it, sipped a little, and then almost pushed it into his hand. "Your health! Much good may it do you!"

* * * * * * * * * * * *

Mr. Tiralla was asleep. They had not even waited until he fell from his chair, for he was still sitting in his place, although his head had fallen on the table. They need not have left the room, however, for they were as good as alone.

Mikolai had gone out somewhat earlier. He had stood a short time at the front door whistling softly, but when the whistling had ceased and Marianna's clatter was no longer heard in the kitchen, the two had nodded to each other with a smile, as much as to say, "We understand," and had also got up from their seats and gone out as the others had done.

They wandered slowly along hand-in-hand. Mrs. Tiralla never dreamt of fearing that anybody should see them; she walked calmly along in her light-coloured dress that could be seen afar off in the flat fields in spite of the twilight.

Martin did not feel so calm. "If anybody were to see us!" he said, as figures, more suspected than actually seen, appeared and disappeared among the corn. "There are still people about."

"Leave them," she said, with a smile. "Come, put your arm round me. Lead me, I should love to be led wherever you want to go. I'll close my eyes, and then I shall neither see the sky nor the fields nor anything more; I shall only feel you." She clung to his arm that was round her. Oh, to wander like this through eternity. Her heart was filled with ineffable rapture; this was better than heavenly bliss. She had now no longer the glowing wish to kiss him as she had done formerly, to press her mouth to his fresh lips, so that neither of them had any breath left; oh, no, she would blush if she were to do that now. The passionate longing which had tormented her until she possessed him no longer tortured her. Now she was his and he hers, now they were like the angels in Paradise, who live in bliss.

He led her into the Przykop. But when he caught her to his heart in a wild embrace behind the first bushes, she repulsed him. "No, not like that." She was no love whom he had picked up in the street, she was his bride, his wife, and when they later on went to heaven, she wanted to stand pure before the throne of God.

Martin Becker was speechless; he did not know what to answer to this. He understood how to kiss, but he did not understand this. It all seemed very strange. Why had she sought him then, hung on his looks? Why had she immediately fallen into his arms like a ripe apple, which only requires a slight touch, if she had become so prudish all at once, as chaste as one whom you have to teach what love is? Why, even little Rosa could not have been more chaste.

He had to sit down on the moss by her side and only touch her hand. The woman looked about her with dreamy eyes; she could see the fields from the edge of the Przykop. It was pitch-dark in the hollow; he would have liked to go down there with her, but she refused; she wanted to look at the stars above the fields, whose twinkling brilliance was reflected in thousands of dewdrops.

"The splendour of heaven has fallen on the earth," she said softly. "You've come to me, and I thank you." And then she told him all she wanted to say about her gratitude.

He felt quite ashamed. How beautifully she could express herself. She was a clever woman and a good one too. What a shame it would be if he were to interrupt her now with amorous speeches and strain her to his heart in a violent fit of passion as he had done on the first evening, when he had been groping in the passage in the dark and had run against somebody soft, who had pressed herself against the wall, and who, when he whispered in an eager voice, "Is that you, Mrs. Tiralla?" had flung her arms round his neck and had let herself be led wherever he wanted. That evening she had been like a heifer that has thirsted for a long time, and has been driven through dusty fields, and that on seeing water rushes at it, so that the restraining rope breaks and it drinks and drinks and cannot get enough. Now she was like a saint.

The young fellow would not have ventured to embrace her, although his arms and all his fingers were tingling, and although the nearness of this beautiful woman and the warmth of the summer evening made his blood surge through his veins. They were quite alone, quite hidden. A deep silence reigned, save for a land-rail piping in the corn, and a deer calling deep down in the Przykop--and still he controlled himself. Everything was so different at Starydwór to what it was elsewhere.

Martin had not come to his age without having held a girl in his arms--as an apprentice at the mill at home and more especially as a soldier--but a woman like this one had never been his. For one short moment a feeling of regret filled his heart at the thought that it might perhaps have been still nicer with Rosa. Besides, he never felt quite happy about this affair. What would his mother have said to it? For this was a woman, a married woman! The blood mounted to his head--his good old mother, who had been so honest all her life. Or was it desire that drove the blood in this way to his cheeks? Oh, how beautiful this woman was, more beautiful than any of the girls he had ever seen in his life. How white her neck looked just where her dress was cut out a little. He could not control himself any longer, he had to kiss it. But she crossed her hands over her white throat and blushed as she whispered, "Not like that, not like that." But when she again and again felt the pressure of his hot lips she could not restrain herself any longer, and clasping him to her bosom with both arms, she cried in a loud, jubilant voice, that echoed through the dark fields, "All the saints be praised. I love you, I love you!"

CHAPTER XI

The Paninka at Starydwór had visions again. Marianna spoke of it in the village, and when she met Jendrek, who was at Mr. Jokisch's, she complained to him of having to sleep in the same room as the girl. It was very unpleasant, and she would rather sleep on the straw in the stables, or anywhere, than be with somebody who talked all night long as if it were daytime, and who carried on a conversation with the Lord as though He were a bridegroom whom she was wooing. Mr. Tiralla had better look round for an earthly bridegroom for his daughter, or give her at once to the heavenly one, so that the dear soul might get peace and not toss about and frighten others with her strange goings-on.

Marianna had also complained of it to Mrs. Tiralla, but she had shrugged her shoulders. Everybody knew that the girl was often very excited. It was on account of her age, and it would be all right in time.

Mrs. Tiralla had not time to think of her daughter at present, for all her thoughts were centred in Martin Becker. The summer was far gone and autumn was approaching, and she sometimes had a feeling as though the man she loved would depart with the swallows. And if that were his intention, then, then---- An icy dread made her shiver.

Mr. Tiralla did nothing now but vegetate, sleep and drink, drink and sleep. He grew more and more dull-witted every day, shunned everybody, sat brooding for hours together with his glass in front of him, now and then had fits in which he would suddenly bellow like an ox that the butcher has just given a blow between the eyes with his axe, then fall down like the ox, clench his fists in rage or agony, foaming at the mouth, and with a rattling noise in his throat, roll his eyes, hit about him like a madman, and at last fall into a deep sleep, dead-tired. He had more than once lain on the ground so rigid and icy-cold that Marianna had buried her face in her hands and howled--now it was all over--and his wife had stood by him with her finger on her lips, her big eyes bigger than ever, and her neck stretched out, listening. But he always awoke again. And even if he felt stiff and weak, and complained of such pains in his limbs that he dragged his legs along as though paralyzed and could hardly walk, he still went on living. He, who had formerly been so stout, now shrivelled up and grew yellow and thin, and was always hoarse, and did not relish his food any longer. Mikolai noticed it, and made up his mind to send for a doctor to see his father, but his stepmother said what was the good of asking his advice? He would not be able to do anything after all. So the young fellow gave up the idea, and preferred to use the money it would have cost to have a doctor to buy a new spencer for Marianna, and a fur cap for himself for the autumn, so that he might find favour in the eyes of all the girls.

They cured Mr. Tiralla themselves. Strong wine was good in a case of great debility, and it was a medicine which Mr. Tiralla would not pour out of the window. And for the weakness in the legs nothing was so efficacious as a bottle of Pain Expeller when well rubbed in. You could buy it at the chemist's in Gnesen, and it would have a good effect if used morning and evening.

But after Marianna, who took care of Mr. Tiralla, had rubbed him the first time, she came running to her mistress in great tribulation. She had hardly uncorked the bottle, she said--true, it had smelt very good, sharp and pungent like strong gin--when the master tore it out of her hand, sniffed it, and then took such a quick, deep gulp of it, that she had been afraid it would harm him.

But the Pain Expeller did not harm Mr. Tiralla, as it could just as well be used internally as externally. So after that he took a gulp of it morning and evening, and sometimes during the day as well, when his legs required an extra rubbing.

* * * * * * * * * * * *

The harvest had all been gathered in, and the wind swept across the stubble, carrying the loosened cobwebs along with it.

Mrs. Tiralla was standing in the gateway looking away over the empty fields at the signs of departing summer. She shivered and wrapped herself up in her shawl; she was filled with a strange feeling of uneasiness. The time had come which she had always feared; the swallows were sitting huddled together on the telegraph wires, gathering together for their flight. To-morrow would be St. Mary's Day, and then they would depart. And he?

The woman pressed her hands together and gazed with terrified eyes at the image of the Virgin in the niche. Martin had gone to confession, for there would be plenary indulgence at the great festival to-morrow. Oh, if only she, too, had gone! She felt sorry now that she had put it off. Then they could have walked to Starawieś and back again together. What a long time it was since they had walked together. He had not had time lately, they had been obliged to get on with the harvest, and he had worked so hard that he was too tired in the evening to do anything but sleep. How often she had fretted to think that she was not strong enough to work in the fields like Marianna and other girls, then she would have walked close behind him, would have stooped continually to pick up the corn he had mown, and would never have felt tired being so near him.

Now the harvest was over and the winter was drawing near, with its days when there is hardly anything to do, days in which you can loiter about and be so happy, *tête-à-tête* with the one you love, but which are awful, awful when you are alone. The woman shuddered.

Why should she always imagine that he intended to leave Starydwór? He had never said a word about it. Nobody had ever said a word about it to her, and still she felt sure of it. She had looked into his heart, and it had lost some of its joyousness. But was there any place in Starydwór where you could feel happy? No, no, no! Her very heart quivered. She often felt as if the old walls were going to fall down on her. And the old pines on the outskirts of the Przykop used to bend their tops at night in the direction of the farm, and groan as though the souls of those who could find no rest were moaning in their branches.

And the rats, too, that had remained quiet for so long in the cellar, had begun again to glide from corner to corner, and through Mrs. Tiralla's dreams like ghosts that were pursuing her. Mr. Tiralla had lived too long. If he were not there she would be happy, for then she could leave the place with Martin Becker, if he would not remain at Starydwór; even though she would have to go on her bare feet, how gladly she would do so!

Mrs. Tiralla looked with longing eyes towards Starawieś, whose church steeple was pointing to heaven like a finger. She would feel easier as soon as she saw Martin again. "For God's sake don't leave me, darling," she would beseech him. It was not his face that she loved so much that she could not live without it even for a few hours, it was not his laugh that had bewitched her, neither was it his light footstep, nor his slender, erect body, but it was his youth she wanted, his heart that was so young, so fresh, so pure, that it carried hers away too to where everything was bright and happy.

"Martin, Martin!" She stretched out her arms as she gave the beloved name into the care of the winds. Then she saw him coming. He was alone, for Mikolai, who had gone to confession with him, had stopped at the booths behind the church. He came quickly along the edge of the field, as though he were in a hurry. The woman smiled--ah, he was longing to see her, as she him. "Martin!" she called once more; a sweet welcome lay in her voice.

But he gave a start. About what was he thinking so gloomily? It was not his wont to frown like that and keep his eyes lowered. And he did not jump over the ditch that separated the field from the road, as he generally did in order to reach the farm gate more quickly; it looked almost as though his footsteps lagged, as he deliberately walked along to the crossing that led into the road further down.

She went to meet him. What did she care if the people from the settlement were standing at the crossroads near the Boża męka on their way back from church, staring at them open-mouthed? She seized hold of his hands and smiled at him. "What are you thinking of, dear?"

"I've been to confession," he said in a low voice, as he drew his hands away from her and put them behind his back, so that she could not get hold of them. He walked beside her, his head bent and without touching her.

How his face used to beam when he saw her again after an hour's separation! How he had wanted to touch her even though it were only her dress! What was it, what could it be? A sudden sense of hopelessness took possession of the woman. Yes, he was going away from her, he was trying to leave her. As she gazed into his face she could discover no sign of joy at seeing her again, but a struggle was depicted on his open features, which had never been able to hide anything. "I've been to confession," he had said, nothing more. Alas, alas, *what* had he confessed? What penance had been laid upon him?

She trembled as she pressed closer to him. "What are you going to do?" she panted.

"I'm going now," he whispered, shaken. "I'm going. Oh, if only I could!" He uttered a deep sigh.

His sigh gave her back her courage. She felt that it was difficult for him to leave, and that made her feel stronger. "You'll not go," she said, smiling amidst her tears, "you'll not leave me. I love you so dearly. And--aren't we husband and wife in the sight of God?" The words came to her like an inspiration. They would calm him--husband and wife in the sight of God. "And those whom God hath joined together let no man put asunder."

"Be silent!" he cried vehemently, raising his hand as though terrified. "You must not interpret it in that way. I've sinned against the sixth and ninth commandments; I know it now." He bent his head very low.

"Have you betrayed me?" she stammered, turning pale and then flushing.

"I've not betrayed you," he said sadly. "But I've betrayed myself, if you call that 'betraying.' How could I do otherwise? I had to confess that I had unclean desires, that I"--he stopped and pressed his hands to his head--"oh, if I had never come here! *Psia krew,* if only I had never seen you." He gave a dry sob as though he were a boy, and ran away from her through the gate and over the yard into the house, banging the door after him.

She followed him with her eyes. What she had had a presentiment of had now happened, what she had never dreamt of at first had come after all. She stood as though crushed. She felt a pain as though there were something in her throat. It was her terror that was choking her, but she forced it down. Clenching her fists so tightly together that her nails dug into the flesh, she threw her head back. She would not give him up--and she need not do so either.

But how, how was she to set about it, how was she to bring about that he remained with her for ever? She stared at the empty fields with lifeless eyes. Then she threw herself on her knees in her terror and distress and deep despair. Here under the sky, that looked like a dome over the flat land, she would pray, she would cry at the door of heaven, so that the saints who were inside might hear her and give her advice and be merciful to her.

She knelt a long time in front of the niche in which the image of the Virgin stood. Ah, the Holy Mother up there knew her feelings, for had she not felt seven swords piercing her heart? She would help her, she must help her. She prayed fervently. And whilst praying, all kinds of plans flashed through her mind. Should she, too, go to Starawieś to confession? But how was she to begin? How should she express herself, so that she betrayed nothing to Father Szypulski, and still was delivered from her agony of mind? She did not know what to do. Her agony was so great, it seemed to grow and grow in spite of her prayers, until it was unendurable. If only she could find peace, peace--but she could only find that when Mr. Tiralla was in his grave.

All at once the woman's lifeless eyes grew animated, and a wave of colour mounted to her pale cheeks. The thought had come to her that if Mr. Tiralla were to die Martin Becker would not hurry away from Starydwór. There would be no need for him to hurry away, for she would be free and could love whom she wished. And nobody would object then, not even Father Szypulski.

She buried her face in her hands and shivered with delight. What a life of bliss displayed itself before her eyes! But--all her misery came back to her once more--but who would help her to this? She had no more poison, and her hands--taking them away from her face she stared at them--these feeble hands could not give him such a push that he, staggering at the graveside, as he did already, could tumble in altogether and stretch his aching limbs in welcome peace. Mr. Tiralla wanted to die, she saw it in his face, she knew it. Had he not groaned, "If only I were dead!" when they had helped him a short time ago out of the ditch into which he had fallen in a fit of weakness, when he had gone out to meet the last wagonful of corn?

It would certainly be best for him if he were dead. Rosa shuddered when she saw her father's yellow face and blood-shot eyes, and smelt his foul breath, and Mikolai felt very annoyed with him, although he now and then laughed at what he babbled in his weakmindedness.

If Mr. Tiralla were not there! Oh, would the children not draw a deep breath of relief when their father was out of the house? It was really true his presence weighed on everybody. He was so repulsive to look at, and his continual coughing and groaning were horrible to listen to. If only she could deliver them all from him, and at the same time give the man his freedom! It would, indeed, be a good deed. But how was she to set about it? Mr. Tiralla had an excellent constitution in spite of everything; he would not drink himself to death quickly enough. Now and then he did not even care to drink, and he would sometimes push his glass away as though he disliked it. But he must drink, must drink more, even if she had to fill his glass herself! Martin must not leave Starydwór, he must remain!

The woman raised her hands to the image, "Help, help!"

All at once she bethought herself of the schoolmaster. What if he were to come more frequently and drink with her husband? He must have somebody to drink with him, so that he got to like it better, so that he felt an eager desire for beer, wine, and gin. Mr. Böhnke had come once a week during the summer, and then Mr. Tiralla had always drunk an enormous quantity, but the man had lately stopped away. He must come again. Not once a week--no, often, often, every day if possible, for--the woman started convulsively--for there were not many more weeks before Martin Becker would be leaving.

If she could delay his departure, only for a little while, for one more month, two months, for then, then--the woman rose from her knees and drew a deep breath--then the difficult task would, nay, must, have been accomplished.

* * * * * * * * * * * *

As they sat at supper that evening, Martin Becker began to speak of going away. You could see that it was very difficult for him to give notice, he could hardly get it out; his face was burning and he kept his eyes fixed on the ground.

Mikolai had just returned from the fair in high spirits, but his good humour now quickly disappeared. What, Martin wanted to leave--what was the meaning of it? That was a nice piece of news! He had never mentioned anything to him about it before. "What's the reason of this all of a sudden, eh?"

He did not care to continue as a farmer, said Martin hesitatingly. He wanted to look about him a little, perhaps look out for a mill.

But that could not be arranged so quickly, said Mikolai, who began to stand up for his rights as master, after he had caught an imploring look from his stepmother. He could not get away from his engagement in that cool way, although they were friends and had always agreed. Was he going to leave him in the lurch just when he had the autumn sowing to do? Mikolai grew furious when he saw all his beautiful plans disappear like bubbles. "It's a confounded nuisance!" he cried, banging the table as he shot a look of fierce accusation at his old father. He, he alone, was to blame for everything going wrong. What other reason could there be for Martin no longer feeling happy at Starydwór? There was no doubt about it; the old man, who was always drunk now, had grown very objectionable. "Stop with us, do stop," he said, returning to the charge, and cordially stretching his hand out to his friend. "I promise we'll alter what you don't like."

Mrs. Tiralla gave a start; now his own son had even said it. "We'll alter what you don't like." She gave Mikolai a significant look and tried to catch his foot under the table; let him urge Martin as much as possible.

So Mikolai, who suddenly thought with dread of having to work all alone at Starydwór, had recourse to begging. Had they not sworn to be like brothers, and not to leave each other if they could be of any use? Could Martin not see that it would be hard work, much too hard work for him quite alone here? "Father's health is failing," he said; "how long will he last?" He cast a half contemptuous, half sad look at the man sitting there so dead to everything; it was hard to see his father like that. "Martin, brother! And I had hoped that we two should always remain together, and that you would marry my Rosa!" he exclaimed in quite a mournful voice.

At that moment Martin, who had listened to it all in silence with his eyes persistently lowered, jumped up so vehemently that he upset his chair. "No, no!" he cried, turning quite white.

Mrs. Tiralla, too, grew as pale as death. They glanced at each other for a moment, almost timidly.

"Let me go," begged the young man. Then his voice grew more energetic. "I must go. I----"

He stopped; Rosa, who had been sitting quietly at the table, so quietly that they had scarcely noticed her, suddenly got up and fled out of the room.

Martin thought he could see that her face was suffused with a deep blush and that she was fighting with her tears. He felt so sorry for her, she was a good girl! But it was better she should think he did not care for her. It would not do--no, it would never do.

He gathered himself together once more, and said in a firm voice, "I'm going. When the first snow falls, we shall have finished the autumn sowing, and until then I'll work like two for you. You shall have nothing to complain of, Mikolai. But I must go. The first of January is the time in this part of the country when everybody changes servants, but I"--his voice was embarrassed, faltering, but he spoke rapidly--"I shall not be able to stand it so long. Let me go, Mikolai, let me go on the first of December. For the sake of our friendship I beg it of you!" He held out his hand. "Don't refuse. Give me your hand."

Mikolai still hesitated--what was he to do to keep Martin? When he begged like that, what was he to do--say yes, or no? But a glance from his stepmother told him to clasp his hand.

December, the first of December! The woman gave a covert sigh of relief; she almost succeeded in smiling in a friendly way. The look of anguish disappeared from her face--bah! it was a long time to December, weeks and weeks, more than two months! All at once she could have shouted with joy; Mr. Tiralla would not be living then.

"Won't you drink something?" she said to her husband, bending over him so as to fill his glass.

But Mr. Tiralla shrank back as though she were poisonous, and when she continued to urge him in a friendly voice he growled, got up from his chair, and stole out of the room.

* * * * * * * * * * * * *

Mr. Tiralla stood outside in the yard blinking in the pale moonlight. It was autumn and the night was cold; he felt so chilly that he shivered and coughed more than ever; he fumbled about with restless fingers. Were the powders still in the little box that he had carried about with him for so long? Were they really there, quite safe? Ugh! Sophia was trying to kill him again!

His teeth, which had grown quite loose, chattered in his terror. If he were asleep and felt nothing? Had she not already once put her hand into his pocket? If she found them this time, he would be done for. But she should not have the chance. A cunning grin distorted his face, which had grown as yellow as it before was red, and the expression of which was now just as weak and malevolent as it before had been good-natured. He would hide the powders in quite a different place, and she should never, never get to know where they had been put. No, never!

Casting a timid glance around to see if anybody were watching him, he tottered across the yard. Nobody was there, nothing but the moon, that looked out from between the clouds above the barn and gave light.

There was not a sound to be heard, neither snorting nor lowing; the horses were standing in front of the rack, sleeping, and the cows were lying in the straw.

There was a hiding-place in the darkest corner of the stables, which he remembered from his boyhood, and where he had hidden many a pilfered apple and pear, and his first cigar, from his father's keen eyes.

Look, the loose brick was still in the corner. If you took it out, you would find a hole three times as big as was necessary for hiding the little box containing the powders.

There, now put the stone into its place again. Nobody would guess what was lying behind it. Now the spiders could again weave a close web in front of it like a veil, and nobody would spoil it for them. H'm, that was very well done, said Mr. Tiralla to himself, with a satisfied growl. Let Sophia look and look until she was blind, she would never find them--ha, ha!

He laughed hoarsely to himself. Then he looked around in the dim stables, in which the lantern only cast a feeble light, and shuddered. If she were to find them after all? He uttered a deep groan and pressed his hands to his head. Oh, how awful it was that this terror never left him in peace. "Ha!" He gave a hoarse cry and shrank back. Was not something rustling? He trembled, he would have sunk on the ground with fright if a strong hand had not seized him by the arm and held him on his feet.

It was Marianna, who had come with her milk pails. She was very frightened herself--what did Pan Tiralla want there, what was he looking for? He was not like the young master, who often used to waylay her at milking time. Poor master! and how ill he looked, it was enough to make your hair stand on end. She felt very sorry for the old gentleman. Were they not all making fun of him? And he had always been so good to her.

So she gave him a cheery smile and clapped him on the back. "You must not fret, Panje. Don't fret because your wife is good friends with Becker." She cast a covert glance at him as she said it, for she was curious to know what kind of a face he would make.

But he did not make a face at all; he only growled, "What's that to me?" Then he pressed his hands to his head again, and rocked to and fro like a bear, and uttered deep sighs.

The maid felt really terrified. Why did the master give such awful, heartbroken sighs?

But Mr. Tiralla would not answer her; no, he would not tell. Who knows what more his wife might do to him if she heard it? He put his finger to his lips, while his eyes roved about in all directions, and said, "Sh!"

But inquisitive Marianna would not let him go. Of whom was he so frightened? Of his wife? It seemed so. Oh, yes--she drew nearer to her master as she whispered mysteriously--but she was certainly a very strange cook. Had not she, Marianna, almost died from drinking some coffee which her mistress had once made for the master?

Mr. Tiralla listened, trembling with horror. Yes, yes, she had wanted to poison him, he had guessed it long ago. And she still wanted to poison him. He hid himself behind the girl like a child. "Protect me, protect me, oh, she's coming!"

Clinging to the girl's skirts, he dragged her into a corner, and, pressing himself in behind her, held her like a shield in front of him. Oh, Sophia was coming, where should he fly from her? He wailed like a boy afraid of the cane.

Marianna had great difficulty in calming him. "Be quiet, Panje, be quiet," she said; "she mustn't, she won't do anything to you. I, Marianna, am here, you know. And if she dares after all----"

"Yes, oh, yes," he broke in hastily, "then you'll go to the police station and say, 'It was she, she, who brought the master to his grave.'"

Yes, by God she would, the master could rely upon her. Marianna gave him many a fair promise and swore solemnly she would do it. That calmed Mr. Tiralla more than anything else.

"Oh, thank you, thank you!" Then he gave her all the money he had in his pocket, and promised to give her much more for herself and children if she would give information as soon as he lay in his grave.

The two wept together in the dim stables, the man with fear, the girl in her good-nature. They sobbed in such a heartbroken way and struck their breasts so loudly that the animals, startled out of their sleep, turned their heads and looked in astonishment at the strange couple. The lantern went out, and no ray of light penetrated the darkness.

* * * * * * * * * * * *

Meanwhile Mrs. Tiralla was hurrying across the fields. She was quite alone. Martin had said good night to her as though it had been for ever. Farewell for ever! If it had been otherwise, he could not have kept his eyes lowered, and his icy-cold hand had remained only for a few moments in hers. She had pressed his, but he had not returned the pressure, rather he had hastily withdrawn his fingers as though hers were burning him, and had not turned round once more at the door in order to return her glance with one equally expressive, as he had always done before. Then an icy-cold fear had taken possession of her, and all the confidence she had just acquired disappeared again. The first of December! There was certainly time enough before the first of December, but who could say that he would really stay until then? Could he not go off secretly in the night, disappear out of her life as suddenly and unexpectedly as he had entered it?

As she dashed across the fields it was as though all the stars were falling from the sky. She was quite breathless, she was running so.

Where did she want to go? To Böhnke, the schoolmaster. He must come, he must help her. Had he not sworn to do so? Had he not sworn without her asking it that he was hers for ever and ever, through all eternity? In her mind's eye she saw his pale face, thin and hollow-cheeked, consumed with passion, and his feverish eyes, feverish with his longing for her. If she implored him to help her, he would not, could not, refuse. So she was hastening to him.

She had run out of the house without being noticed. Alas, how quickly Martin had at other times followed her steps! He had always heard her softest footfall, her very breath in the dark passage, every movement of her hand as it glided over his door. To-day nobody had followed her. A feeling of bitterness overpowered the lonely woman; without knowing it hot tears ran down her cold face, that was already wet with dew. Was there nobody who really loved her? She, the pious woman, could no longer understand how the Sacrament of Penance could strike terror into any one. And even if she were never to obtain forgiveness, and were to be lost for ever, she would never give up her love nor her lover. Away to Böhnke; he would, he must help her.

The dogs barked in the village as the woman tore past. She rushed along past the sleeping cottages like the wind's bride, her skirts fluttered, her hair had come undone owing to her hasty flight, and the cold breath of autumn beat against her face. Nobody met her; it was already late for the people in the village, and there was hardly a light to be seen anywhere. If only he were awake! And if he were not awake? Then she would thump on his door, or knock at her window so loudly with her fist that he must awake.

There was the house in which he lived. She had never been there, but he had told her that his room was on the left side of the front door. She found his window easily, it was still lighted up, and the shutters were not closed. God be praised, the saints were with her! There he was!

She stood on tip-toe and looked in at the low window. He was sitting at the table, just as she had pictured him to herself, pale and hollow-cheeked, his face ravaged with passion. The lonely man had a bottle and glass in front of him, and he filled his glass and drank it off in one gulp, and filled it again, and then buried his face in his hands and brooded like Mr. Tiralla used to do.

She knocked, but he did not hear her. Then she thumped with her fist so that the window panes rattled.

He started up and came to the window. He uttered a suppressed cry in his fear and joy at seeing her standing there. He tore the window open, and his hands trembled as he stretched them out. She had come, come to him? He stared at her with glassy eyes, his breath smelt of drink like Mr. Tiralla's.

She was afraid of him, and still her distress drew her nearer and nearer to him. "I've come to you--you," she said in a swift whisper. She seized his hands imploringly. With a little help from him she swung herself up, and stood beside him in the room.

There was his bed, there his sofa, there his desk and all his books. She stared around with eyes in which, however, there was no interest. She only wanted help, help, and she thought of nothing else.

He had closed the window and he now closed the shutters too. A gleam of prudence had returned; what would people think if they saw her in his room at that hour? He drew her to the old sofa, and she let him do so; he ventured to kiss her and she allowed him to do that too.

Something rose within her; in her shame and anguish she longed to thrust him back, but--she had need of him, she had need of him. She held her breath so as not to smell his. She suffered him to kiss her, her lips tightly compressed, but when he drew nearer and nearer to her in his intoxication she repulsed him. Then she recollected that she would have to put up with it, for she dared not offend him, she must bind him to her. She tried to find an excuse for her repulse; had he not deceived her once before with the dish of mushrooms? Could she really trust him again?

He swore solemnly that she could, glowing with desire.

Then she said, "Pan Tiralla must die, and you, you must help me."

"I--I?" he stammered, all at once sober. He was sorry for the man, he had been punished enough. Why should he die?

She did not notice his hesitation. "You must drink with him," she whispered hastily; "drink every day with him at our house, so that he drinks more, much more than he does now. He doesn't drink enough at present. You must be with him, you must fill his glass without his noticing it, you must entertain him the whole time, tell him what he likes to hear, put him in a good humour by saying, 'Your health!' and 'Much good may it do you!' so that he goes on drinking and drinking. You must help me in this way." She looked at him imploringly.

He avoided her eyes; no, he could not do that, he did not like to. Mr. Tiralla was rather fond of him, but how much did she care for him, eh? Not *so* much. He snapped his fingers in her face. She preferred another man, Becker; oh, he knew it very well, and that was the reason things were not going quickly enough for her. No, he would not give her a helping hand to that, never, never, he panted, excited to fury by his passionate jealousy, and let his hand fall with a bang on the table, "Never!"

She trembled and seized hold of his clenched hand; she must win him, he must help her, he had no right to refuse her his help, what should she do then? Thoughts flew like lightning through her brain; the first of December, the first of December, oh, Martin would run away from her much earlier than that, he was even now like a young bird trying its wings, and she would soon not be able to hold him any longer. Martin, Böhnke--Böhnke, Martin, all ran together. She could not think clearly, she was beside herself with terror. She threw her arms round the schoolmaster's neck and, putting her lips close to his ear, sobbed, "You must, you must, I implore you!"

Her face, which in spite of hot tears and cold dew was still so alluring, so dazzling, was quite close to his. Then he caught hold of her with all his strength. "You've made me a drunkard," he jerked out, from between his clenched teeth, and strained her to his heart, so that she lost her breath, "and you're making me a murderer--but by God, I love you, I love you!"

CHAPTER XII

Winter had come during the night.

Even yesterday the gossamer had flown across the fields and hung fast to the bare bushes and tops of the few remaining turnips; to-day the first snow lay on the ground. There was not much of it, but still it was wet and cold.

The young men, who were sowing the last seeds, finished their day's work in silence, a silence that was as heavy as the grey, lowering sky overhead, and as sad as the damp, sullen-looking fields in November. They had nothing pleasant to say to each other. Martin's thoughts were far away, he was longing to leave Starydwór, leave it far behind him; and Mikolai was also deep in thought.

The happiness that Mikolai had felt during the summer was a thing of the past. Although a farm of one's own is not to be despised, he would much rather be servant somewhere else than master at Starydwór. How awful his father was! Why, he was out of his mind! If only he could catch that fellow Böhnke by the throat, he thought to himself, clenching his fists in fury. Why did he come creeping to the farm day after day, locking himself in with his father? They never let anybody in, but they would drink and drink, until they had not as much sense left as the cattle. Mikolai swore to himself as he thought of it. And then his stepmother even expected him to put the horses in and drive that drunken rascal home when he felt too tired to have a chat with Marianna. Let him sleep himself sober in the first ditch he came across; it was quite good enough for him. But instead of that he had to be hoisted up into the cart and driven at a walking pace along the pitch-dark road, so that he, Mikolai, was frozen and wet to the skin and felt thoroughly annoyed. What could she see in the schoolmaster to make her so patient and calm that she put up with his visits, which were certainly not doing his father any good?

The young fellow felt very surprised, and now and then something like suspicion awakened within him. How could his stepmother always be smiling? Was it not rather a thing to cry about? But who could know if her smiles came from the heart? She was, no doubt, to be pitied too. It was wrong of Marianna to speak so unkindly of her mistress. She ought not to shrug her shoulders and make faces, but it was just like a servant. That was another cause of annoyance to the young man. If there had been anything between the schoolmaster and his stepmother, he would, of course, have noticed it of his own accord, he was no longer a foolish boy. Rosa gave him much more to think of than that. He felt very uneasy about her, she was so strange. He could not dissuade her from that confounded wish of hers to go into a convent. She persisted in it more than ever. He had already tired himself out with talking to her about it. She would listen quietly, with her eyes fixed on her hands lying idly in her lap, and then, when he knew of no other argument to bring forward, she would say softly, but more decidedly than if she had spoken in a loud voice, "I shall go into a convent, all the same."

What a pity the girl was so holy. "Holy," that was what Marianna called her. If only Becker and she had married, how nice it would have been. Mikolai still harped on this, and it was this disappointment that grieved him most of all. Why did Martin not care for Rosa?

As they were returning home together in the early twilight, Mikolai once more took courage. He was certainly not going to offer Rosa again to Becker--he felt too sorry for her to do that--but he wanted to hear why his beautiful plan could not be realized. So he said, "The snow has come, now you'll soon be going," and cast a covert glance at his friend to see what he would say to it.

Martin answered quite simply, "I shall soon be going."

"There's still a fortnight," said Mikolai.

"There's still a fortnight," repeated Martin, and then gave a deep sigh of relief as one who again breathes light, fresh air after it has been sultry and oppressive for a long time.

Mikolai sighed too. *Psia krew*, how difficult it was to sound the fellow. Although he thought he had introduced the subject so cunningly, he saw he would have to be still more explicit. So he continued, "Only a fortnight longer, a very short reprieve. We shall all miss you, Rosa especially. Well, well!" He paused for a moment, and then cast another covert glance at Martin.

The latter's face, however, was inscrutable; it was as though it were hewn out of stone, and he could learn nothing from it. But what was that? It seemed to Mikolai as though his friend's pale face had suddenly flushed. Then he turned his head from side to side, as if his collar were too tight, and swallowed a few times as if he were gulping something down, and then the corners of his mouth drooped as though something were grieving him. At last Mikolai could no longer restrain himself. Why this dissimulation? He put his arm round the other's shoulders and said in a low, cordial voice, "Marry my sister, do. She's good and pretty and has also expectations. We three will be very happy together. Take her, Martin, I beg of you."

"Let me go!" cried the man, pushing Mikolai away as though he had said something more than unkind. Then he strode over to the other side of the road and kept his head obstinately turned towards the field. He did not look at his friend again, so that Mikolai, who was completely nonplussed, grew silent too.

So they walked along in silence through the soft mud and deep ruts, each on his side of the road. Mikolai's eyes suddenly felt wet. The deuce, what was that? He rubbed them angrily, but they were wet the next moment again. Here, here they had driven last summer--only a few months ago-- with hay and flowers on the wagon, and had been so gay. And now? His lips trembled, he felt unstrung. At last he had really seen that things must take their course.

When they reached the farm the house lay in darkness. There was only a light in Mr. Tiralla's room to the right of the passage; they could see it shining through the closed shutters.

What, was that confounded Böhnke there again? If you had a sharp ear you could hear somebody speaking in a subdued voice, almost a whisper, and a gurgling sound as though they were drinking quickly and then putting their glasses down. Mikolai flew into a rage; he felt just in the humour to pitch the fellow out. It was not exactly the thing he cared to do, for a guest is sacred; but that cad was no guest, he was a monster. He was ruining his father entirely. Mikolai lifted the latch angrily, but the door did not yield, it was locked. Then he shook it in his fury, "Hi, open the door!" He banged and scolded. But everything remained quiet in the room, nobody answered and nobody opened the door.

Then he rushed out of the house and into the barn in his anger, threw himself down on the straw, clenched his fists and wept aloud until he fell asleep.

When the schoolmaster left the farm at a late hour that evening Mr. Tiralla was quite drunk. He had only enough sense left to whisper in a tender voice, "Little Böhnke, friend, take care. If Mikolai catches you, he'll chop you into small pieces, perhaps with the hatchet, perhaps with the chopper. Ugh! he's a brute--they're all brutes here--ugh! my friend, you don't know what brutes they all are. My dear, beloved friend." Mr. Tiralla fell on the other's neck, kissed him and stammered in a hiccoughing voice, while he stroked his cheek, "If I--I--ha--hadn't you--God--bless--you--it would--b--be all--up--with me."

Böhnke left the room filled with a strange emotion. He was not so drunk as Mr. Tiralla--he could still collect his thoughts, if he took the trouble to do so--and he was thinking of the man who loved him as a friend and son. But very soon Mrs. Tiralla took entire possession of his thoughts. He looked around and listened for her step, and strained his eyes so in the dark that they watered. Was he to leave the house without a single kiss? *Psia krew*, he would not do that. He swore in an undertone, for he had suddenly grown brutal. He would be paid, paid for every visit. It was no pleasure to him to get drunk with that fellow. If she did not come now, then---- There was still time to go away and never come back, to become again as he had been before. If he were to ask to be removed and left the neighbourhood, and never more put his foot inside the door at Starydwór? Let Mr. Tiralla drink himself to death, alone. But if he were never to see this woman again?

The fresh air in the yard cooled his brow as he stepped out of the house. "Ah!" He drew a deep breath; air, thank God. There was still time, still time.

At that moment he heard the rustle of a dress in the dark passage, a furtive whisper of "Pan Böhnke!" and turning round he stretched out his arms in a transport of delight. "My darling, my sweet one!"

She did not respond to his kisses, but he did not notice it in his joy; and he did not see either in the dark how she pressed her eyes together and screwed up her face. All he heard was her whisper in his ear, "How are you getting on? I hope you've filled his glass frequently? How is he? Please tell me, will it still last long?"

He did not answer her; he had buried his mouth in her hair, and his lips were glued to its silky waves like those of a thirsty man. When she wanted to free herself in her impatience, "Speak, why don't you tell me, how much longer?" he clasped her still more closely without replying. There was no escape for her. They were standing like a pair of lovers, almost melted into one; her head was lying on his breast as though welded to it by the pressure of his arms. Thus her eyes and ears were closed, and he--he only felt her.

At that moment the door of Mr. Tiralla's room was gently opened and the old man stuck his head out timidly. Had his little Böhnke, his friend, succeeded in escaping?

The sick man was tortured by the idea that they wanted to kill the schoolmaster just because he was his, Pan Tiralla's, brother and friend, his only friend. If they were to do something to him? If they were to attack him in the dark yard? His terror on his friend's account had given strength to his shaking limbs, and he had been able to stand upright and walk.

He peered around like an owl that is dazzled by the glare; the light from the open door fell on the passage. Ha! who was standing there? The murderers! the murderers! Save yourself, little Böhnke. He was on the point of crying out aloud for help when his voice suddenly snapped--why! it was only Marianna. A grin full of pleasant memories appeared on his wrinkled face--ha, ha! it was Marianna standing there with a lover. But all at once the pleasant grin turned into a terrified grimace; it was not Marianna after all, it must be Sophia, and with her?

The idiot's eyes had suddenly become clear, and he had recognized his friend, his brother. Böhnke was holding his wife in a close embrace, and they were standing like a pair of lovers, breast to breast. Alas, alas! Mr. Tiralla fell back as though a gleaming knife were pointed at his face. The two were talking away so busily, so softly, that they had not noticed him. What were they whispering about? His teeth chattered. Murderers, murderers! Ugh! they were taking counsel together how they were to kill him--little Böhnke and Sophia--Sophia and little Böhnke. Little Böhnke! His friend, his only friend!

The man's wrinkled face shrivelled up more than ever, and his figure became quite small. Closing the door carefully and bolting it in trembling terror, he shuffled back to the table, groaning.

His little Böhnke, his friend, his only friend!

The man looked round the empty room with a wild glance, as though his terror were pursuing him. There, there, there! He stared at the chair near him; his friend, his only friend had just been sitting there, close to him.

Then he began to cry bitterly, that is to say, his red eyes could no longer weep tears, but he puckered up his face like a whimpering child, and a hiccoughing sob raised his chest in jerks. And then he drank what remained in all the bottles.

* * * * * * * * * * * *

Mikolai started up out of the straw in bewilderment--what was he doing in the barn, why was he lying there? He had had such awful dreams. Was it evening, night, or already morning? It was no good looking at his watch in the dark. He got up, and rubbing his swollen eyes staggered out of the barn. The moon was already high above the farm; it must be near midnight. Who was that creeping off to the gate?

"Stop. Who goes there?"

Could that be Böhnke? *"Psia krew!"* All at once the young fellow recollected how miserable he had been.

"Heigh, stop!" He set out in pursuit of the man who had just gone out of the gate.

Böhnke heard neither the calls nor the panting man who rushed after him. He was staggering across the fields as though intoxicated with joy, repeating the words, "My darling, my sweet one!"

At that moment somebody caught hold of him by the nape of his neck, and as he was walking very shakily, he fell down without any show of resistance and without a cry, so that Mikolai, who had whirled him round and was now kneeling on his chest, had an easy time of it. "It's I, Mikolai," he panted. "I'll teach you!"

Mikolai had hardly ever given anybody such a thrashing before; it was such a relief to him to get rid of his misery in this way. He flogged the man until his arm was stiff, and then threw him into the ditch at the side of the field and went home satisfied. He whistled as he walked back to the farm. There, now he had given that fellow a good reminder; he would have a few bruises to show. And if he felt inclined to bring an action against him, then let him; he would never repent of what he had done. He felt much brighter now. He looked about for Marianna; how tiresome, she was no doubt sleeping upstairs by now. He went round to the gable and began to whistle, but nobody opened the window, and no eager "Yes, yes!" reached his ear. How tiresome! The woman was sleeping like a badger in his hole. He would have to enjoy the thought of his successful stroke by himself, then, and he pressed his fists against his mouth and hopped about on one leg with joy.

When he came round to the front door again he noticed a light gleaming through the shutters in the big room. What, was somebody still awake? Was his father not asleep yet? Perhaps in his drunken condition he had forgotten to put out the lamp. Then it would be smoking the whole night through, as it had done a short time before, when the smelling thing had only gone out for want of paraffin. Did the old fool really want to set fire to the whole concern? How dreadful it would be to have a fire with all that straw in the barn. The man cast an anxious look at the streak of light which found its way through the shutters; it seemed twice as broad as usual. What was the old man up to? He would be doing some mischief some day, that was certain. Seized with an unaccountable uneasiness, Mikolai groped in the dark passage for the door-handle. *"Psia krew!"* Of course, it was locked on the inside. He knocked; then he called, "Father!" He rattled the handle. "The deuce, why can't you open?"

Still no answer, and no bolt was withdrawn.

He shook the door with all his strength. "I shall break the door open if you don't unlock it at once."

The door creaked and groaned, and Mikolai's loud voice echoed through the house, so that one would have thought it would have awakened the dead--bat there was no sound in the room.

Then a fear gripped him; what should he do now? He was still pondering when he heard his stepmother's voice.

Mrs. Tiralla had gone to bed, but she had not slept. Her face had burnt like fire, for she had been rubbing and washing it, so as to wash the kisses off which she had been obliged to put up with in the dark passage. Her forehead pained her as though there were a fresh scar on it, for the man had strained her so forcibly to his breast that his watch-chain had left a mark there. Oh, that stigma! She passed her hand over it again and again, but however much she rubbed it did not disappear. She wrung her hands in impotent fury. But then she clenched her teeth; no, no complaint, for she had done it for Martin's sake. Was it not a joy in spite of all this agony to think that she was suffering for his sake? Who could sympathize with her feelings? No one except the Lord. He had wrestled in the Garden of Gethsemane; He had endured Judas's kiss.

"O Lord," she raised her hands in the dark to the picture on the wall of the Saviour holding His flaming heart in His hand, "Thou art acquainted with every suffering, Thou seest my sufferings, have mercy!"

It was probably the first time in her life that Mrs. Tiralla had not used the prescribed form of prayer, that her heart had cried out in its own words. Then she whispered, "Martin, Martin," as if the beloved name were a form of conjuration, and stretched out her arms longingly in her cold, dark room. Oh, how warm and bright it had been at Starydwór! Suddenly a smile spread itself over her troubled face; it was as though a feeling of sweet peace had come to her from afar, and had told her that it would be warm and bright again. The certainty of this in the near future consoled her and made her patient. She pressed her hand to her heart--hope, hope!

Then she grew calmer, the burning sensation in her face had become less acute, she had said her prayers for the night, and prepared herself for sleep with her hands folded across her breast like a child. Soon, soon! The smile was still on her face.

At that moment the loud noise in the passage had startled her.

What could it be so late at night? She ran out of the room in her petticoat with no shoes on her feet; she was seized with a sudden fear--Martin, if it were Martin who wanted to run away. She must go to him, take hold of him, cling to him, he must not go! But then the thought struck her that there was no need to fear, he would not be leaving with so much noise. But still, if Mikolai were holding him, if they were quarrelling, struggling with each other, the one wanting to go, the other endeavouring to hold him back? Hark, what a noise! How Mikolai was shouting!

"What is it, what is it?" cried Mrs. Tiralla, as she stood in front of her stepson, panting. Mikolai had lighted a kitchen lamp, and they gazed at each other in the dim light with haggard faces.

"Where, where is he?" She caught hold of her stepson's arm. But then she bethought herself. Martin was nowhere to be seen, and this was not his bedroom door; this was Mr. Tiralla's, on which Mikolai was thumping, and before which he now stooped down and tried to look through the chinks.

"I don't know, I don't know," cried Mikolai, shaking the handle once more. "There's a light burning in the room; but everything is so quiet, and father isn't snoring."

"Oh, leave him!" It was no longer a matter of any importance to her, and she was going upstairs again. "He's fast asleep, that's all."

But Mikolai held her back in his fear. "Do stop," he begged, and there was a strange note of anxiety in his voice as he added, "Father always snores so at other times. I wonder if he could have had a stroke?"

Could it be possible! The woman's cold face grew hot.

"Father!" cried Mikolai once more, rattling the latch with all his might, but the bolt did not move. "I'll fetch a hatchet," he whispered; "we shall have to break open the door. You wait here and look out." He ran to the shed, where the axe lay by the block.

She remained standing in front of the door, whilst an eager desire to learn her fate almost tore her asunder. Her eyes nearly started out of her head. Everything was as quiet as death in there--at other times he always snored so--what would she see in there? God be praised! She could hardly await the spectacle.

She threw herself against the door with all her weight; she pressed her hands and knees so firmly against it that she, the weak woman, succeeded in doing what the strong man had not been able to do. The rotten framework gave way, and the door, lifted off its hinges, fell with a dull crash into the room. The woman fell with it.

At first she saw nothing, stunned as she was by the fall and blinded by the dust from the rotten wood. But how soon she saw it all!

There was Mr. Tiralla hanging from the hook in the centre beam, which had once been destined to carry a chandelier, close to the table with bottles and glasses. The man had made a noose of his handkerchief; the ceiling was low and his toes almost touched the chair, but still he was dangling.

"O God!" She uttered a heartrending scream and sprang forward. There he was, dangling, quite blue in the face and with his tongue hanging out of his mouth. How awful, how terrible! She did not give herself time to consider whether he was alive or not, or whether he would recover; all she did was to look round for help.

At that moment Mikolai returned. He stood motionless, staring with open mouth, the hatchet in his hand. The woman tore it out of his hand, swung it like lightning, the sharp edge cut the noose--and Mr. Tiralla fell on the floor with a dull thud.

* * * * * * * * * * * *

It was a terrible night at Starydwór. Everybody had come running, awakened by the noise of the falling door and Mikolai's cries.

Marianna howled as though she were out of her mind; both she and Mikolai had lost their self-command. Rosa had only given one short scream, and then, with upraised hands, had fallen down in a deep faint.

Mrs. Tiralla was the only one who remained calm. She had helped the two men to put the body on the bed, and now she stood looking on, mute and motionless, whilst Martin rubbed the stiffened limbs and moved the man's arms up and down, as he had been taught to do when he was a soldier. Was Mr. Tiralla dead?

"He's not dead yet." It was Martin who spoke, and she heard what he said without answering a word. She closed her eyes; how compassionate his voice--the beloved's voice--sounded. Did he feel sorry for her--or himself? No, he only felt sorry for Mr. Tiralla.

She opened her eyes wide. "Fool, idiot!" she could have shouted to him in her fury. But then she hid her face in her hands and staggered to a corner, where she broke down and groaned. She was the fool, the idiot, for she had cut him down herself. Why? She did not know.

* * * * * * * * * * * *

Martin carried Rosa upstairs. Mr. Tiralla was breathing again, and now the young man had a feeling as though he would have to fight once more for a life--but a young and innocent life this time.

He carried the unconscious girl tenderly in his arms. She had only very little clothing on, and he felt how thin and slender her limbs were. Her bushy mane--not smooth and silky like his love's beautiful hair-- tickled his cheek, but there was a perfume about her dry locks and about her whole person that reminded him of the perfume of the fields in spring-time, which he was so fond of ploughing. He carried her as carefully as though every movement could harm her, as though she were a soap-bubble which disappears if over-curious fingers touch it. And still he clasped her tightly. Once he thought he could feel her nestling against him; but it must have been imagination, for she had swooned and she hardly breathed.

On reaching the door of her room he entered almost timidly. A light was flickering there. There was no help for it, he had to lay her down on her bed, for the people downstairs had lost their heads, but he did it shyly. There she lay, and as he bent over her--was he dreaming?--she flung her arms round his neck.

She dragged his head down to her lips and he felt her hot breath as she whispered, "Always united--many years--and many children--my Saviour, my Redeemer--oh, my beloved one, come, kiss me."

Her whispering made him shudder. Why did she mix so strangely what was in the Prayer-book with what lovers whisper in the dark? Would she be saying any more? He could not help it, he had freed himself, but he remained standing at her bedside, listening.

"Oh, I know, I know it very well," she wailed. Then she gave a deep sigh, "Alas, alas, how beautiful you are, mother--Mary, Holy Virgin--alas, so lovely, a thousand times more beautiful than I. If only I were dead--dead like daddy." She was crying softly, and her hands were locked as though in pain or prayer. "I shall go into a convent." Then she wrung her hands and cried in a loud voice, "Have mercy on me, have mercy on me! Mary, Holy Virgin, help me, let me hold the Christ Child on my lap! Oh, don't turn away--help, have mercy on me!"

She stretched out her hands--oh, dear, was she going to catch hold of him? How her hands trembled, how red her pale face had become.

Martin heard no more, he fled in horror. Oh, this Starydwór, this Starydwór, if only he were hundreds of miles away from it!

CHAPTER XIII

What had happened at Starydwór soon became known in Starawieś. How could Marianna have kept silent about it?

She had told Jendrek with many sighs the very next evening behind the stable door, when he had rushed over for a quarter of an hour from the settlement, and her apron had been quite wet with tears. The dear, good master! Jendrek really ought to have seen how the poor man hung. Like that. And she turned up the whites of her eyes and let her red tongue hang loosely out of her mouth, so that the inquisitive man still shuddered when he thought of it.

Ugh! But how did Mr. Tiralla look now?

Oh, just as usual, you could not see that anything had been the matter with him. He crept about again as he had always done, yellow and thin. But the strangest thing of all was that he did not know anything about it.

Did not know anything about it? Jendrek would not believe that. How can a man hang himself and afterwards know nothing about it?

That astounded everybody. People came running to see Mr. Tiralla and press his hand in mute condolence whilst they gazed at him with curious, disappointed eyes. There were so many visitors the next and following Sunday as Starydwór had not seen within its walls for many a day.

Mr. Jokisch and Mr. Schmielke came, as well as the forester and the gendarme and all their friends from Starawieś and Gradewitz. Even the priest was there. The big room was quite full of visitors. Refreshments were brought in, Tokay and beer, and Mrs. Tiralla herself smilingly handed everybody a glass of gin, which was very welcome in that cold, unhealthy weather. Mikolai offered cigars, and soon the room was dark with thick, blue clouds of smoke, through which every now and then a quick glance was cast at Mr. Tiralla, as though the men suddenly recollected why they had come to Starydwór. There was much laughing and talking.

Mr. Tiralla sat staring in front of him without saying a word, or taking any interest in what was going on. It was as though he were no longer one of them.

Yes, the man was in a bad state of health, they all saw that. What had the doctor said?

They had not had one so far, said Mrs. Tiralla, casting down her eyes. Then she added softly, with trembling lips, that up to now she had only prayed and prayed.

The priest nodded. But when he soon afterwards left and she accompanied him to the front door, he took hold of her hand in the passage and pointed out to her that it was her duty to send for a doctor. "My dear Mrs. Tiralla," he said, "invoking divine help is certainly--h'm"--he cleared his throat, those wide-open, staring eyes made him quite confused--"divine help is certainly the chief thing, but human help is not to be dispensed with. Your husband seems very ill, really dangerously ill, why won't you have a doctor? You must absolutely send for one."

She followed him with her eyes as he walked away and there was a peculiar smile on her face. So--so he said that? Surely he did not believe that a doctor could change what had been decided upon in heaven? Very well, she could, of course, send for a doctor. But the man might prescribe whatever he liked, Mr. Tiralla would still be tottering to his grave with every step he took.

* * * * * * * * * * * *

"A strong-minded woman," remarked the visitors, as they walked home across the fields. "Terrible," they said then, and shivered as though they felt cold.

The wind whirled round them, and a flock of ravens, startled at their approach, flew out of the furrows screeching and cawing just over their heads. What a horrible noise! The men stood still involuntarily. Look, look! they all flew back to Starydwór and settled on the roofs. Those birds of ill omen!

Psia brew, how awful it must be there at present, to be every day with that man. Why, he was quite idiotic. Mr. Tiralla had never been very bright, and he had always had a hankering after drink. Well, well, your sin is sure to find you out. Poor woman! She was the only one who deserved to be pitied. It was really admirable how she kept up her courage.

"H'm, it's taken a great deal out of her, nevertheless," remarked Mr. Schmielke with a long--drawn whistle. He had suddenly grown very cool in his feelings towards her. "Sophia Tiralla's reign is over and done with. Did you notice the hollows in her cheeks? And then her eyes, how sunk they were. H'm, that lanky, red-haired girl, who dared not show herself at her mother's side a short time ago, is almost nicer-looking now. She's really not at all bad."

"You had better keep your fingers off her," said some one. "She's going into a convent."

"Tut, tut, don't talk nonsense. She--with *those* eyes?"

But the gendarme knew it for a fact, for the priest had mentioned quite a short time ago that the Ladies of the Sacred Heart at the Wallischei had been told of Rosa Tiralla's coming.

"Very well then, I shan't," said Schmielke. He made no more of his frivolous remarks, but grew silent as the others had gradually done. They all felt out of tune, thoroughly depressed. Starydwór seemed to be running behind them, now that they had left the place. In their mind's eye they continued to see the black birds on the gloomy-looking roofs, and the man who had hanged himself and was still alive, and the woman who had cut him down and who still smiled.

All at once they hastened their steps, and not another word was spoken until they reached the first house in Starawieś.

Then they began to speak of the schoolmaster. That was another of them, he and Tiralla were a couple. Both of them were being ruined by drink. But it was a great shame of Böhnke, for he ought to be a pattern to the children, as the priest very rightly had said. How could such a fellow teach children, a man who drank so much that he had been found in the ditch like a tramp, his clothes torn, and bleeding and dirty? It was a great disgrace.

The gendarme could tell a tale about that. He had many a time seen the schoolmaster coming home at dawn, and had watched him trying to poke his key into the lock; he had many a time had to help him to open the door. But when he had picked him out of the ditch on his way home from a round in the Przykop, looking no better than a drunken vagabond whom you look up, he had felt obliged to speak about it. Father Szypulski would perhaps have preferred him to have hushed it up, but it surely would not do for the village schoolmaster to be found lying drunk and bruised in a ditch. It would have been found out sooner or later, and then nobody would have any respect for him. Of course, the man could not stop at Starawieś, and who knows, perhaps he would have to give up being a schoolmaster altogether. The priest, who as a rule was so loquacious, had never said a word about it.

As they came past the house where Böhnke lived, they looked at it askance. What did the man feel like? He had not shown himself for days-- had he already left? The priest had said "as soon as possible."

They all felt they had never liked the schoolmaster; he had always been so conceited, so proud of his learning. Here you could plainly see it, "Pride goeth before a fall."

They knocked at the door. The shutters in front of the schoolmaster's window were closed. Had he really left, or was it because he felt so ashamed of himself?

The schoolmaster had indeed left, so the old woman, his landlady, who lived on the other side of the house, told them. Oh, dear, she complained, now her lodger had gone, and she had not got another one. "And what had he done?" she cried, clenching her fists in her fury. "Let those be struck by lightning who have slandered him. Dear, dear, how he wept. When I said to him, 'Don't weep, Panje Böhnke, my husband, the *stas*, also drank himself to death,' he did nothing but repeat, 'Oh my mother, my mother!' and groaned so that he made my heart come into my mouth. His mother is said to be a schoolmaster's widow and very poor. She won't be pleased when her son comes home like that. God have mercy on us all. Oh, Mr. Böhnke, Mr. Böhnke, what a good lodger he was." And the old woman began to sigh and weep so for her former lodger that the men got away as speedily as possible.

How disagreeable everything was, and then the weather was so raw. The only thing for them to do would be to make themselves comfortable at the inn. And they did so.

* * * * * * * * * * * *

Marianna carried the news to her mistress that the schoolmaster had been turned out of Starawieś in disgrace, in a voice full of malice and scorn. Pan Böhnke had gone to the devil, what did the Pani say now, eh? She cast a covert glance at her--what would she look like, pale or red, happy or sorry?

But Mrs. Tiralla looked quite unconcerned. At any other time she might perhaps have rejoiced, but now it did not even surprise her. So the schoolmaster was no longer in her way? Good. She knew that her guardian angel was keeping his wings spread over her.

She felt so calm at present that she was often surprised at it herself. Her heart no longer throbbed and ran riot as it had formerly done. She had been a fool and even a sinner, when she had caught hold of her guardian angel's arm, and had cut her husband down when he was dangling; but she felt that the saints had already forgiven her. She saw more plainly day by day--almost hour by hour--that Mr. Tiralla was drifting quickly, uninterruptedly to his end. She often longed to fold her hands in her exceeding gratitude; she went about the whole day with prayers of thankfulness on her lips.

Marianna was rather astonished to find that her mistress took the schoolmaster's departure so coolly. Had there never been anything between them? Neither formerly nor lately? Anyhow, she seemed very indifferent about it. Now Mr. Mikolai had a much softer heart, for he was very much cut up when he heard that the man had left. At first he had opened his eyes in surprise, but then he had pressed his hands to his head and groaned, "I would never have thought it; oh, dear, if I had only known it!" What a good fellow Mikolai was. He would in time be just what his father used to be. And Marianna was more attentive than ever to him.

Meanwhile Mikolai went about looking very troubled. He had certainly not wanted to do that, he had only wanted to give Böhnke a reminder when he thrashed him and threw him into the ditch. It also grieved him bitterly for his father's sake; the old man had been so fond of the schoolmaster, who used to spend hours with him like a friend. And now his little Böhnke would never come again. He felt so sorry for his father that he thought he must speak to him about it.

But Mr. Tiralla listened to his son's stammering excuses without understanding them. "Schoolmaster--schoolmaster?" He shook his head. "I don't know any schoolmaster. Friend--friend? Have--no--friend."

Mikolai shuddered when he looked at his father. There he sat with loose, hanging lip, and eyes the eyeballs of which looked as rigid as though he could not move them any more. He was not like a human being any longer. Did he not remember anything? He seized the old man by the shoulder and shook him, "Father!" Then Mr. Tiralla shrunk together in his corner like a hedgehog when you put the tip of your finger near it, and shot nervous glances at his son, glances in which there was malevolence as well as fear.

Mikolai felt desperate; the man only answered with a grunt now, it was impossible to explain anything to him. He felt as though something were choking him, he was obliged to run out of the stuffy room into the biting north-east wind that swept across the yard from the open fields and whirled the straw and chaff and feathers about that were lying around.

How terrible it was! The old man was spoiling both house and farm for him. He clenched his fists and a sigh of indignation was wrung from him; why, it would have been better if his stepmother had not cut him down!

He made the sign of the cross as though to confirm the thought. Then he turned to go indoors again. What could he do out there? There was no work to be done, a grey, heavy November mist hung over everything. What had become of Martin? He could no longer understand his friend. How well they had formerly assisted each other to kill time during these dark days. But now Martin could find no rest at Starydwór, he took no pleasure in anything, all he thought of was the first of December, when he was to leave them.

The lonely man shivered. Rosa would also be leaving after Christmas; even now she sat in her room upstairs as if it were a cell, and she was happy only when praying alone. She hardly ever appeared downstairs, she seemed to shun everybody. How different it all might have been, how splendid! But his father had ruined everything, everything.

The man uttered a curse as he entered the house. He went in search of his friend. Martin, however, was not pleased to see him; he had begun to turn his drawers and looked up disagreeably surprised when Mikolai came so unexpectedly into the room.

"What do you want?" he asked in an angry voice, hastily throwing a bundle of clothes into his box which he locked.

"Are you already packing?" inquired Mikolai. Then he added, "I suppose you can't await the day of your departure? But it hasn't come yet."

Martin cast an uncertain glance at his friend. "I know that," he said softly, and then added hastily and in a louder voice, as though he wanted to convince himself and friend of the truth of what he was saying, "I'm not thinking of it either. There's plenty of time; I'm not in any hurry."

Who believed that? Mikolai no longer believed his friend; why did he not look him in the face? *Psia krew*, something had come between Martin and him which he could not fathom, but it was there, nevertheless.

He felt very dejected as he left the room, the walls of which had so often echoed with their laughter. Now no laughter resounded within the thick walls of the old house. He stumbled up the dark stairs to Rosa's room; he would go to her and say, "Come, laugh with me, Röschen, or at least talk to me. I can't bear it any longer."

But when he suddenly burst into the room his sister jumped up with a terrified, eager look. She had been sitting near the low window, through whose curtained panes there hardly came a gleam of light. Some needlework had been lying on her lap, but it had slipped down and lay on the floor, and there was a flushed, expectant look on her face. Who was that?

"Oh, it's you." It sounded as if she were disappointed. She grew pale, and her lids drooped wearily, but she forced herself to smile. "Good morning, Mikolai."

"Good morning, sister mine." He took hold of her hands and gazed at her. She seemed so tall--or had she looked like that for some time? "Pretty girl," he said playfully, and pinched her cheek that felt like velvet.

"Don't talk nonsense." She freed herself indignantly and her face darkened. But when she noticed that he looked put out, she smiled a wan smile, and whispered as she clung to him, "Don't be cross. I must be preparing myself, you know, and such things are no longer for me."

"What rubbish, what nonsense." He grew seriously angry. "I've had enough of these goings-on here. The old man drinks the whole day, you pray the whole day, and there's not a bit of happiness in the house. *Psia krew*, let the lightning----"

"Sh!" She laid her hand on his mouth soothingly. "You mustn't swear, Mikolai," she begged softly, "it's sinful. Come, sit down."

She drew him with her to her chair near the window, the only seat in the narrow room except the stool beside Marianna's bed. Her delicate fingers forced him down and he squatted in front of her, whilst she put her arms round his neck.

"When I shall no longer be with you--it won't be long now, only three, four, five weeks more." She counted and then sighed, "No, still six."

"So you count like Becker," he interrupted her angrily. "You're longing to get away like he is. Nice love and friendship that, I must say."

She had flushed when he mentioned his friend's name, and a restless look had come into her eyes, but she soon grew calm again. She gazed at her brother with eyes full of love as she said, "You'll miss me, Mikolai, I know that very well. And I shall miss you too. But I'll pray for you. Oh, dear"--her voice was very sad, and big tears began to trickle down her cheeks--"I have to pray for so much, for so many." She wrung her hands. "My life will not be long enough for it all."

"Oh, yes, for father," he said in a low voice, and his head drooped.

She nodded: "And for mother too."

"What do you mean?" He looked at her in surprise. "She'll earn her seat in heaven by her own merits, she won't require your prayers."

"Who knows!" There was an expression of doubt in the girl's pure face, and she stared straight in front of her as though she saw something that others could not see. She trembled, and her voice was full of agony as she continued, "Who can know for certain that she does not require anybody to pray for her? Look, look!" She seized her brother's hand, and he shuddered at the peculiar expression in her eyes, that had become even more fixed than before. "I see mother in a white dress--oh, how beautiful she looks--I see her flying up to heaven--but look, look! There are spots on the hem of her dress. All those dark spots--do you see them, Mikolai?--are dragging her down. I'm not sure of it, not sure of it"--she shook her head, and there was a troubled gleam in her eyes and a terrified look on her face--"I love her so, I love her so, but there's something." She passed her hand over her eyes. "I can't wipe it away, it's there and it tortures me. Mikolai, brother!" She threw her arms round his neck, sobbing bitterly, and her tears wetted his cheek. "You must love me, love me dearly."

Her trembling lips sought his and imprinted a long kiss on them. He kissed her tenderly in return; his dear little sister, and she wanted to leave him?

"Speak to the old man," he begged. All at once he felt convinced that his sister would be able to alter everything. "Talk to him," he said ingenuously, "remonstrate with him, point out to him how wrong it is to drink, and he won't do it any more. Then all will be right. And you needn't go into a convent."

"I'll speak to him. I'll remonstrate with him. But I shall go into a convent all the same," she added in a low voice.

He did not hear her last words, he was too happy at the thought of her speaking to their father. Yes, there was some truth in it, there was something holy about Rosa, she could convert heathens, he felt sure.

He whistled as he went downstairs.

Martin Becker gave a start when he heard his friend's clear tones. How happy he seemed to be. An embarrassed smile crossed his face; to-morrow by this time Mikolai would not be whistling so contentedly, for he, Martin, if God were merciful to him, would be away over the fields, far away, almost there where the setting sun had left a yellow streak in the sky. "Mikolai will have to forgive me," he murmured, and went on with the occupation in which he had been disturbed before.

He had secured himself against interruption now, for he had bolted the door. He was packing his belongings. He had arranged and hung up his things in the room as though he had intended remaining at Starydwór for ever. But now he tore down his parents' photographs and those of his sisters and brothers, which he had hung up over his bed, and the picture of Mikolai and himself as soldiers, and the gay-coloured calendar which had looked so nice on the wall--no, he would have to leave the calendar, Mikolai would miss it too much.

He squeezed everything into his wooden box, and, as it would not close at once, sat down on it impatiently. How fortunate it was that it was no bigger, and that he could carry it comfortably on his shoulder!

He used to awake every night when the old clock in the passage struck the hour of midnight. What had become of his blessed sleep? To-night he would wake as usual, and then he would lie with open eyes and listen--one o'clock, two o'clock--and when everybody was lying in that deep, sound sleep which comes in the early hours of the morning, he would quietly put on the rest of his clothes--he would not undress himself entirely--and steal out of the room in his socks with his boots in his hand and his box on his shoulder. Softly, very softly. But that would hardly be necessary, for Mikolai always slept soundly, and there was nobody else downstairs except Mr. Tiralla, and he no longer counted, of course. So he could easily get away, for the key was in the front door and the farm gate was quickly opened. Then he would run across the fields--it would be dawn by that time and he would be able to see the path--away, away to Starawieś. And then through Starawieś, where everybody would still be asleep, away, away to the station in Gradewitz. The first train left at eight o'clock, he could easily catch it. And when he was in the train, then--the man drew a deep sigh of relief--then God had been merciful to him, then he was saved.

Martin did not take into consideration that he was treating his friend badly. True, the thought had occurred to him for a moment that he had given Mikolai his word and hand, but his duty to himself seemed of more importance to him. His everlasting salvation was at stake. He had felt that since the last time he had gone to confession, and he felt it daily with renewed pangs of conscience. But he also felt that he was paying a high price for his salvation. How she crept round him with her soft footsteps, making the circles smaller and smaller. Had she not brushed past him in the passage the day before, and whispered so close to his ear that her breath had tickled him, "Are you coming?" If she were to repeat that again and again, would he continue to have sufficient strength of will not to follow her? She knew how to talk and make excuses. How sweetly she could talk. Had she no anxiety about her own salvation? On thinking it over, he could not remember ever having heard her say anything irreverent or impure. When she sat opposite him at table, quieter now than she had ever been before, and mutely raised her big eyes to the ceiling, she looked exactly like the pictures of the Virgin Mary whose heart is pierced with seven swords owing to her grief for her Son. Oh, no, she was no bad woman, she was a good woman--and still, it was a sin to remain near her any longer.

Martin had lain awake a long time the night before, for the words, "Are you coming?" still rung in his ears and made his blood course through his veins like fire. There was such a pricking restlessness about him, that he felt as if he could not remain in bed any longer. But when he had at last fallen asleep after tossing about for a long time, he had dreamt of his dead mother.

She had appeared to him, and that portended something. And she had held up her finger as if in warning--or had he only thought of that later on? He could not be sure, but next morning, when he felt as tired, as heavy, and as worn-out as though he had been dragging something that had been too heavy for him, it came over him like a divine inspiration; this could go on no longer, he would have to leave at once and not wait for the time that had been fixed. His mother had come to fetch him, her anxiety for her child left her no peace at the throne of God.

And Martin felt that he would have to go away secretly, without any leave-taking. If she were press her lips to his, if her tearful eyes were to implore him with a look like that of a wounded hind, if she were to say, "My sun, my love, remain in my sky. It is God's will that the sun shall remain in the sky, for otherwise it would be dark night, and then I should die"--then he would not go. He would remain, and then--well, then? He uttered an incoherent prayer. He was sorry for Mikolai; he felt a stab in his heart when he heard him whistling. But he was glad he had not seen Rosa that day. If only he did not see her again.

Martin shunned Rosa. He did not know himself whether the feeling he had for the girl was a pious awe, because she was destined for the convent, or an awe in which there was something like shame, shame because he had listened to her when she lay on her bed and whispered her innermost thoughts aloud.

The man sighed as he passed his hand over his brow on which the sweat was standing. How deeply he had sunk, more deeply than in the deepest pond in the Przykop. The only thing that could help him now would be to tear himself away from Starydwór by force, without any consideration for anybody.

He remained in his room the whole morning, but when he heard the rattling of plates and Marianna's call to dinner he stole past the sitting-room door and out into the yard. He did not care to eat. He stumbled about among the trees in the Przykop where nobody could see him, and gave a start every time an animal stirred, or a dry leaf fell to the ground. His heart felt broken, but the hope of salvation shone feebly before his eyes. He would soon be away. If only this day were over!

* * * * * * * * * * * *

It was a short day in November, but still it seemed endless at Starydwór. Mrs. Tiralla was full of anxiety and impatience. Martin had spent the morning in his room, and he had not come to the midday meal. Where was he? She had sought him everywhere and had not found him. She was trembling--

where could he be? The calm which she had lately acquired had all at once disappeared; she forgot that the saints held her fate in their hands; all she could think of was that Martin had gone away without a word. Was he coming back?

She wandered about in an agony of fear, she could not remain a quarter of an hour in one place. She ran up and down stairs, from her room down into the passage and then up again, then out into the yard, where she stood at the gate without cloak or shawl, and where the cutting wind caught hold of her apron and spread it out like a sail, whilst she looked about for Martin. But she could not find the one her heart was longing for.

The fields lay desolate, the Przykop yawned like a grave in which there is no living thing to be found Where had he gone? She sought his footprints, as a dog seeks those of his master, but the rain and snow had obliterated them, and her eyes, full of tears, soon saw nothing but a grey, impenetrable mist.

She ran back into the house and began to question Mikolai. Where had Martin gone? He must know, for between him and his friend there was always a perfect understanding.

Her stepson stared at her in amazement. Why was she so angry? Becker would be sure to come back when it grew dark. Maybe he had gone to the village; it was long since he, Mikolai, knew anything about his whereabouts.

That did not add to the woman's peace of mind. So Martin kept away from Mikolai too. He was separating himself more and more from them all. "O God, have mercy! let him come back, let him come back!" She was like a hunted hind that is seeking a place of shelter.

So she ran to Rosa. It was long since she had been to her room; she had not found time to go. But why had Rosa kept away from her? Surely it was more fitting for the child to come to her mother than the mother to her child? Now, however, in her great anxiety she fled to her tender-hearted daughter.

At first Rosa was somewhat reserved. There was something shy and strange in her behaviour towards her mother, but the latter did not notice anything; all she wanted was a soul, a friend to share her anxiety.

"I don't know where Becker is," she began. "It's already dark and he hasn't returned yet. He has never gone away like this before, never stopped away so long without saying a word. O God, surely nothing can have happened to him?" she cried, pressing her hands to her temples with an expression of dread. "Oh, this fear, this fear!"

The woman no longer thought of hiding her feelings; there was a look of wild terror in her eyes, and her agitated voice was full of despair.

Rosa's face had flamed when her mother came into the room, but she turned deadly pale now. She did not answer, but she gazed at her mother as though she were trying to read her soul.

A shot was heard in the Przykop. Mrs. Tiralla gave a shrill scream.

"A gamekeeper is shooting," said Rosa.

"They surely can't have hit him? Oh, if he were in the Przykop and they had wounded him? But that"--Mrs. Tiralla gave an excited laugh--"would not be the worst. If only he comes back, if only he comes back! Do you think he could go away without saying good-bye?" she asked her daughter eagerly, casting an imploring glance at her. If only the girl would say, "He'll come back, mother, don't grieve, he'll come back to you." If only Rosa with her innocent lips would beseech the Almighty to give him back to her.

"Pray, my child," stammered Mrs. Tiralla, as she pressed her daughter's folded hands between her own. "Pray. Let us pray together."

A convulsive movement passed over Rosa's pure face. It looked as though she were going to thrust her mother away. But the struggle only lasted a moment. Fixing her eyes on a crucifix that she had hung over her bed, she said with shining eyes, "What shall I say?" just as she had spoken as a child, when her mother, tortured and full of hate, had knelt in the evenings at her bedside and wakened her with her tears and sighs.

"Pray, pray."

But Rosa's voice had lost its childish cadence; the clear, silvery ring had gone, and there was something austere and coolly calm in it now. "What do you wish me to say?"

"Oh, you know," groaned her mother. "Pray for him--oh, my fear, my fear. Pray that he may return to me. Child, my child, pray for me."

Freeing herself from her mother's clinging hands Rosa began to repeat the *Salve Regina*. "Hail, Queen, Mother of mercy. Thou our life, our sweetness, our hope, hail!" Her voice gradually rose and lost more and more of its cool austerity, as though she were intoxicating herself with the sweet beauty of the words, until it became warm and soft and melting as she said, "To Thee we call, to Thee we sigh, as we grieve and weep in this vale of tears." And then passing from the Salve to another prayer, she raised her voice in fervent supplication until it almost became a cry, "Be gracious to him! Spare him! Deliver him from all evil, from all sin!"

"Be gracious to him--spare him--deliver him!" repeated her mother mechanically. She did not know what she was praying, she did not understand that the words her daughter had been repeating were from the litany for a departing soul.

"We, poor sinners, pray Thee to hear us." The mother and daughter mingled their voices in fervent prayer, whilst the words, "Martin, Martin, what has become of you?" echoed in their hearts and rose like a twofold cry from the narrow little room that was gradually growing darker and darker.

"Stop, stop!" The woman sobbed aloud, she could not pray any longer. She threw her arms round her daughter's neck and wept. "Rosa, Rosa, he's not coming back. Rosa, darling,"--she pressed wild kisses on her daughter's face that was uplifted so piously--"pray, pray--how am I to thank you? No, don't pray any more, rather tell me--hark, there he is!"

In a second she was on her feet, and had rushed to the door, which closed with a bang behind her.

Rosa remained alone in the darkness.

She heard Martin's voice downstairs, and then Mikolai--and then her mother's happy laugh.

But Rosa continued to pray fervently; it was as though she were holding fast to the words of her prayer. The stars had long ago come out above the farm, the new moon was just over the gable, but she still lay on her knees praying. But now it was a soft whisper to the Lord, a blissful communing with the Bridegroom of her soul.

* * * * * * * * * * * * *

It was night at Starydwór. The moon had disappeared, and black clouds, driven along by the boisterous wind, were chasing each other over the house-top and hiding the stars.

Mr. Tiralla was sitting alone in his room. It was really time for him to go to bed, but there was nobody to assist him; Marianna had not come, and he was unable to go to bed alone. At first he had moaned and growled, but now he was calm. The few thoughts he had left were creeping after the servant. Ha, ha! how she was racing; she was running to meet a sweetheart. It amused him to picture her to himself.

What a good thing it was that his thoughts were his own, that they had not taken them from him as well as everything, everything else. He made a grimace as he clenched his fists. "That woman!" There she had stood--there at the writing-desk, and had wanted to steal his money--no, not his money, the powders, his powders. They were worth more than money. She had wanted to get him out of the way by the help of them. Ha, ha!--he chuckled to himself--but he had hidden them well, she would not be able to find them now.

Next time little Böhnke came he would show him where he had hidden those dear, precious things--no, he would not even show little Böhnke, for who knows, perhaps they would make his mouth water, and he would kill him so as to get them, and then eat them all up himself.

"Now, now, little Böhnke," said the man, shaking his finger at an imaginary person in the corner of the room. Then he added, "No, I'm not angry with you, in spite of your not having been to see me for so long. Take a seat, brother, there, sit down." He dragged a chair nearer with his heavy foot, and smiled at the schoolmaster, who was sitting near him with such a pale face and such hollow eyes.

"Drink, friend, drink," said Mr. Tiralla, as he seized his glass and finished it in one gulp. "Pooh!" He made a gesture of distaste. It did not taste at all nice--or did it taste nice? "No, no!" He raised his fist and struck the glass so hard that it broke into pieces. There, that did him good. Now *that* enemy could not harm him again.

"Ha, ha!" He chuckled to himself again, and did not notice that the blood was trickling down his finger. "Why are you so quiet, little Böhnke?"

No answer. But the wind moaned round the house and rushed down the chimney screeching, "Oo-hoo, oo-hoo," like an owl.

The man had been accustomed all his life to this wintry music round Starydwór, but now it terrified him. He attempted to make the sign of the cross and glanced round timidly. The schoolmaster had gone, he was alone, quite, quite alone.

"Who's there?" He started up in terror; he wanted to scream, but he could only utter a few inarticulate sounds. Somebody had opened the door. He blinked and tried to discover who the intruder was, but his eyes had grown very dim. Somebody was coming in, but it was not little Böhnke. Who else could be coming to see him? A man--a woman?

"You?" he shouted, seizing hold of the bottle so as to defend himself with it. What did Sophia want? Was she coming to kill him now in the night? He hurled the bottle and it broke into bits on the floor.

"It's I, father," said Rosa, and she knelt down and collected the broken pieces of glass.

"Oh, it's you." He drew a long breath. Yes, now he could see it, it might be Rosa. The lamplight fell on her curly, reddish hair, and he bent a little forward as she knelt before him and took hold of it. "No, it's not Sophia," he said with a sigh of relief. But he was still suspicious. "What--what do you want?" he stammered.

She was glad to think that he at least recognized her. How unutterably heavy her heart felt. She had knelt in her room until her knees had ached, and had prayed and prayed. There had been no Marianna to groan on account of her everlasting whispering and sighing, for the girl had gone out. And when she had at last finished her prayers, she had sat down on her bed with her hands folded and waited patiently until there was not a sound downstairs. She wished to speak to her father quite alone, without being disturbed by any one. And if he had already gone to bed, she would sit down on his bed. How often she had had to do that as a child, and he had always been so affectionate to her in those days. Then she would say "Daddy," and stroke his hair as she used to do. Oh, she was quite sure it would be all right, for she had been praying for it so fervently.

But when her father stared at her with his dull, yet fierce eyes, she lost her assurance. "I wanted--I----" she stammered. She would have liked to cry aloud, he looked so awful. No, that was not her daddy, whose hair she had smoothed, on whose cheeks she had imprinted kisses--first on the right cheek and then on the left--her daddy who had called her, "My star, my little red-haired girl, my wee birdie, my sun, the key which is to open the door of heaven for me, my consolation."

She did not know how to begin, so she sat on the other chair near the table and gazed at him intently with her sad eyes. She had thrown the pieces of glass, which she had collected in her apron, into the peat basket near the stove, and now she wrapped her apron round her hands, for she shivered with cold, although the room was so stifling. What she had undertaken to do was too difficult after all; oh, it was her dread of him that made her feel so cold. She had never, never seen anything so horrible as this man who was her father. He used to be big, but now he seemed to have grown small; his coat was much too large for him across the shoulders and hung round him. A horrid grin made his lips droop, and his purple nose positively shone in his pale face, that was of a dirty yellow colour. The rims of his eyelids were puffy and turned outwards. But the worst of all was his eyes. Oh, those eyes!

Rosa felt as though she must protect herself from that well-nigh lifeless glance, which at that moment, however, had something glittering, even brutish, in it.

What was her father thinking of? Whom did he take her for? She gave a start. "Ha, ha! Marianna," he chuckled, stretching out a shaking finger towards her.

He touched her. "Ha, ha!--hope you're enjoying yourself--ha, ha!"

She had to keep a firm hold of herself so as not to scream aloud, and her hands closed over each other tightly under her apron. The mere fact of folding her hands calmed her. She had so often prayed for strength, and she was sure that He would not forsake her now. She felt as though she were the maiden whom she had been so fond of reading about in the book of holy legends, who had entered the fierce lion's cage undismayed, and had gladly given her blood for the sake of her Heavenly Bridegroom.

"Lord Jesus," she cried loudly and fervently, then, pressing her folded hands to her heart, she smiled at her father. "Daddy, my daddy."

For a few seconds the old man's grin grew even broader, but then his face became calm. Daddy? He looked at his daughter in astonishment and stammered, "Little Böhnke has gone--who's speaking--so kindly?"

"I, Rosa."

He shook his head peevishly. "Don't want her."

A happy thought struck her. Laying her trembling hand on his, she said in a low, persuasive voice, "It's I, Röschen, your little star, your red-haired girl, your wee birdie, your----" the tears welled into her eyes; she gulped them down bravely, but her voice choked.

Then he continued, "My sun, the key which is to open heaven's door for me--ah!"--he smirked as though he remembered something, and then added as tenderly as he could in his husky, faltering voice, "my consolation." He looked at her, felt her hair as he had done before, and passed his hands over her as she stood before him tall and slender, for she had jumped up from her knees in her bitter, painful emotion. "Too big--too big--you're not my wee one, not my little daughter--Röschen--my sun--my consolation." And he looked down at the floor and smiled, as if a tiny little girl were standing there, who was not yet big enough to reach up to the table.

"But I *am* Röschen," said the girl quickly, as she seized hold of his hands with her feeble ones, and pressed and shook them as if she wanted to bring him to his senses in that way.

He continued, however, to speak to an imaginary little child on the floor, as though he were mad or intoxicated. "Are you coming to daddy? Poor daddy is always alone, quite alone since little Böhnke has gone." Then he added in a mysterious, almost unintelligible whisper, "Sophia is going to kill him--they'll all help to kill him--poor Mr. Tiralla." He shook his head miserably.

"Father, I--I'm with you--I'll stop with you," cried Rosa, shaken by his plaint. What awful things he imagined, poor, unhappy man. "I'll help you. And the Lord will help you, and His most Holy Mother Mary," she added solemnly, and made the sign of the cross on his forehead and breast as well as on her own. "May the Lord help you and us." And then she said resolutely and courageously--what was the good of hesitating? Had she not promised Mikolai to do it and also prayed about it?--"What you've been saying is not true, daddy. Nobody is going to do you any harm, neither mother nor anybody eke. You're not kind to mother. You're talking nonsense. Look, here is your Röschen, feel my hands." She put her dry, burning hands round his wrists. "As true as I stand here, I swear that you've nothing to fear, we all lov----"--no, she must not lie, so she quickly corrected herself--"we all mean you well. Daddy, oh, my daddy!"

She let go of his wrists and impulsively pressed her hands to his cheeks, as she had so often done when she was small and her fingers had seemed no bigger than the legs of a fly that played about on his fat cheeks. "Oh, my dear daddy, if only you would stop drinking. Everything, everything would be better then. Then mother would no longer"--she suddenly stopped and the colour mounted to her brow; she did not mention her mother again. But her voice sounded so honest and convincing as she continued, "Then you would never have cause to fear any more. You would see then that nobody wishes you ill. And how happy Mikolai would be if you were to go into the stables and fields again, and talk to him about the work on the farm. Poor Mikolai, his friend is going away and he'll be so lonely. And you would feel much better yourself. You wouldn't cough so much--Marianna says you spit blood--you would be happy again; you wouldn't sit alone in this room any more, and you would see the wheat and the oats and the red clover that smells so sweet. Just think of it, daddy!"

She grew quite hot in her eagerness; at that moment she forgot all about her convent and that she would not be at Starydwór to see the improvement. And then as the last and best promise she said, "And you would still be saved, daddy; God in heaven would forgive your sins." Her eyes shone as she looked at him, as though she wanted to infect him with some of her own radiant happiness.

But his eyes did not shine. He was looking down in a dull-witted way and merely muttered, "Yes, you're Rosa."

Ah! now he knew her. The saints be praised, that was a big step forward. Putting her sweet face close to his, and without shrinking back from the poisonous breath that almost suffocated her, she whispered, "And Rosa will love you again, daddy; love you so dearly if you'll only leave off drinking."

She pointed to a full bottle standing on the table next to an empty one, and some of the holy fury of the converters who used to fell oaks and shatter idols came over her. Raising her voice till it sounded almost triumphant she cried, "Throw it away, so that it breaks on the floor like the other bottle! Then the horrid gin will run between the boards down into the earth, down into hell, where it belongs. The evil thing will have gone, and we, father, we'll pray and give thanks."

"Listen!" She fell on her knees beside him and piously raised her hands. "Do you hear? The angels in heaven, with your guardian angel at their head, are shouting, 'Hallelujah'."

Mr. Tiralla mumbled something unintelligible.

Rosa did not hear it; she heard nothing more, for her soul had taken wings and flown out of the stifling room. God had heard her, the Lord was with her. The joy she felt almost overpowered her; her cheeks were wet with the tears of sweet exhaustion that comes when every nerve has been strained. What were all the joys of the world compared to the joy of saving her father and of delivering his soul from perdition? She buried her face in her hands, and a tremor passed over her.

There was silence in the room, but the storm was whistling and howling outside.

Mr. Tiralla had seized the bottle, but not to hurl it on the ground as Rosa had bidden him; he clasped it nervously to his breast, as if it were a priceless treasure that must be taken care of.

So they even wanted to rob him of that, the last thing he possessed? He would not let them take it from him, he would rather die. *"Psia krew!"* He swore so loudly that he startled his daughter.

Awakened out of her trance of bliss, Rosa saw with horror that her father was holding the bottle to his lips and drinking, drinking, hiccoughing and groaning, until he could drink no more, until the gin ran out again at the corners of his mouth. He sighed when he had to leave off; but he did not put the bottle on the table again, he hid it under his jersey.

"Go--go, girl," he growled angrily, and glared at her with malevolent eyes. "What do you want from me? My precious bottle"--he patted the place where he had hidden it--"you're the best friend I've got now. Come, my love, don't cry," he said, pinching Rosa's cheek as she sobbed. His spirits had improved since he knew the bottle was safe.

"My darling girl,
Why are you weeping?"

he croaked huskily. Then he grinned. His Rosa would soon get married now, would soon have children, many little grandchildren-girls as small as this one, and he gazed once more at the floor. There she was, the little girl who could not reach up to the table. He had long ago chosen a fine, handsome husband for his Rosa. "Look out, he'll soon be coming now." He nudged his daughter with his elbow, and blinked at her with the same expression in his eyes as when he had been thinking of Marianna. Then he chuckled to himself. What a joke, what a joke! He tried to slap his knee, but he could not; all at once his arm felt paralyzed, as heavy as lead, and his tongue obeyed him even less than his arm. He stretched it out after every sound, but the sounds would not form themselves into words; his furred tongue trembled the whole time.

Oh, what did her father want? Rosa was terrified. How horridly he looked at her with his blood-shot eyes, and why did he wag his tongue like that? "Speak!" she implored him in her terror. "What did you want to say? Do speak."

But he took no more notice of her, his eyes were fixed on the door. The man he had chosen for his little daughter must come that way. He stared and grinned, and then turned up the whites of his eyes. At that moment something cracked either in the wall or stove that sounded like a knock. Aha! he was knocking already.

"Come in." All at once Mr. Tiralla's tongue again obeyed him. Look! was that not Becker, slender and nice-looking, who embraced Rosa with a bridegroom's impatience?

The drunken man sat grinning, as one picture after the other flashed across his sick brain. "Very good, very good," he mumbled, smacking his lips. He gave Rosa a push, "Come, kiss him too, it's Becker, you know. Handsome fellow, good fellow, isn't he? Sweet little bride. I'll look the other way." He gave a hoarse laugh, that came from his throat like a hiccough, and put his hand to his eyes; but he peeped underneath it. "Young Martin, young Rosa--many little ones--one--two--three." He made a fearful grimace as he showed their heights a little above the floor. "Grandpa Tiralla is glad-- many, many--little Martins, little Rosas--all going to console him--aha!"

He attempted to pat Rosa and draw her on his knee, but she thrust him away with a cry of shame and aversion. Pressing her hands to her ears and closing her eyes tightly she rushed out of the room.

The madman followed her with astonished eyes. Who was that? "Hi, hi!"

No answer; he was quite alone.

Ugh! what was that? He stared at his fingers, on which there were several bloody scratches, which he had got from the broken pieces of glass. He suddenly felt that they hurt.

"Blood--blood!" he stammered, terrified, holding his hand up to his swollen eyes. They had wanted to murder him. "Help!" He screamed and stamped about the room.

* * * * * * * * * * * *

Martin Becker heard the cry for help as he sat up in bed with open eyes. Where did it come from? But he did not attempt to find out, he felt as though he were rooted to the spot. A strange horror paralyzed him. He had not even been able to sleep until midnight, he had lain awake for hours listening, and his nerves were so excited that he could hear all kinds of things. What was that stealing softly down the stairs? Had it not stopped outside his door--or had it crept further along the passage? Oh God, it was she, she, and she would not let him go!

What was it crying so, sobbing, whimpering like a terrified child, and groping along the walls? Hark, something was crunching the sand in the passage, the stairs were creaking. Was that the front door that rattled? Something was moving about the whole time.

"All good spirits!" The man made the sign of the cross as he murmured the words, and then crept further down under the feather bed. Why, it could not be half as bad as this in a battle. Much rather face a cannon's mouth than that eye--the eye he imagined was fixed on him in the dark.

"Mikolai!" he called, but his friend only muttered in his sleep. How soundly he was sleeping. It would have been so easy now to get up and go away, Mikolai would not have heard, and he could have escaped so easily-- and still. Martin lost courage, he dared not do it. Rather leave in the daytime, in open defiance if it must be, by force, than go into that dark passage where there were ghosts and whisperings.

Martin did not know what it was to fear a human being, but he feared ghosts at night. And they were spirits of darkness that raged in that house, he felt sure. So he remained in bed with anger in his heart at his own cowardice, and still not able to conquer it. He would go next day in broad daylight, even if he had to leave his box behind with everything it contained, his dear keepsakes and precious belongings. He would leave Starydwór next day. He stuck his fingers into his ears; the whole house, the night, all the air seemed to be filled with meanings. God be praised--at last! Then he fell asleep, and heard nothing more.

* * * * * * * * * * * * *

Mr. Tiralla had moved along by the walls of his room. He ran like a restless animal in a cage; not quickly--he could not do that--but to and fro as though in despair. "Rosa, Röschen," he called in a loud voice. It seemed to him that she had been with him, but he did not know for certain. And that was what he was pondering over now. How awful it was not to be able to recollect anything! She had been such a dear little girl--she had once been his little daughter--but she was that no longer, for she, his consolation, had thrust him away from her. Alas, alas! It was very sad.

He puckered up his face and began to cry. Now he had nothing to console him, everything was gone. "Everything dr--dru--nk up," he stammered, sobbing. All at once he understood things clearly; no, he had nothing more in this world.

Where was Starydwór? It had not belonged to him for a long time, he neither went sowing nor reaping, it was not his any longer.

He had no wife, no children, no friend, and no God. The Almighty would not have anything more to do with him. He had forgotten all, all his prayers; he had ceased to go to confession; he belonged to hell.

"Poor Ti--Ti--Ti----" he said sadly, as he struck his breast with his trembling finger. He could not even recollect his own name--that had been forgotten too. He had nothing, nothing whatever.

Oh, yes, he had. He put his hands to his shaking head, that never kept quiet for a moment. He had saved something, hidden something like a dog his bone. He would go to it now. And even if his father were to beat him afterwards and say, "Boy, why do you eat unripe fruit?" still, what was hidden behind the loose stone in the wall would taste good.

Mr. Tiralla walked to the door; he had suddenly recovered the use of his limbs. He shuffled and staggered, but still he went on. It was a wonder that he succeeded in opening the front door, which was looked, but all at once he had become possessed of strength in his fingers and strength of will too.

The wind in the yard knocked him down. He fell full length, but picked himself up again. "*Dalej, dalej!*" Quiet, very quiet--no lamenting even if he had hurt himself on the stones--so that his father should not come and seize him by the collar, "Tell me, my son, where are you creeping off?"

"*Dalej, dalej!*" He was longing to get there. A bright streak in the sky already cast a faint glimmer of light around. The man looked about as he groped along. Aha, there was the stable! Aha!

Then Mr. Tiralla was happy.

CHAPTER XIV

Marianna was humming a song, although she had been up all night and the words almost froze on her lips in the calm, cold, wintry air.

"Black eyes in her head,
Just like me, just like me.

Golden hackles on her shoes,
Just like me, just like me.

In her pocket not a coin,
Just like----"

"Ah!"

She yawned and then tried to dance a few steps. How tired she was. But it had been very nice with Jendrek, he was the best of them all in spite of everything.

She rattled her milk pails merrily as she glided nimbly across the slippery yard to the stables in her low, creaking shoes.

The light was still faint and the air was cold, bitterly cold. A hard frost had come at daybreak, the first that year, and had touched everything with its blighting finger. The pools in the unpaved yard, from which as a rule the rain, dirty water, and melted snow flowed in rivulets to the big pond in the centre, were now united and formed a single white mirror.

The house was still dark and quiet. Marianna's eyes twinkled; aha, they were all still asleep. Good! then none of them had heard that she had only come home at six that morning. She had not been up to her room yet to take her best dress off, but it would not harm it, even if she were to wear it whilst milking for once. Hark! how the cows were lowing. They were waiting impatiently. But how they would stare when they saw her in her beautiful, new, red dress, with its many pleats, which she had got on purpose to do the thing in grand style with Jendrek, and her spick-and-span new shoes, in which she had danced last night for the first time.

The vain girl tittered as she skipped into the stables where the cattle were lowing dully. "Quiet, quiet there," she said, groping about for the lantern in order to light it, as it was still rather dark. "Yes, yes, here she is, here's Marianna. *Psia krew*, hold your tongues." At that moment the lantern cast a light around. "Good God!" Breaking off in the midst of her chatter, the servant let the milk pails fall to the ground with a shrill scream. Why, the master was lying there! She stood as though rooted to the spot. Oh dear, how frightened she had been. What was he doing there? What did he mean by going to sleep there, and frightening people who came unsuspectingly into the stables out of their wits?

"Panje, Panje Tiralla," she called. "Do get up, *gospodarz!*"

She had come up to him now; he did not move. She gave him a slight push with the point of her new shoe; how tipsy he was. "Wake up, master," she said. "Finish your sleep in bed, I'll help you into it." What pleasant dreams he was having. It seemed to her that there was a smile on his face.

She bent over him. "Panje, Paniczek!" She looked at him a little more closely, she felt him--then she began to scream so that the walls resounded with it; she mingled her screams with the lowing of the cattle that had started afresh; she screamed still louder, so that she dominated the lowing, screamed so that it sounded across the yard to the sleeping house like a trumpet. Mr. Tiralla was icy-cold; he was dead.

She tore her hair and behaved as though she were mad--her master, her good master! Then rushing out of the stables and across the yard she shouted and shrieked, "Pani, Pani, help! Help, Mr. Mikolai!"

Mrs. Tiralla came immediately. She had lain awake the whole night. How could she have slept when her heart trembled between fear and hope, when at one moment it had seemed to her as though the events of the afternoon had only been a prelude, as though Martin were going away at once and for ever, and the next as though he had been given back to her, and Mr. Tiralla were going away for ever? She had wept and called on the saints. But when the maid's cry for help brought her downstairs, there was no more fear in her heart. She surmised that the decisive hour had come, but all she felt was eager curiosity.

"What--what? Where--where?" she cried, seizing Marianna by the arm with a convulsive grip, as the latter came rushing up to her.

"Dead, dead!" stammered the girl trembling.

"Dead?" Was Mr. Tiralla dead? But tell me then. The woman shook the screaming servant with wild impatience.

"Oh dear, oh dear, my good master is dead," howled the maid. "He's lying in the stables without saying a word."

"Show me."

They rushed over to the stables. There lay Mr. Tiralla as the maid had left him; he had not moved. Marianna made the sign of the cross over him and wanted to fold his hands, but Mrs. Tiralla pushed her aside--"Leave him!" What had he got there? The woman's eyes dilated; he was clenching a small box in one hand, a box she knew very well. The lid had fallen on the ground, and the powders wrapped in paper had been torn out and were lying beside him near a brick on which there was a cobweb. She stared open-mouthed--rat poison! Look, there was the grinning death's head above the cross-bones!

In the other hand the dead man was still holding an empty paper, and some grains of sugar still clung to the wild-looking stubble on his sunken chin.

"Jesus! Mary! Joseph!" The widow threw herself on her knees, made the sign of the cross, and bent her forehead to the ground. "I give his soul to you." Her lips continued to move in prayer, whilst her thoughts flew on. So he had got some of the poison after all? He had kept it hidden--*she* had not known where--he had taken some of it himself--pilfered some of it like a boy pilfers sugar--he had died of it.

She made the sign of the cross again and again. "Holy Mary, reconcile him to Thy Son, commend him to Thy Son, bring him to Thy Son." The saints had willed it, the saints had been gracious to him--and to her too.

Mrs. Tiralla could not help it, but she no longer felt the slightest animosity towards the man lying there. She touched his forehead with her lips, then folded his hands and tried to close his eyes, "May he rest in peace."

Then she sent the weeping servant to fetch his children whilst she remained on her knees alone with the dead. She felt no fear. It was as though a light had risen for her in the dark stables, and as though she must thank the dead man for it as well as the saints.

Mikolai was not so calm, the calamity had affected him deeply. His father, his old father. And he had died in all his sins without the consecrated candle, without a priest, and without absolution. He could not compose himself, he sobbed so.

He and Marianna vied with each other in weeping. He and she had carried Mr. Tiralla into the house, and their tears had fallen on him like warm rain, drop by drop, a constant flow.

* * * * * * * * * * * *

The sun had risen over Starydwór when Martin Becker awoke, disturbed by sobbing and wailing. He had slept very heavily. He had been so exhausted by emotion and the decision that he had arrived at after a long struggle that he had not heard Mikolai run out of the room when the maid's loud screams had awakened him, but had slept on like a peaceful child. He finished dressing. He was still so sleepy that he could not understand why he had gone to bed in trousers and socks. But then his eye fell on his box that stood packed and corded. Then he remembered everything. He braced himself up and left the room to announce his intention to Mikolai. Why were they weeping and wailing so?

Marianna ran past him in the passage. She pointed to the door leading into the big room with a convulsive sob, "Holy Mother, holy Mother!" What was the matter with her? What had happened? An accident? The blood suddenly rushed to his head; had anything happened to Mrs. Tiralla? Of course not--he shook off the sense of oppression which was overpowering him--she did not know yet that he intended leaving that day.

He went into the room from whence the weeping came. It was half-dark, the shutters were closed, and the only light in the room came from the candles burning on the table. He distinguished some dark figures kneeling by a bed, and on the bed an outstretched figure under a white sheet. He started and pressed his hand to his brow; he felt terrified. Who was dead?

At that moment Mrs. Tiralla came towards him with outstretched hand. "Mr. Tiralla is dead," she said.

"Dead--dead?" he stammered. Her voice had sounded almost triumphant. He did not grasp it all at once, it was not a thing that could be turned over in the mind so quickly. He shuddered, and swiftly made the sign of the cross. A dead person in the house! And the woman could say it so calmly, and gaze at him with such a radiant look that the black in her eyes illuminated the darkness like a sunbeam.

The young fellow had a feeling as though he must turn round and run away. He was still hesitating when the woman drew him forcibly towards her, and he felt her icy-cold fingers gripping his wrist.

"Martin, Martin," she whispered softly in his ear, "he's dead, now you needn't go." Her voice was only just audible, for Mikolai and Rosa were kneeling at the bedside.

But Martin had not noticed them. "I shall have to go all the same," he said aloud, without looking at her. "When Mr. Tiralla is buried, I shall go. Holy Mother, pray for us, now and in the hour of death!" Making the sign of the cross he stepped up to the bed, knelt down beside Rosa without noticing her in his consternation, and quickly repeated a silent prayer.

Whilst kneeling there he heard an angel praying softly. That must be Rosa. Now he saw her. And when he had finished his prayer and made the sign of the cross, he pressed her hand and then Mikolai's.

The three put their heads together like the terrified lambs of a flock over which a storm is raging. "Eternal rest give to him, Lord," whispered Rosa, and the two men murmured in response, "and let perpetual light shine upon him."

Then Martin got up from his knees and went to the door. He longed to be doing something, for there is always much to see to in a house where death has entered, and he had once more a warm, living feeling of how good Mikolai had always been to him, and how much he liked both the sister and the brother. Somebody would have to run to the village to tell Father Szypulski first of all, and if possible bring him quickly to the farm, and then--but the woman barred the way.

"Where are you going?" Her voice no longer sounded firm, it was trembling.

He tried to pass her without answering--no, she should not hold him again.

But she followed him into the passage, where she again seized hold of him. "I shall not let you go, tell me first where you're going."

"Into the village. Let me go, I tell you," He turned his head aside defiantly, so as to avoid her eyes.

"Swear that you'll come back," she whispered hoarsely, "swear by God Almighty, by Mr. Tiralla lying dead in there."

"I will not swear." He pushed her away.

Then she threw herself on his breast, and her arms held him like chains. "'Look at me, why do you turn your dear face away? Look at me, it's I, darling, I, whom you love so. Mr. Tiralla is dead."

She no longer spoke in a whisper, she no longer took care that her words should remain inaudible to others, and her voice sounded loud in the echoing passage. "I'm a widow now. I'm free now. Don't go! All I possess shall be yours. And it's no sin if we love each other. I beg of you, I implore you, don't go! Stop, my darling, my Martin, stop!"

She slid down and embraced his knees, sobbing; she pressed her face that was wet with tears against his clothes. "Why are you so cold; why don't you speak to me? What have I done to you?"

He stood like a tree without bending. "You've not done anything to me," he murmured at last, gloomily. "Not to me, but----" "I've not done anything to him either," she cried, jumping up eagerly and pointing to the door. Then she raised her fingers as though taking an oath. "I swear that I'm innocent, quite innocent; he, he took it himself. I swear by God I've not----" "Don't swear." He caught hold of her raised hand and pulled it down. "You must not swear."

"Why not?" She stood erect before him with sparkling eyes and head thrown back. "Ask Marianna, ask Mikolai; he, Mr. Tiralla, took the poison himself in the stables; we found it still in his hand. I--I"--she struck her breast and again raised her fingers to swear--"I'm innocent of it. The saints have willed it."

He looked her full in the face scrutinizingly, as though he would pierce her with his eyes. "The saints have willed it," he repeated, then, as though reconciling himself to the fact. But when she attempted to seize his hand in her elation--ah, he still loved her after all, he could not leave her--he shook his head and looked away from her in fear. "Even if it were heaven on earth here, I would not stop," he whispered. "I see that man"--pointing to the door--"the whole time before my eyes. He must separate us, so help me God. Good-bye."

He held out his hand to her, although he could hardly bring himself to do it. All at once he feared her hand, it was as though something were dragging him away from it. "I prefer to go immediately. Mikolai is there, he'll arrange everything for you. I cannot--cannot stay any longer." And he rushed out of the door and into the yard.

She stood there as if turned to stone, and her eyes were fixed. What, he was going after all? Mr. Tiralla was dead and yet he was going to leave her?

"Martin!" she screamed shrilly, rushing after him. He ran like a stag and she like a hind. "Martin, Martin!" But she could not reach him.

Purgatory and Hell were flaming behind Martin Becker and Eternal Salvation was beckoning to him. So he ran as he had never done before, without coat or hat, and but thinly clad for such a raw day. He would let everything remain behind, box and belongings, everything he called his own, he did not want anything more from Starydwór, for sin was cleaving to it, sin that clave like blood.

He ran through the fields like a boy who has lost his way and is trying to get home to his mother.

She saw him ran, but she could not follow him further, she sank down at the gate. She crouched in the frozen snow with a low cry. How red everything looked. Was it blood that had been spilt? She shuddered as she gazed around like one demented. Or was it the wintry sun that had dyed everything red? Yes--she drew a deep breath--oh, yes, it was only the sun. The whole sky was aglow, and it was that which made the glistening snow look red.

She would implore the saints to help her. But she could not rise, her ankles felt broken, so she slid on her knees to the grating in the wall, behind which stood the image of the Holy Mother with her Child. The withered wreath was still there, which she had made of corn and flowers and clover, and hung up on a happy day.

"Bring him back, oh, bring him back," whispered the woman beseechingly, and then burst out sobbing. The saints had helped her once, why should they not do so again? Innumerable tears rolled down her cold cheeks and turned to ice on her bosom. She prayed and wrung her hands. She begged for the return of the one as she had formerly begged for the death of the other. One prayer had been granted; Mr. Tiralla was dead. And she knelt there guiltless--for who, who could say that she was to blame?

She looked around with wild eyes. At that moment she saw somebody standing before her, between heaven and earth, accusing her.

"No!" she shrieked, stretching out her arms. How dared he accuse her? Was it she, she, who had given Mr. Tiralla poison? And even if she had attempted to do so before, the poison had no longer been poison in her hands, for the mushrooms had not harmed him, and the corn had not harmed the poultry. "No, I'm innocent, quite innocent of it." The saints had willed it, they had put into his mind to take some of the powder and swallow it. And they had willed that he should die of it. So his death had been decided upon in heaven.

Folding her hands once more the woman prayed in a whining, fervent voice; would the saints not fulfil her second prayer too, and bring back the man who had fled from her?

Her thoughts grew more and more confused. Now she saw Martin Becker, now Mr. Tiralla, and then the angel with the flaming sword. She cowered; alas, alas, was he going to punish her with its sharp edge?

But suddenly the sword fell from the angel's hand, and lay gleaming in the snow. He laid his cool hand on her burning brow--oh, that was no longer the cherubim who drives sinners out of the Garden of Eden, that was Rosa, Rosa's hand, and that was her dress.

"Help, help!" cried the woman, clinging to her daughter as though she were awaking out of a frightful dream. "You help me. Shall I be lost? Oh, speak! Help, you help me!"

And her daughter answered, "I'll pray for you day and night. Calm yourself, mother, I'll intercede for you." She laid both her hands on the woman writhing in despair, and it was as though a soothing stream, as though a mighty saving flood, proceeded from those delicate, yet firm hands.

That was no longer Rosa, her young daughter, the delicate girl, who now stood with erect head before the sinner imploring help, and seemed to be visibly growing bigger and bigger. And that was no longer Rosa's voice. It was a more powerful voice, which dominated the howling and whistling of the wind.

That was the Bride of Christ. But not the humble, longing maiden; it was the Bride of Christ, the powerful Church herself, whose voice resounds over the plains as far as the church steeple in Starawieś, and further, much further, resounds powerfully throughout the whole world:

"Ego te absolvo a peccatis tuis!"